WALES
HISTORY OF A
NATION

In the long run an ideology can survive only if it facilitates the smooth and efficient functioning of the economy. If it hamper that, the society – and with it the ideology – must perish in the end. But the reckoning may be long postponed.

V. Gordon Childe, *What Happened in History*

We are still here! We are still here!
Despite everyone and everything
We are still here!

Dafydd Iwan, *Yma o Hyd*

WALES

HISTORY OF A NATION

DAVID ROSS

WAVERLEY
BOOKS

Picture Credits

The publishers gratefully acknowledge the following picture sources for their images:

The National Museums and Galleries of Wales
Pages 29, 42, 56, 128, 183, 224

National Library of Wales
Pages 112, 210, 235, 237

Photolibrary Wales
Pages 45, 75, 93, 100, 104, 139, 146, 162, 174, 199, 249, 255

Wrexham County Borough Museum
Page 223

PhotoDisc, Inc.
Pages 24, 134, 145

IMS Communications
Page 191

Mark Mechan
Pages 252, 253

The Illustrated London News Picture Library
Page 219

Charles Knight's *The Popular History of England*, 1864
Pages 65, 119

***Welsh Pictures from Victorian Times*, 1892**
Pages 21, 61, 78, 81, 98, 114, 170, 195, 205

This edition published 2010 by Waverely Books,
144 Port Dundas Road, Glasgow, G4 0HZ, Scotland
First published 2005 by Geddes and Grosset
Reprinted 2006, 2008

© David Ross 2010

ISBN 978 1 84934 049 6

Printed and bound in Finland

Contents

Fact Windows

Foreword

In the spring of 2010, the people of Wales, along with those of many other countries, were contemplating a future in which tax rises and cuts in social services loomed large. For a time it had seemed as if Wales might ride out economic recession more successfully than other parts of the United Kingdom, but by late 2009 unemployment had climbed to 8.7% of the working population, compared to a UK average of 7.8%; and further cuts in industry and local government payrolls seemed inevitable. Though Wales's modest-scale financial institutions were not exempt from charges of risky trading, there were no scandals and bailouts compared to Ireland and Iceland, two independent nations whose economic success had often been eyed with a degree of envy. Wales's economy in the past fifty years has become increasingly dominated by the 'services' sector, which accounts for two thirds of the gross annual product, with manufacturing diminished to 32% and agriculture, mining and forestry contributing only 1.5%. But the Welsh were not going to prosper by taking in one another's washing. The only positive factor was that the decline in the value of sterling might attract more foreign visitors.

Within the constraints of British and European government policies, the Welsh Assembly government struggled to encourage outside investors to hold on and to promote new initiatives. After the elections of 2007 gave no party a clear majority, Labour and Plaid had set animosities and old grudges aside, for the time being at least, and under the rubric of 'One Wales' formed a coalition, with 6 Labour and 3 Plaid ministers in the senior posts. Its broad statement, 'Our ambition is no less than to transform Wales into a self-confident, prosperous, healthy nation and society, which is fair for all' could have been used with equal validity by the other main parties. Both governing parties committed themselves to a further referendum (to be held by 5 May 2011) on whether full law-making powers within Wales should be devolved from Westminster to the Assembly.

One might ask why, in 2007, a hundred years on from when David Lloyd George was Chancellor of the Exchequer, Wales was not already all the things that 'One Wales' seeks to achieve. The answer emerges at least partially from the pages of this book. Politicians and people alike are aware of the range and scale of the problems affecting the country. Urban blight, rural decay, anti-social behaviour often encouraged by 'role models' in sport, entertainment and (sometimes) politics, the growing divide between the affluent and the impoverished, the difficulties of integrating new arrivals into old communities, are only a few of them. As in other Western-type societies, the Welsh are living longer, and the proportion of elderly citizens is steadily increasing. People drink more, their children are often unhealthily fat, and despite a range of social services, domestic labour-saving devices, and opportunities for pleasure and self-gratification which would have been the stuff of fantasy in 1907, they complain more. Today in Wales, the expectations of the individual, from life and society, have never been higher (like the average debt level), and as elsewhere, the ethos is firmly focused on the demand for satisfaction here and now.

There is, of course, another side. Wales remains a country with a strong sense of community at national and local levels. More is being done to come to terms with climate change and to promote the production of sustainable energy than in the rest of the United Kingdom. Tidal estuaries, bare hills, wind and rain have their advantages here, though pressure to conserve the existing environment is also strong. Initiatives have been launched, like the 'Welsh Bac', an effort to widen the experience and value of school education. Efforts continue to decentralise administration from Cardiff and the M4 Corridor to the west and the North. A vibrant spirit exists to preserve the things that hold and express the identity of Wales, while still aspiring to make it a model 'small nation' that participates and shares in helping to resolve the urgent problems of the wider world.

Introduction

A LONG, BREATHLESS MOMENT

In the year 1405, during the long summer days of late August, the inhabitants of the fertile lands around Worcester should have been busily occupied getting in the harvest, as in every year since time immemorial. But in this particular part of England, in this particular year, things were not the same as they had always been. A Welsh army was drawn up, ready for battle, on Woodbury Hill, ten miles north-west of Worcester city, where the fine perpendicular-style tower of the cathedral, at that time additionally heightened by a tall wooden spire, could be seen rising above the low roofs. The city had already been stormed and looted by the invaders. Strengthened in manpower and morale by French support, the Welsh force had surged through south Wales from Milford, winning battles at Haverfordwest and Carmarthen, crossing into England unopposed.

Eight hundred men-at-arms, six hundred bowmen and twelve hundred foot soldiers had been sent from France to form part of the force. But its main strength lay in its native Welshmen, whose numbers were put at around 10,000. Long famed for their tenacity, fierce courage in battle, and their fighting skills, including the deadly art of the crossbow, the Welshmen were a formidable enemy. The threat of an invasion from Wales was something to strike fear across the rich lands of the English Marches. And now it had happened. This was no hastily mustered and ill-armed group of rebellious farmers and peasants. It was made up of men seasoned in battle, with notable victories already behind them. And it was a national army. At its head was the Prince of Wales, Owain Glyndwr. For five years he had resisted the might of England, ranging the strength of all Wales behind him, making treaties with the kingdoms of France and Scotland, acting as a sovereign in his own country. Now he had brought the war into England. It was a long, breathless moment.

On Woodbury Hill, Glyndwr had marshalled his army as if for defence. But there was no sign of an enemy in arms. Henry IV, King of England, did not bring or send an army against the most serious invasion from Wales that England had ever experienced. Glyndwr might have advanced further. The way east across the Vale of Severn and the Cotswolds was open. Oxford was only three or four days' march away; and London was two days from Oxford. There was no lack of enthusiastic Welsh prophecies to foretell the sight of a Prince of Wales riding in triumph over London Bridge. He had hoped that among the Englishmen who had supported the murdered Richard II and regarded Henry IV as a usurper, he would find enough recruits to give his forces the patriotic aspect of an army out to restore legitimacy in England. But recruits were sparse in the extreme. Eventually, when one morning he gave the order to break camp and set out on the march again, it was for a return to Wales. The invasion was over. Apart from the booty of a provincial town, the allies had won nothing. Owain Glyndwr, who two years before had plotted with his allies, Mortimer and Northumberland, to divide the realm of England among themselves into three parts, with himself lord of five English border counties as well as Wales itself, returned to Aberystwyth with nothing to show for either his diplomacy or his military prowess.

Henry IV resumed his slow, relatively ineffectual but dogged invasions of north Wales. That other Prince of Wales, Henry of Monmouth, later to be Henry V of England, defeated another Welsh force at Grosmont, near Hereford, in March 1406 and a few weeks later Glyndwr's brother was killed and his eldest son taken prisoner at Pwll Melyn, after a failed attempt to take Usk. Although Glyndwr's hold on Wales itself lasted another four years – and even after his last great stronghold at Harlech was lost, his guerrilla resistance continued from 1409 to 1413 – the retreat from Worcester marked the climax of his extraordinary career and the start of its decline.

The invasion of 1405 marked the last attempt of the Welsh to assert by force of arms their right to be a separate nation, in coexistence with the vastly larger and richer neighbouring kingdom, but with their own prince, parliament, church and laws. Glyndwr's reasons for ordering a retreat have often been pondered over, but beyond the bare fact of his action, there is no evidence to show what prompted it. He was a complex man, very far from being a simple-minded mountain warlord: experience, strategy, international politics, astrology all played a part in his decisions. Nevertheless, in his decision there has often been seen an essential hesitancy – a holding back at the very brink – in the Welsh endeavour to be free. It was as if, despite all their ardour, their sense of being a people with a language, a culture, a tradition to sustain them, there was some lack of will that prevented them from grasping the vital moment.

Perhaps, even as he looked out over the broad Vale of Severn and the blue countryside stretching away to the horizon, Glyndwr became fully aware of the sheer size and wealth of the power that he was assailing. Even a weak king like Henry IV could summon formidable captains and far greater armies than Wales could muster. More than a thousand years of Welsh history had led to this moment, and the loudest among the ringing messages that tolled from this long period were those that said: 'Hold on to what you have, lest it be taken from you.' There also rang the high call of national fervour, of the urge to take back some at least of what the Saxon had grasped, the voices of Emrys and Myrddyn promising that one would arise who would chase the invaders back to the sea:

> I will prophesy –
> It will be truth!
> From Aber Taradyr
> The Cymry will be bound
> Under one warlike leader
> Of the line of Gwynedd.
> Usurpers of the Prydein
> He will overcome.

But against this, and deeper and stronger, was the note of hard experience, the memory of defeat, of bloody reprisals, the infliction of alien laws, the subjugation of Welsh people to English lords and their arrogant, greedy henchmen.

To know and understand the forces at play in 1405, and which still continue in various forms into the third millennium, it is necessary to go back to the beginning.

CHAPTER ONE

Pre-Celtic Wales

THE SHAPING OF WALES

Human occupancy of the north-western tip of Europe was sparse and sporadic for thousands of years in the long era labelled as 'prehistoric'. The oldest evidence of people in what we now call Wales is from around a quarter of a million years ago. A single human tooth found in the Pontnewydd Cave in the Elwy Valley has been dated to this era. At that time there was a relatively warm interval between the glaciations which for long periods covered all or most of the country during the most recent geological era, the Pleistocene. During these interglacial periods, the land, with a regenerated plant and animal population, was the terrain of small nomadic bands of hunters, armed with stone weapons, who used caves or makeshift shelters. Around them, in a way imperceptible to the passing and short-lived generations, a landscape was evolving. Great changes occurred. Sea level rose and fell and rose again, fluctuating in a range of some 100 to 150 metres (300 to 450 feet). For long periods the British Isles were not isles at all, but part of the European landmass. Other hints of human habitation have been found in Wales, in caves near Laugharne, dating back to around 90,000 years before the Common Era. Still in a vastly remote human past, caves at Pontnewydd and Ffynnon Beuno in the north, and Coygan and Paviland in the south, are believed to have been inhabited off and on during a long 'warm' interval of some 20,000 years between 60,000 and 40,000 BC. Greater evidence is found from the Upper Palaeolithic or Old Stone Age. This epoch of human culture lasted until around 8000 BC. One of its best-known representatives is the 'Red Lady' unearthed from the Goat's Hole Cave at Paviland, in Gower. This skeleton, at first believed to be that of a female, is that of a young man, ceremonially buried with a number of ornaments and an elephant's head, under a covering of red ochre. It was excavated by William Buckland, antiquary and cleric, whose dating of it to the Roman era, despite the prehistoric animal bones, was probably influenced by his belief – shared by most at the time – that the world was only 4,000 years old. The 'Red Lady' has been dated to around 24,000 BC. The nature of the interment shows that the people inhabiting, or visiting, the terrain of Wales had achieved more than a basic subsistence on the earth's surface. They had beliefs and traditions, and the resources to symbolise these.

After that, the ice returned. The final thrust of the ice sheet did not cover all of

Wales; the south-western tip remained clear, though it would have been a bitterly cold and empty stretch of sub-Arctic tundra. A large icecap was centred on Snowdonia, and its glaciers and subsequent melting had a major effect on the geography of north Wales and of the western midlands of England. As the ice receded, the Irish Sea and the Bristol Channel or Severn Sea rose, and the now-familiar outline of Wales, with its two peninsulas and the deep gulf between, became clear. The rising sea invaded the ice-deepened rift valley, north of the Snowdon massif, that now forms the Menai Strait, and Anglesey became an island.

From around 9000 BC, plants, birds and animals began their return to a renewed landscape. Now the mountains, plateaux and valleys that we still see had assumed, or been reduced into, their present shapes. There was thick forest cover of birch, pine, hazel and, later, as the climate grew wetter, oak and alder. The tree line was high, around 750 metres (2,500 feet) so that only the higher peaks rose above it. Rivers much steeper and stronger than their present-day descendants bore away the meltwater and glacial debris from icecaps and glaciers, creating such spectacular scenes as the Devil's Bridge, the Pass of Aberglaslyn and the Wye gorges.

The humans who ventured into this new landscape had acquired new skills and techniques, evolved far to the south and east, where their development had gone on steadily, uninterrupted by climatic change. In the words of Jacquetta Hawkes: 'On what had been open grassland or tundra with a scrub of dwarf birch and willow, forests spread, stocked with the appropriate forest animals – red deer, aurochs (wild ox), and wild pig. With the withdrawal or extinction of the great herds on which they had preyed, the economic basis of the hunting societies was cut away and their carefully adjusted culture made obsolete. This was one of the moments when early man was able to prove the full advantage of his self-made equipment over the biological specialisation of the beasts.' The forest was a wild place – wolves and wolverines prowled there, and bears. Hunters needed effective weapons as well as skill.

Their equipment took the form of the tools and weapons of the Mesolithic cultures. The big, crude flints of earlier times were replaced by 'microliths', enabling finer and more precise work to be done by sharper blades. They developed stone axes that could cut down substantial trees; and used wood for many purposes, including the making of dugout canoes. The population was still very sparse and seminomadic: hunting and foraging were its means of finding food, and every little group must have required about thirty-five or more square kilometres of ground (around twenty square miles) in order to have enough resources to survive. Further changes were on the way. Very slowly, generation by generation, new ways of doing things spread westwards over the continent of Europe. The Mesolithic period lasted about twice as long as our Common Era

The Pass of Aberglasyn in Victorian times

so far has done, from around 8500 to around 4500 BC. By the later stages, many communities were practising a form of pastoralism. Long observation, deduction, trial and error led to gradual progress. From the original wolf strain, dogs were bred and trained. Wild pigs may also have been domesticated. Certain plants were long known to be productive of food and efforts would be made to preserve and conserve them.

EARLY SETTLEMENT

Important changes came about when grain-growing was introduced. New groups of people, from continental Europe, spread slowly across England and into Wales. Some may have come directly by sea to the Welsh coast. They had learned how to sow and grow grain, how to harvest it and convert it into nutritious and storable food. From the grasslands of the continent they brought sheep, horses, goats and cattle, and this was much more significant in Wales, which has always been a stock-rearing rather than a grain-growing land. These people were farmers, who formed permanent or long-term settlements. As their numbers increased, so the Mesolithic period gave way to the Neolithic or New Stone Age. From now on, Wales was no longer an uninhabited landscape, superficially exploited by roving bands. It was seen as a homeland. But it was also joined by economic and perhaps social links to other places. The inhabitants of Stone Age Europe knew where the best resources lay, and would travel great distances to secure them. Flint, for example, was rare in lowland Wales, and quality flints had be imported. Specialised tools, like heavy axes, were also made in specialist workplaces and traded. At Graig Llwyd, on the slope of Penmaenmawr, there was an important source of fine-grained hard stone, with a workshop that sent its products as far away as Essex. The 'factory' spoil heap and chippings can still be seen on the hillside. From such activities arose the basis of trade and economic contact. From its mountain regions Wales also had pelts to offer, including white winter pelts, as well as workable bone and horn, and decorative feathers.

With the development of farming, the population could begin to grow. New techniques could support more people. From about 2200 BC, the method of saving seed corn to enable annual planting was well known, and regular crops of early kinds of wheat – club wheat and emmer – and barley were grown. The need for suitable tools was answered by the development of the hoe and the digging stick. Grinding of the seeds was done between two hard stones, one large and one small. With use the larger stone developed a hollow, making the process easier, and from then the shape of the quern, or stone grinding basin, was defined. Pottery, at first very simple and undecorated, was made to store dry food, water and milk. At this time, the country probably showed a varied pattern of habitation, between the most 'modern' settled communities and others which were still largely focused on the old hunting-gathering methods. It is impossible to assess the degree to which these communities were – or regarded themselves as – a single people. Before this time, the population was tiny. The earlier-established Mesolithic inhabitants may have been killed off by the more highly organised newcomers; or they may have eventually died out 'naturally' as their lifestyle became less and less easy to maintain. There may have been a degree of absorption. The inhabitants of Wales around 2000 BC may have spoken a variety of different languages, but there is evidence of cultural homogeneity.

This is seen in the earliest stone buildings of Wales. Some of the chambered tombs, known as cromlechs, were already more than a thousand years old. Their distribution, with its greatest density in Anglesey, Llyn and Pembroke, reinforces the theory that life in Wales in this era was much more formed by influences coming in from the west, by sea, than from the east, by land. The Stone Age agricultural communities were the first to make their mark upon the landscape, with constructions that rank among the oldest in Europe. Evidently they had acquired the techniques necessary to build substantial stone structures. Equally important, they could support the huge number of man-hours necessary for such building. Slave labour, which would continue to be used in Wales throughout the Celtic era, may have played a part; but even slaves have to be fed, and there must have been a substantial surplus of produce over and above the subsistence level. Another feature of this society which the cromlechs reveal is the depth and intensity of a belief system that prompted the investment of so much wealth and energy into the burial of the dead. As a cult it is comparable with that of the Egyptians, at much the same time; though the monuments of Egypt are the work of a much older, more continuously evolved and vastly more wealthy civilisation. It has been suggested that the development of these monumental graves was the result of a cult that spread northwards, up the western side of Britain, following the route of trade and colonisation, perhaps uniting peoples of different origins and language tradition.

PRE-CELTIC CULTURE

The chambered tombs were used only for the burial of a small number of people, suggesting that there was a social hierarchy in place. It has been further suggested that they were also centres of ritual in other ways than burials, with the implication that a priesthood of some sort existed. There were other sites for ritual assemblies, perhaps other kinds of assembly too, like army musters or seasonal trading fairs. These are the henges, circular open spaces defined by a dyke and a ditch, and often with standing stones at the entrance and in the interior space. Scanty remains of contemporary art can be seen in stonework of this time, mostly simple geometric forms and cup-marks whose symbolism is lost.

Just as 'advanced' and 'primitive' groups coexisted at the end of the Old Stone Age, so the same thing happened as the use of metals slowly spread. For about a thousand years, metal and stone tools were used together; in fact stone and bone implements went on being used in some places well into the Roman era.

Bodowyr Neolithic burial chamber, Brynsiencyn, Anglesey

The first metal items in Wales were made of copper, imported around 2500 BC. These were rare and precious, status symbols perhaps more than usable objects. Copper deposits were being mined not far away in Ireland; and with the opening up of the Cornish tin mines, Wales was quite favourably located for the development of bronze tools and weapons. Prospectors learned how to look for the right kind of rock formations. Small deposits of copper and gold were found in the Welsh mountains, and contributed both to native metalworking and to the export trade.

In recent decades there has been a revolution in the thinking of historians of ancient history. The notion that the British Isles suffered a succession of invasions by technically more advanced peoples, who displaced or disposed of the already-established inhabitants, has been largely abandoned. This change of view is based partly on archaeological discovery and partly on a change of ideology which has left the 'imperialist' invasion-based version of history outmoded. Much more emphasis is placed on steady evolution and gradual change. Such changes flowed in on the back of trading contacts, through knowledge passed on from point to point over a lengthy period, and through small-scale immigration, perhaps of high-status family groups. As a result of all this, the once-important arrival of the 'Beaker Folk' in Wales has been very much played down, and the changes once associated with their invasion, including the abandonment of monumental graves for individual burial sites, and the use of a more decorative kind of 'beaker' pottery, have been ascribed to long-term cultural change within the settled communities. The developments in Wales were much less striking than those which occurred not far away in what is now Wiltshire, where the extraordinary structures of Silbury Hill, Avebury and Stonehenge were raised by a wealthy society known as the Wessex Culture. But Wales played a significant part, since the massive bluestone monoliths of Stonehenge were removed from an already established monumental site in the Preseli Mountains of Pembrokeshire, probably by boat for as much of the way as possible. To quote Jacquetta Hawkes again: 'The journey of at least 200 miles gives insight alike into the unexpected possibilities of prehistoric transport and the great sanctity which must already in Wales have hallowed the bluestones to prompt such a prestigious undertaking.' Stone circles, or their remains, on a smaller scale, can be found in many Welsh moorland locations.

More intensive exploitation of resources included use of the land itself. The advantages of manuring were identified and put into action, increasing productivity in the small fields and promoting the stability of the settlement. Social hierarchies became more developed. The establishment of an aristocratic chieftain-led society is clearly seen in the Wessex Culture, and is likely to have been paralleled, on a more modest scale, in the settlements of Wales. Bronze gave humans the sharpest edge yet found, and they were not slow to employ it in weaponry. As communities became larger and wealthier, and less preoccupied by the sheer need to provide themselves with a subsistence living, they became more aware of one another. Rivalry, envy and fear played part in their relationships. The mobility and speed of the horse, the improvement of weapons, the evolution of a warrior caste who need not trouble themselves with the basics of farming – all encouraged the development of a society which was preoccupied by warfare. Although in fact the amount of actual warfare was probably very small, its cultural importance was relatively much greater. Its effect would be to bring isolated communities into larger groupings, either by conquest or by combining for defence. In these Bronze Age communities, we can perceive the origins of the Celtic society that the Romans would encounter, though that meeting was still more than fifteen hundred years away.

The communities themselves, even if settled in a particular district, were still mobile in one vital way, as indeed they would remain for many centuries to come. Farming was chiefly pastoral, and the movement of stock between the deep valleys and the upper slopes and high plateaux was a major consideration. At least until around 1600 BC, the uplands were inhabited to around 400 metres (1,200 feet) or higher in sheltered places. Many graves are found at this level. After this time, there was a progressive deterioration of the climate. This was particularly marked in Ireland. An important source of trade in earlier times, it now saw a serious reduction in population and much land went back under forest again. A similar pattern in Wales is detectable from a number of sources. Colder, wetter and windier weather drove the population, human and animal, downhill. Use of the uplands became much more seasonal, with a transfer to the high ground only for the summer months. Archaeological remains suggest a degree of impoverishment, with little to be found between around 1400 BC and the advent of iron use. Burial sites are hard to trace and their contents are scanty.

CHAPTER TWO

Celtic Wales

WHO WERE THE CELTS?

The development of Celtic culture in Wales was formerly identified with the arrival in the country of Celtic colonists, who brought with them not only a language and customs which had developed in continental Europe, but also the secret of ironworking. Their possession of this latest step in human technology enabled them to achieve dominance over the already established inhabitants. Since the abandonment of the invasion theory, this rather neat explanation has had to be reconsidered and a somewhat more complex picture emerges.

From 1200 BC or earlier, there was a people, or peoples, who lived in south central Europe and who were later identified by both Greeks and Romans as 'Celts'. This was a very broad definition, comparable with that of 'Scythians' for the peoples who lived to the north of the Celts, in a band of Europe stretching from Scandinavia far into Russia. There are few references to the Celts before around 400 BC.

The language, or languages, that they spoke belonged to the Indo-European family, as did Greek, Latin and the later Germanic tongues. There were a number of resemblances between it and the Italic group, though whether these were caused by two sets of language speakers living in contiguity with each other, rather than any kind of joint descent from a single ancestral Indo-European language, is a matter for speculation. By around 1000 BC early forms of the Celtic speech had evolved, and by 600 BC were being spoken in the Iberian Peninsula, in Ireland, and in North Italy.

Around the year 1200 BC, historians of the ancient world have identified a period of dramatic change. In a relatively short space of time the east Mediterranean civilisation, which included the wealthy and advanced kingdoms of Minoan Crete, Mycenae, and the Hittites in Asia Minor, entered a state of collapse. The result of this was a disruption of many channels of trade and international contact, and an eventual shift northwards of the dynamic centre of power and trade to central Europe. The culture of this area was labelled the Urnfield Culture, since one of its most traceable characteristics was large-scale burial sites with the burnt remains of the cremated bodies placed in urns. From other archaeological records it is known to have been a warrior society, with the strong emphasis on personal display that is almost invariably found with such a system: 'The great bronze cauldrons, bronze and gold cups decorated in repoussé style and the elaborate weapon sets of the Urnfield period are the outward and visible signs of these otherwise hidden social systems' (Chadwick, *The Celts*, p. 25).

As the Urnfield civilisation spread, so its demand for imported raw materials grew greater and its own influence radiated out across a vast extent of northern and north-western Europe. Such influence was generated not only by its commercial demands but also by its innovations in art and social life. In all fields, including religion, its prestige would have been great, and there would be much respectful and enquiring interest from far afield in the way of life exemplified by the increasingly flamboyant courts of the magnates. Probably few individuals travelled from Wales to these places, or made the trip in the opposite direction. Much of the trade was organised on a sort of pass-it-on basis, from community to community, until the goods reached their destination. Knowledge was handed on in much the same fashion. The process of language expansion went along the same lines also, perhaps stimulated by enthusiasm to acquire the new speech. In the words of Professor Barry Cunliffe: '... if the socio-religious package of Urnfield practice, with its attendant infrastructure of language, was thought to be desirable as a mode of élite expression, then it would have been quickly assimilated into the culture of the Atlantic communities' (in Chadwick, *The Celts*, p. 28). Wales, of course, formed part of this Atlantic zone.

In the later Bronze Age, during the eighth and seventh centuries BC, a dynamic part of the Urnfield culture arose in the Austrian mountains, supported by the wealth generated from the salt deposits of Hallstatt. Salt was already a precious mineral resource, vital in food preserving and preparation. In addition to bronze, iron began to be worked here, perhaps from the eighth century, the techniques imported from further east. A Hallstatt sword was a powerful totem as well as a dangerous weapon, and from the later Hallstatt period, swords were exported as far away as Ireland. Local smiths copied the designs and the Hallstatt pattern was reproduced in many places. The cemetery site at Hallstatt, when excavated, revealed remarkable burials of high-status goods, including a wheeled cart and much horse gear. The wheel had been known for a long time, but the invention of the metal tyre, shrunk on to the rim, appears to have been made by the Celts. Metalworking had always been a highly specialised craft, practised by a small number of workers and no doubt closely supervised by the rulers. The advent of iron enhanced this specialism. The new metal was so much more effective, adaptable and durable than bronze that it might have been seen as having magic qualities even without the deliberate creation of a cult around the activities of the blacksmith (who would become an important and honourable figure in the Celtic community). By the later centuries BC, with the expansion of Greek colonies and the rise of Republican Rome, the centre of continental Celtic culture had moved further west. It is typified by the site of La Tène, on Lake Neuchatel in Switzerland, close to the north–south trading route that stretched between the Greek city of Massilia (Marseilles) on the Mediterranean Sea, and the coasts of north-west Europe. The La Tène culture arose around the fifth century and lasted until the first century BC and the Roman invasions of Gaul. La Tène was to have an influence on 'insular Celtic' art in Britain and Ireland long after it had been subsumed into the Gallo-Roman civilisation, and numerous artefacts in this style have been found in Wales.

The Cerrig-y-Drudion 'bowl' – a Celtic decorated artefact found in a stone-lined grave in the county of Conwy in 1924

THE EARLY CELTS IN WALES:
THE EVIDENCE OF LANGUAGE

The inhabitants of Wales were of course on the periphery of this thousand-year flourishing of Celtic language and Celtic art within the heart of Europe. Not only that, after about 600 BC, there is very little evidence of the kind of links that had been kept up earlier. This has been related to a period of severe climatic deterioration which reduced populations and limited any sort of contact with the wider world. This was again particularly serious in Ireland, and these centuries of relative isolation have been linked to the preservation there of a more archaic form of Celtic language than that of continental Europe and of Britain. What language or languages were spoken by the inhabitants of Wales before they adopted a Celtic form, we do not know, any more than we can be certain of the process by which the Celtic form spread through the population. We can surmise that this happened first with the upper levels of society and was gradually picked up, generation by generation, by the rest. It is notable, though, that in the first century the Romans found essentially the same language was spoken throughout the whole of Britain south of the Forth–Clyde line in Scotland. The process was not limited to Wales. Such uniformity of speech suggests close connections between the tribal groups of Wales, as they emerge from prehistory, and those of south Britain. This pre-Welsh language has been labelled Brittonic or Brythonic. It stems from the 'Common Celtic' that also evolved into the Gaulish language. Both share the linguistic changes that Irish Gaelic never adopted, notably the change of the *k*- or *q*- sound into *p*- . Thus 'four' in Welsh became *pedwar*, whilst in Gaelic it was *ceithir*, closer to the Latin form *quattuor*; 'head' in Welsh became *pen*, whilst in Gaelic it was *ceann*; hence the often-found references to the languages as being *p*-Celtic and *q*-Celtic respectively.

It is important to bear in mind that Brittonic came to be spoken by the same people whose ancestors had lived in Wales for many generations previously. Any admixture of colonists from Europe was likely to be so small as to be of imperceptible influence. Incomers from Ireland – unless, as is possible, there were groups in Ireland who spoke a *p*-Celtic language – are also unlikely. To what degree Brittonic spread into Wales from the tribes of south Britain is harder to gauge. The inhabitants of Kent and Sussex were much closer and more immediately accessible to the coast of Gaul than were those of Wales. On the other hand, in the first century BC, transport into Britain seems to have been virtually the monopoly of the Veneti tribe, living on the coast of what is now Brittany. To them, Cornwall and Wales would have been readily accessible, and there was a long-established trade route by sea down to the mouth of the Garonne and inland from there. Language dissemination could have passed through Wales in an eastward and north-eastward direction.

It is an interesting footnote to Welsh history that the language, which in latter years was to become the very bastion, gauge and banner of Welshness, should be an import by origin, albeit one honoured by long history and usage. As most scholars are nowadays concerned to stress, it is only in the area of language that the word 'Celtic' has any real objective meaning.

HILL-FORTS, WEAPONS AND TOOLS

Among the concepts imported into south Britain from the Hallstatt culture was that of fortification. Prior to the seventh century, it is likely that the inhabitants were more concerned to protect their settlements from the attacks of wild animals than from the attacks of other communities. Wood was the chief, probably the only, building material, apart from daub, straw and leaves. No stone dwelling from before the Iron Age (around 500 BC) has been identified in Wales. A simple palisade of stakes is likely to have been the protection of most homes. In central Europe, however, where riches and rivalries were at a far higher level, protection from one another became more important. Hill-forts, surrounded by massive ramparts, were established, often with whole 'towns' inside for the population to reside, or seek protection, in. Hill-forts had already been established in Wales, perhaps as early as 1000 BC, but in the middle of the millennium, their numbers increased rapidly. Of the more than five hundred hill-forts identified, many are relatively small, the majority being of less than five hectares in extent, and some two hundred being under half a hectare: refuges for an extended family group and their animals rather than true forts. The builders of these forts were principally pastoralists, though they also cultivated wheat, barley and flax in small fields where shelter allowed. Evidence of metalworking has also been found at some fort sites, such as Dinorben in Denbighshire and Breidden in Powys; at these forts the patronage and protection of a local chief or king allowed the bronze- and tin-smiths to practise their craft in security. Many forts were used only on particular occasions, such as special assemblies for trade or ritual, apart from serving as refuges. Over the centuries they were often rebuilt, extended or reduced.

Hill-forts were built throughout Wales, though they are fewest in the most mountainous regions. Their concentration is greatest in the south-west, though the majority here are small. Often they are coastal features, utilising the ridges running seawards by having a wall placed across the neck of the resulting promontory. Anyone walking the Pembroke coastal path will come across 'cliff castles' of this type. Larger forts are more common on the eastern side, where a sequence follows the line of the Black Mountains and the Berwyns, overlooking the Wye and Severn Valleys. Among the largest is Llanymynech, in a district where copper was mined. In the same region, Oswestry Old Fort is one of the best preserved in site and outline, its rampart walls and ditches still sharp and steep in profile. The huts within the forts, ranging in number from one or two to 150 or more, were round houses. A thick wall of stones and turf, with a single entrance, provided a base for a pitched roof of thatch, with a central smoke-hole for the fire. The building of hill-forts effectively came to an end with the Roman occupation.

Until recently, historians linked the introduction of ironworking into Wales with the arrival of a 'Celtic' people, whose iron weapons and tools were an important factor in their achieving domination over the inhabitants who were still practising a Bronze Age technology. The notion of the sudden importation of iron has been abandoned in favour of that of a much more gradual process, similar to that which also transmitted changes of language and culture. The oldest iron artefact found in Wales is a sword, from Llyn Fawr, in the mountains above the Rhondda, dating from about 600 BC. At such a time, it would have

---

WELSH MYTHOLOGY: THE *MABINOGI*

The oldest traditions of Welsh speakers are preserved in this collection, its full title *Pedair Cainc y Mabinogi* ('The Four Branches of the *Mabinogi*', which may mean 'tale of youth'). The branches are the tales of *Pwll*, *Branwen*, *Manawydan* and *Math*; although the surviving manuscript sources belong to the fourteenth century, the tales clearly belong to a much older period. First collated in the twelfth century, their origins go far back in the oral tradition, linking the stories of mortals to those of divine or semi-divine beings. *Pwll* deals with the exploits of a ruler of Dyfed, who travels to the Otherworld, marries Rhiannon, and is father of Pryderi. *Branwen* tells the story of the offspring of the sea-god Llyr, and brings Ireland into the action, recounting how the giant ruler of Britain, Bendigeidfran (Bran), whose seat is at Harlech, gives his sister Branwen in marriage to the Irish king Matholwch, but invades Ireland when Matholwch treats Branwen dishonourably. *Manawydan* recounts how the brother of Bendigeidfran retrieves Rhiannon (whom he has married after Pwll's death), and Pryderi from a magical spell. *Math* is the son of Mathonwy, and rules Gwynedd. The story that bears his name is a complicated but highly exciting tale of heroism, love, adultery and vengeance. Among its characters are Gwydion the magician, his sister Arianrhod ('Silver Disc'), mother of the twins Dylan and Lleu Law Gyffes ('fair one of the steady hand'); and Blodeuedd, the woman made from flowers who forsakes Lleu for the hunter Gronw Pebyr.

The most authoritative manuscript form is in the *Red Book of Hergest*, compiled between c.1382 and 1410, largely by the scribe Hywel Fychan fab Howel Goch o Fuellt, which also contains other ancient texts. The *Mabinogi* stories, plus others, are also recorded in the *White Book of Rhydderch*, written down around 1325, probably at a site in Deheubarth. Fragments are also found in other fifteenth-century manuscripts. The first English version was Lady Charlotte Guest's *Mabinogion* of 1838–49, which also included other legends from the *Red Book of Hergest*, including *Culhwch ac Olwen*, *Breuddwyd Rhonabwy* ('The Dream of Rhonabwy'), *Breuddwyd Macsen Wledig* ('The Dream of Magnus Maximus'), and other tales which combine historical and mythical characters.

been among the first and very few of its kind. This remarkably preserved weapon, probably made in Britain, is of Hallstatt style in such details as the chape, or base-plate, of the scabbard. An iron sickle, made on the model of an older bronze one, was also found, as well as bronze spearhead and axeheads, and two bronze cauldrons. Some writers believe that the Llyn Fawr items were thrown there for hiding, by raiders caught with their booty; but they may also have been placed as sacrificial offerings.

For a long time, iron remained a prestige metal, and bronze, stone and bone also remained very much in use. From this era grew the legend of the smith-god Gofannon, incorporated into old Welsh mythology as a son of the mother-goddess Don, and who in the *Mabinogi* sharpens the plough of Amaethon for Culhwch.

During World War II, when the runways at RAF Valley were being extended in connection with the defence of the Western Approaches, a remarkable hoard of ancient weapons and other artefacts was discovered at Llyn Cerrig Bach. This was almost certainly a cult area, where these items, including many iron pieces of harness, were offered to the gods. Some may have been made locally – clearly Anglesey was a rich and heavily populated island in the early Iron Age – but others have been traced to workshops in Ireland and different parts of south Britain. Many of them show clear influence of the La Tène style in their design and decoration.

THE TRIBES OF WALES

By the end of the first century BC, the population of Wales had formed itself, or been formed, into a number of distinctive tribal groups. Their names, awarded by the Romans, may have been based on their own names for them-selves, or their own names for one another. In the south-west were the Demetae; east of them the Silures; in the north-west, perhaps including Anglesey, were the Deceangli; the region stretching from Snowdonia towards Pumlumon was occupied by the Ordovices; and the eastern side along the Severn river was the home of the Cornovii. These groups may have been further subdivided into smaller tribes and chieftaincies, but if so, nothing is known of them, and the Romans found it possible to treat with each of the five as a single autonomous unit.

Their organisation corresponded with that of the tribes living in what is now England, although at this time no Angle had yet landed there. The entire terri-tory was inhabited by Brittonic-speaking tribes. Little is known in detail of how the tribes in Wales functioned. Some signs can be gathered from the archaeo-logical record. The many small forts of the Demetae, for instance, suggest a tribal structure based on small groups, probably members of an extended family, and without a strong central authority. Whilst small forts are found in the territories of the other tribes, they are dominated by larger ones, suggesting both a larger overall population and more important centres of authority. No site is known definitely to have been that of a tribal over-king, though Llanmelin, in the lands of the Silures, is a strong candidate for their principal centre. It was deliberately replaced by the Romans with the cantonal centre of Venta Silurum (later Caerwent).

If the tribes of Wales shared the same laws and customs as those in south Britain, like the Iceni and the Brigantes, then at times they may also have had ruling queens, like Boudica and Cartimandua in the latter tribes. The extent to which comments made about other Celtic-speaking tribes and nations, over a very long period of time, can be applied to those of Wales is difficult to judge. Many writers have commented on the consistency of Celtic culture. John Davies points out that: 'Their culture had a tenacious longevity. The characteristics of the Celts, as described by the classical authors, can be clearly discerned a millennium later in the laws and the myths of the Irish; half a millennium later still the same characteristics may be seen in the society portrayed in the *Mabinogi*, and in centuries yet later still there is more than an echo of them in the social order praised by the Welsh poets.' This has the truth of a general statement, but 'Celtic' societies showed a good deal of variety within their sameness, and it would be rash to apply more than the most general qualities to the tribes of Wales. Nor did the customs and habits of the peoples remain static. To mention only the most dramatic cultural change, the advent of Christianity, with its theology, its view of our place in the world, and its concept of an afterlife, brought a radical alteration in the attitudes to life and death of the pagan Celtic-speaking peoples. Contemporary details of pre-Christian culture in Wales are virtually non-existent, though there is one striking and lurid exception. The earliest written records in Welsh are all from much later.

Quite apart from any doubt as to how far the classical references to the Celts can be said to apply to the Celtic-speaking tribes of Wales, those references themselves need to be treated with care. The great majority are from Roman sources. In the last centuries BC and the early centuries AD, Rome, first under the Republic and then under the Empire, was a vigorously expanding mercantile empire with a strong militarist philosophy. It was the Roman army that built the roads which later were also used for trade and commerce. The Roman army achieved the conquests which brought vast new provinces under Roman rule. Law and order, learning, all the aspects of ancient civilisation, followed on, but only in the wake of the most efficient terror and killing machine that human ingenuity had yet devised. A Roman army, armoured, trained, thoroughly drilled, armed with the best and latest weapons, was unbeatable except in the most exceptional circumstances. It could take on and defeat greatly superior numbers of 'barbarians' with small losses to itself. The Romans brought war wherever they went, until they obtained the surrender of those who stood in their way. Some of the more thoughtful Roman writers, including Tacitus, who came to Wales with Agricola's army, knew this. But others, writing propaganda, or obsessed by a notion of Rome's Imperial mission to rule the world, failed completely to note who was the aggressor. For such writers, the Celts were 'war mad', because they fought back against invaders who took their land, stole the treasures from their temples, raped their women, took them as slaves, and imposed a harsh and alien rule which included heavy taxation. The benefits of Roman civilisation, real as they were, were also dearly bought. To justify their own invasions, and the rapine which followed, the Romans were happy to brand the Celts not only as obsessed with fighting, but also as the practitioners of dark and horrible cultic rites.

In his *Gallic Wars*, Julius Caesar records of the tribes he encountered in Gaul that:

> *The whole Gallic people is exceedingly given to religious superstition. There-fore those who are suffering from serious illness or who are in the midst of the dangers of battle, either put to death human beings as sacrificial victims or take a vow to do so, and the druids take part in these sacrifices; for they believe that unless one human life is given in exchange for another the power of the almighty gods cannot be appeased. Sacrifices of this kind are also offered for the needs of the state. Some tribes build enormous images with limbs of interwoven branches which they then fill with live men; the images are set alight and the men die in a sea of flame.*

These vast wickerwork cages, assembled in rudimentary imitation of a human form, and turned into holocausts of human beings, exercised a powerful influence on the Romans' imagination. Other writers mention them. But even Caesar, often so precise, does not say which tribes made them, or that he himself saw such things occur. Whilst they may have happened, it is also possible that such stories, received as true by later centuries, are fabrications or exaggerations. The demonising of the enemy side in warfare is probably as old as warfare itself.

CELTIC SOCIETY

It is reasonable to assume that Celtic society in Wales was aristocratically organised. An upper class of warriors and priests formed its leading citizens. From a small number of families, a king or chief could be chosen, by virtue of his descent and his abilities. It was necessary for him to be of royal descent – son, nephew, grandson or great-grandson of a king. The chief ability was that of being able to impose or enforce his own ambitions above those of other claimants. Following a very ancient tradition, the king would unite the warrior and the priestly aspects of the tribe's life in his own person. He would play an important part in many of the rites performed by the druids. He would also lead the warriors in battle. An important function of later kings – the making of law – may not have been part of his role, although the maintenance of established law and practice would have been. Amongst the upper class, but also forming a group of somewhat lower status, was a range of professionals, including law men, doctors, carpenters, smiths, boatwrights, and, not least, scholars and poets. Such functions were probably largely hereditary, though promising boys from the lower orders may have been brought in, particularly if there was a shortage of talent.

Although by the last century BC some of the tribes of Britain were using coinage, this does not seem to have been true of the tribes of Wales. Gold objects were highly prized, but the true measure of wealth was in cows. This reflects both the importance of the by now long-established tradition of stock-rearing, and also the ultimate significance of the land itself. It was the land that sustained the herds. In return the people did much to express their gratitude, anxiety and devotion to the life-giving soil. Seasonal rituals, sacrifice and cere-mony were practised for many centuries before the mundane effectiveness of manuring – another contribution from the cow – was also found to be helpful. The landworkers formed another segment of society. Probably as bondmen to members of the warrior class, they tilled the soil and cared for the animals. They were not required to fight, although from this group may have come chariot drivers – in the era up to around AD 100 when war chariots were still in use – and other supporters required by a noble warrior on the battlefield, such as spear-carriers. All these groups participated to a degree in the life of the tribe, sharing its traditions, its sense of identity and its aspirations, if any. Even in the hierarchic structure, a strong sense of kinship is possible, as seen in the Scottish clans up to the eighteenth century. Below the landworkers was a group with no rights or involvement – the slaves. Prisoners of war or victims of raids, they no doubt accounted for much of the hard work, like stone-carrying and earth-moving. Their numbers are impossible to assess. Mortality among them is likely to have been higher than among the regular tribespeople, though successful raiding could always increase the numbers.

Even before the Roman geographer Strabo characterised the Celts as war mad, there is plenty of evidence of them having been engaged in warfare in different parts of Europe. However – apart from times of outside invasion, as when the Romans came to Wales in the first century BC – it is not at all clear that the ancient Celts waged war among themselves in the same way that European nations have done from the medieval period onwards. Although not much of the evidence comes directly from ancient Wales, it would appear that war between, or even within, tribes was a largely ritualised affair. Large armies are mentioned in ancient Irish literature, yet much of the fighting is done by individual champions, or small groups of champions, belonging to the warrior class. Such combats probably had a set form. Closely involved was the well-attested cult of the head. They were headhunters, not in an indiscriminate way, but prizing the decapitated skull of a noble and worthy enemy above almost any other possession. The gates to a fort or the doorway of a house might be decorated by such trophies; the best ones were decorated with gold and kept in ornamental chests. The 'common people' of the tribe may scarcely have been involved in such activities, other than in religious rites before and after such contests.

Feasting, gift-giving, and opulent display played an important part in the lives of the leaders of these tribal groups. Both within the tribe, and among the tribes, it was important, and expected, for a king or champion to display his riches. It was however a society in which wealth basically flowed upwards: the distribution of gifts did not represent a distribution of wealth through the tribe. Rather, the efforts of the lower echelons enhanced the 'capacity-for-display' of the upper one without altering their own lot by very much.

It has often been speculated that the warrior-priest class may have been a different people to the others; that they – rather as the Normans were to do later – were able to establish dominance over larger groups of earlier inhabitants. This in turn has been related to the 'Celtification' of Wales, on the supposition that such small groups may have imported the language and its attendant traditions. There is insufficient evidence either to prove or disprove such a theory; on the whole, scholars are sceptical of it. It is quite possible for the aristocratic society, forms of which are found also among the Gaels of Ireland and the Picts of Caledonia, to have developed rather than to have been imposed.

Thus we can look, at the beginning of the Common Era, at a society long-established in the land, with ancient traditions and a strong conservative strain. Apart from Pictland, it was in essentials the same throughout the island, from western Wales up into the southern uplands of Scotland, across to the Wash and down to Cornwall. Their world for long had been a settled one, with no one to molest them but one another. At this time, however, there were signs of change. In the south-eastern part of south Britain, for a hundred years or more, large numbers of new arrivals had been coming in from northern Europe, settling, and disputing land and borders with the old-established tribes. These were Belgic tribesfolk, speakers of a Gaulish language quite similar to Brittonic.

Displaced partly by war with the Teutonic peoples to the east, they were also refugees moving away from the steadily advancing front of Roman conquest. The ambitious, brilliant and ruthless Roman general, Julius Caesar, was pushing out the frontier of the Roman Empire, setting up his new province upon the dead bodies of a million Gauls.

CHAPTER THREE

Roman Wales

THE CONQUEST

It was not in Caesar's time, however, that the tribes of Wales were to experience the advance guards of Roman civilisation. His brief exploratory invasion of 55 BC was not followed up until long after his assassination and the subsequent turmoil which ended with the establishment of the Roman Empire under his nephew, Augustus. Ninety-eight years later, in AD 43, another Roman invasion was launched, and this time it was intended to result in permanent occupation of the British island. By 47, the south-eastern part was under Roman rule from a capital set up at Colchester. This had been the land of the Catuvellauni, a Belgic tribe headed by Cunobelin (Cynfelin in Welsh tradition). One of his sons, Caratacus, fled to the Silures, the powerful tribe whose main base was Llanmelin. Persuaded by him as to their likely fate as Roman expansion continued, the Silures and Ordovices attacked the new colony. But there was no unity among all the still-independent tribes of Britain. Such large neighbouring tribes as the Iceni had not been displeased to see the threat of the Catuvellauni neutralised. At first they were favourably disposed towards the Romans, but when the Romans set out to disarm them, they became hostile. The Roman army had to defeat the Iceni before it was in a position to concentrate its efforts on the hostile tribes of the west. The task was not easy. In the words of Professor Sheppard Frere, the historian of Roman Britain: 'The Silures in south-east Wales, guided at first by Caratacus' brilliant leadership, were to prove themselves the toughest and most successful opponents which the Roman army was to encounter in these islands' (*Britannia*, p. 62).

Ostorius Scapula, the governor and general in charge, identified the means by which not only he but also later strategists would seek to neutralise any threat from Wales. He moved into the Cheshire Gap, the area of relatively flat ground between the upland regions of north Wales and the Pennine Chain of England, though here he had to be careful not to antagonise the tribal federation of the Brigantes under their queen, Cartimandua. In 48 he is recorded as receiving the submission of the Deceangli: with this entry in Tacitus' *Annals* Wales comes into written history. From this time dates the importance of Shrewsbury (originally as the Roman town of Wroxeter) as a control point on the corridor into Wales though the Llangollen Valley. An entire legion would eventually be based here. The other key area was the lowland route from Gloucester into south

Wales, and in 49 a fortress was established at Kingsholm near present-day Gloucester, followed by a permanent military colony. Roads were built to link these key points and to join them to the safer regions to the east. It is likely that there were also naval operations along the south Wales coast and up the Bristol Channel. Caratacus, around 51, moved to the wilder and more broken territory of the Ordovices. In guerrilla-type attacks, the tribes could harass the Romans, but not strike a deathblow. But in a pitched battle, they did not have the weight to break the Roman armour and discipline. In a battle in the hills, perhaps at a site west of Caersws, Caratacus tried his fortunes in such an encounter, and was defeated. He was able to flee to the Brigantes, where his presence was a serious embarrassment to Cartimandua, trying to preserve an uneasy alliance with the Romans. She had him captured and handed him over to the grateful Romans. He was sent to Rome and put to death, but his memory remained green among the tribes; his name was an inspiration, and Caer Caradoc, Caratacus' fort, still rises above the valley between Wenlock Edge and the Wrekin. The struggle continued. Scapula died in 52, and before his successor Didius Gallus arrived, the Silures defeated a Roman legion – probably the Twentieth – in open battle, a remarkable achievement. It was not the kind of thing the Romans normally forgave, but, under orders from Emperor Claudius in Rome, Gallus consolidated the frontier rather than making a punitive invasion, and was able to hold the Silures at bay.

In the year 57, under a new emperor, Nero, and a new governor of Britain, Quintus Veranius, the policy of containment no longer sufficed. Under Veranius and his successor Suetonius Paullinus, the Roman army took its revenge on the Silures. They were subdued, if not wholly conquered, and by 60 Paullinus was master of the north. He had crushed the Deceangli and was preparing to mount an attack on Anglesey. This great island was important for a number of reasons. It was a source of wealth from its copper mines, and its fields grew grain that fed the northern tribes. It was also a centre of great spiritual and political import. Writers of the time named it as the centre of the druidic cult.

THE ROMANS AND THE DRUIDS

The concept of the druid, radically changed though it is nowadays, never quite went away in Wales. At the time of the Roman attacks, the druids were clearly seen by the invaders as a power that must be smashed, before their own authority and their own systems, including their system of worship, could be introduced. As a result of this, what Roman writers say about the druids should be treated with some caution. Julius Caesar leaves us in no doubt about their importance among the Gauls: 'The druids are concerned with the worship of the gods, look after public and private sacrifice, and expound religious matters. A large number of young men flock to them for training and hold them in high honour. For they have the right to decide nearly all public and private disputes and they also pass judgement and decide rewards and penalties in criminal and murder cases and in disputes concerning legacies and boundaries' (*Gallic Wars*). Caesar may have been confusing the role of druids and lawmen here, though at that time a clear separation of functions may not have taken place. Dr Anne Ross in *Druids* notes that: 'The words used for this tripartite order, which is found in Europe and in the British Isles, are Gaulish as recorded by the classics: *Druides*, "priest-philosophers", *Vates* or *Manteis*, "diviners or prophets", and the *Bardi*, "panegyric poets"' (p. 16). The Welsh for 'druid' is *derwydd* or *dryw* (Dr Ross notes that this latter word also means 'wren', a bird sacred to the druids). Religion was a central element in the society of the Celtic-speaking peoples, and the druids, with their arts of divination, their management of ritual, and their high social rank, were among the leaders.

Anglesey, or Mon, was a great centre – perhaps at this time the principal centre – of the druidic cult. Its fertility and long history of habitation were probably the main reasons. From all the sources available, it is clear that the cult was very much based on sustaining and celebrating the productivity of the soil. Its great seasonal festivals occurred at times significant in the agricultural year. It is likely that there was a college of druidical teaching on the island. There must also have been a great temple site, perhaps associated with the great deposits of weapons, bones and artefacts found in the lake at Llyn Cerrig Bach. The influence of the druids of Mon stretched as far as Gaul. The first-century Roman writer, Pliny, noted that druidism was a practice that had crossed the ocean (by which he may have meant the sea between Britain and Europe) and that: 'At the present day, Britannia is still fascinated by magic, and performs its rites with so much ceremony that it almost seems as though it was she who had imparted the cult to the Persians' (*Natural History*).

For the Roman military, the important thing about the druids was that their cult sustained the independence of the Celtic-speaking tribes and their priests were leaders in organising the resistance to Roman occupation and rule. To attack and destroy their chief centre was therefore a prime strategic aim. A few blood-curdling stories about gory rituals helped both to whip up the ardour of the troops and to keep home opinion favourable. In his *Annals*, the Roman historian, Tacitus, memorably described the confrontation on the shores of the Menai strait: 'On the shore stood the opposing army with its dense array of armed warriors while between the ranks dashed women in black attire like the Furies, with hair dishevelled, waving burning brands. All around, the druids, lifting up their hands to heaven and pouring forth dreadful imprecations, struck

Iron Age metalwork from the time of the druids of Mon, including slave chains, found in the lake at Lyn Cerrig Bach in 1943

fear into our soldiers by the unfamiliar sight, so that, as if their limbs were paralysed, they stood motionless and exposed to injuries. Then urged by their general's appeal and mutual encouragements not to quail before a troop of frenzied women, they bore the standards onwards, smote down all resistance, and wrapped the foe in the flames of his own brands. A force was next set over the conquered, and their groves, devoted to inhuman superstitions, were destroyed. They deemed it, indeed, a duty to cover their altars with the blood of captives and to consult their deities through human entrails.'

THE RECONQUEST OF WALES

Almost immediately, the Romans were distracted by the uprising of the Iceni under Boudicca, which almost lost them their new colony. By the end of the year, the tribes knew that the Romans had regained control, but Wales, though much ravaged, was not yet conquered. It was more than a decade before the legions reappeared in force. Governors of Britannia had first to reinstate their shattered province. They were also troubled by hostility among the Brigantian tribes of the north. On their western flank, the tribes of Wales remained a dangerous threat. It was in 74 that operations to neutralise this threat began, under the governor, Sextus Julius Frontinus. From a new fortress at Gloucester, and harbours between there and Bristol, he launched a major attack, probably seaborne. Strong points were established on the Glamorgan coast, to act as bases for operations into the valleys; and at least thirteen 'marching camps' – short-term, ditch-protected sites – have been located. Evidently a very large Roman force was engaged, perhaps the greater part of three legions. Frontinus also launched a heavy onslaught on the Ordovices further north. By 79 the great fortress of Deva (Chester), intended as the headquarters of a legion, was under construction. In the north-west the Deceangli had never recovered from the savage battering from Suetonius Paullinus's army in 70; and it seems that the Romans were mining lead in their territory at least from 74. Anglesey, however, had been lost to the Romans, and was not reconquered until the new governor, Gnaeus Julius Agricola, regained it in 78. Agricola's campaign across the north was close to genocidal. The Ordovices had stormed a Roman fort and defeated a cavalry regiment, and the subsequent Roman reprisals were savage. In the south, too, the war was ferocious. 'The Silures were not easily quelled. Neither lenity nor rigorous measures could induce them to submit,' wrote Tacitus (*Annals*). By 79, however, the Romans could regard the conquest of the Welsh tribes as all but complete, and with his flank secured, Agricola pressed on with his campaigns to the north.

The tribes had been forcibly subdued rather than brought into the famous *pax Romana*. Agricola established around twenty forts to keep control, holding around 10,000 troops. The pattern was clearly established. To the east, the three great legionary centres at Gloucester, Wroxeter and Chester controlled the ways out and in, and were themselves linked by a north–south road. Another large fortress was established at Isca (Caerleon), with a road along the coastal plain to Cardiff and on to Carmarthen, another, known in Welsh as Sarn Helen, inland; and yet another running up the Usk Valley to Brecon and on to link with a western road running north from Carmarthen to Pennal, where it met a road coming in from Wroxeter via Caersws. Roads between Chester and Caernarfon looped around the Snowdonia mountains; at the latter place, engineering works included aqueducts to ensure a water supply. The tribes were well and truly boxed in. Only in the south-west, the territory of the Demetae, were there no Roman forts (apart from Carmarthen, their former tribal centre), suggesting either that they had made peace, or perhaps that they had been largely wiped out. Fifty years after Agricola, in the reign of Emperor Hadrian, there were still at least fourteen forts in use, garrisoned by around 9,500 men. Sheppard Frere notes evidence of unrest in Wales in the mid-second century: '… unrest or rebellion in Wales would seem to be suggested by certain troop movements. The second forts at Leintwardine (Herefordshire) and at Walltown in the Marches may belong to this period, and forts were rebuilt also in Wales about this time at Forden, Coelbren and Caernarvon' (p. 146). How far tribes in Wales kept contact with those north of the Roman colony is not known. At least one tribe to the north of Hadrian's Wall, the Votadini or Gododdin (who would have strong links with Wales in times to come) were allies of the Romans almost throughout the whole Roman occupation of Britain. There is evidence of further fighting in central Wales at the end of the second century, but the occupiers did not lose control. In the south-east, however, the Silures gradually accepted Roman rule, and their territory became the most Romanised part of the country.

LIFE UNDER THE ROMANS

By the reign of Emperor Diocletian (284–305), Wales was part of a province known as Britannia Prima, whose civil government was based at Cirencester (Roman Corinium). There are signs of civilian settlements as well as military forts: at Carmarthen, the Roman town of Moridunum, which probably began as a trading site outside the army depot, was established in the mid-second century, with a little grid of streets and a public amphitheatre; at Venta Silurum, where a town (Caerwent) built as a settlement of veteran soldiers also became a centre for the semi-Romanised Silures, there is further evidence of civic construction, including water pipes.

By this time, the town of Venta Silurum, like others in Roman Britain, had also been recently surrounded by walls – an indication of internal insecurity. Although a modest town even by the standards of the time, with a population estimated around 2,500, it did not lack amenities. Frere notes that: 'One of the compartments in the forum of Caerwent produced remains suggestive of an oyster bar' (p. 251). Like Moridunum, it also had an amphitheatre for gladiatorial and other shows.

Outside the Roman forts and townships, the Celtic-speaking tribesfolk carried on living in much the same way as they had always done, at least in terms of accommodation and style of agriculture. Raising cattle and cultivating the little rectangular fields with primitive implements like digging sticks and hand-ploughs, continued. Round houses were still built, though under Roman influence some were put up on a rectangular plan. Most people perhaps still lived at a level which did not require the coinage in circulation. Close to the centre at Caerleon were quite different settlements, Roman-type villas: more like large country farm-estates than anything else. As well as the landowner's house, built round its courtyard in standard Roman fashion, it had outhouses, sheds and barns to accommodate the work, the workers and their produce. The famous villa excavated at Llantwit Major, with its own bath-house, is the best-known example. Estates almost as large were founded in the vicinity of the fort and Roman town at Carmarthen. Slaves were the basic workforce on these estates. The Romans were keen exploiters of what-

Roman ruins at Caerwent (Venta Silurum)

ever the land could offer, so long as it was worth a merchant's investment, and they were mining gold at Dolaucothi, near Carmarthen, on an industrial scale, using water power, and employing both open-cast and tunnelling techniques. Such enterprises were under strict Imperial control, though contractors might have been employed to do the work. Lead and silver were extracted in the north, around Flint, where coal was also mined for the smelting furnaces; and copper continued to be mined in Anglesey. Although the great bulk of mineral product was removed to Britannia, or further afield, native metalworking still persisted outside areas of Roman influence, and brooches and ornamental metal wares decorated in the La Tène style continued to be made.

Although the Romans sought to stamp out the cult of the druids, or some aspects of it, this was more because of the powerful part played by the cult in nourishing a sense of independence, than because of any specifically religious practice. So long as religion remained within certain bounds, and did not offend the Romans' not very highly developed sense of propriety, they were quite happy for a whole variety of cults to flourish. Their chief requirement – certainly for anyone aspiring to Roman citizenship – was that the Imperial cult should also be honoured. Its was the chief temple in any Roman town, and civic dignitaries like the *decuriones* of Caerwent were compelled to support and officiate in the cult of the deified emperor and his ancestors, at least if these were also of Imperial blood. Consequently, pagan Celtic and pagan Roman worship went on side by side, and each often borrowed or blended aspects of the other. The Romans had a tendency everywhere to assimilate local deities to their own pantheon. Julius Caesar claimed firmly that the Celts worshipped Mercury, Apollo, Mars, Jupiter and Minerva, when in fact he meant that they worshipped gods whose aspects corresponded to some aspects at least of those classical deities. The gods worshipped by the Celtic-speaking tribes were a less easily identifiable group than those of Greece and Rome. They varied from tribe to tribe, with not only a change of name, but often other partial changes as well. In the developing mythology there was a whole range of intermediate figures, part-god, part-human. A cult of the human head continued well into Roman times, and numerous stone heads found in Wales come from this period. The religion of the Welsh tribes resembled that of the Romans in that it was one of ritual observance rather than personal dedication. The gods were an impersonal force who did not demand impassioned and exclusive commitment. This enabled both forms of paganism to coexist and intermingle.

Such was not however the case with the new 'mystery religions' which had arisen on or beyond the eastern fringes of the Roman Empire. By the second century there were already Christian 'cells' in a number of Romano-British communities. Tiny groups in a vast sea of heathendom, they had a mission, indeed a compulsion, to proclaim and gain recruits for their faith. And to adopt their faith meant to shun all other gods, even the deified emperor. Roman officialdom saw this as political subversion of the most sinister and dangerous kind, undermining the very basis of Imperial society. The first Christian martyr in the British Isles was St Alban at Verulamium, but two Christians, Julius and Aaron, were recorded as martyred at Caerleon during the Diocletian persecution of the late second century.

By 313 the subversive and suspect religion of a tiny minority had become strong, flourishing, and officially allowed by the edict of Milan. By the end of the fourth century it was the official religion of the Roman Empire and able to exclude other religions through laws and sanctions operated by the same officialdom that had previously persecuted its followers throughout the empire from Caerleon to Judaea.

But in the far north-western territories of the Imperial domain, Christianity would suffer severely from the long, slow haemorrhage of Roman power as the western empire gradually collapsed in front of pressures which it had neither the resources nor the inner authority to withstand. The decline was gradual and interrupted by periods when it seemed as if the old *status quo* were permanently restored. The tribes of Wales, like all the other subject peoples, had a finely tuned ear for the heartbeat of power. Some, like the Romanised Silures and

Deceangli, feared for what would happen on the departure of Roman legions and auxiliary forces from Britannia to fight yet again on the continent for some jumped-up soldier who wanted to make himself a regional emperor. Others, the Ordovices perhaps, who had never quite bowed to the colonial scheme of things, waited hopefully for the chance to break out. They were very much on the Imperial periphery. It was events on the European mainland that determined the fate of the empire, as the Teutonic tribes, in vast numbers, spilled across the long frontiers and overran the villas, farms, and comfortable towns of Gaul and Italy.

Franks, Goths and Vandals seemed a long way from the land of the Silures. A more immediate threat was seen to the west. Ireland, uninvaded by Rome, its society still in most respects an Iron Age one, had been isolated, literally and figuratively, for centuries. Now, with the consolidation of tribal kingdoms into provincial over-kingships, its leaders were beginning to look further afield. Two processes contributed to this. Increase in population numbers was putting pressure on land use. The political consequences of inter-tribal rivalry could mean the ousting of a family or family group, who might try their fortune by settling in the land across the sea. There were also opportunities to raid. Semi-legendary Irish kings, like Niall of the Nine Hostages, led their fleets along the coasts of north and south Wales, looking for booty from the rich villa-farms. The old Roman fort at Dinorben was re-garrisoned in 260. During the fourth century, new coastal forts were established at Holyhead (Caer Gybi), Caernarfon and Cardiff, and the legionary fort at Chester was also reinforced; and in the late third or early fourth century the Roman town of Wroxeter was set on fire and rebuilt, perhaps as the result of an Irish or Ordovician raid.

PAX ROMANA AND ROMAN DECLINE

In the century from 250 to 350, there was wealth and relative peace. Despite the uncertainties of life, and the usurpations of adventurers like Carausius, who proclaimed himself Emperor of the West in 286, and lasted until his defeat in 293, the British provinces of the Roman Empire flourished. Between 350 and 353 rule of the western empire was briefly seized by the soldier Magnentius. Although he was defeated far away in Pannonia, he took large numbers of troops from the British garrisons, gravely weakening the provincial defences. Raiding from Ireland and the tribes to the north of Hadrian's Wall intensified. In 360 an Imperial army was sent by Emperor Julian to restore order, but raids resumed soon after its departure. Between 365 and 367 the raids were so frequent and large in scale that historians have assumed a concerted plan made by the outsiders. A further attempt to restore the position was made in 368 when the military Count Theodosius arrived with four regiments and drove the Picts and Scots (at this time still coming from Ireland) out of the provinces. Among the provisions made by Theodosius for greater security was to confirm the Votadini or Gododdin as formal allies: their chief, Padarn or Paternus, was made an Imperial officer, and took the name Padarn Pesrut, 'Padarn of the red cloak'. Theodosius' dispositions extended to Wales, and the fleet base at Caer Gybi and the rebuilt fort at Caernarfon may date from this time. In 370, it seemed as if Imperial rule was firmly re-established, and for some years, the earlier prosperity resumed. In 383 there was another military rebellion, under an officer known as Magnus Maximus, who was probably the general in charge of the army in Britain. He found many supporters in Britain, where the Romanised inhabitants were coming to realise that the western emperor, Valentinian II, based at Trier, was far more concerned with barbarian incursions across the Rhine into Gaul than he was with the fate of the British provinces. Magnus took his army across to Gaul, removing troops from Chester and the Welsh forts. Wales was left severely depleted of troops, though some forts like Caernarfon may have held their garrisons, but Maximus hoped to keep the peace by claiming the allegiance of the tribes. It has been surmised by historians that daughters of Maximus may have been married to tribal kings, and several Welsh royal lines would claim their pedigree from Macsen Wledig, Emperor Maximus, but these claims are all from a much later date than the fourth century. Nor could Maximus obtain the co-operation of the Irish tribes. Settling in the Llyn peninsula, in Pembroke and in Gower, they established substantial Gaelic-speaking communities. In 388 Emperor Theodosius I – son of the general – defeated and killed Maximus, but without re-establishing control of the British provinces. Only in 396 did another Imperial army – the last one – land there, under the orders of the Vandal general, Stilicho, effective ruler under the youthful Emperor Honorius, and again drive the invading Picts and Scots back. Between 406 and 409 three successive 'emperors' were set up by the army in Britain; the last of them, Constantine, removed virtually all the remaining troops to support his bid for power. He was executed by Honorius in 411, and Britain was again nominally in the Imperial domain.

In actuality, the provinces were on their own. The writer Zosimus records of this period: 'The barbarians across the Rhine attacked everywhere with all their power, and brought the inhabitants of Britain and some of the nations of Gaul to the point of revolting from Roman rule and living on their own, no longer obedient to Roman laws. The Britons took up arms and, braving danger for their own independence, freed their cities from the barbarians threatening them …'

The revolt from Roman rule presumably reflects the desperation of a people still led by Imperial officials but with no support from Imperial resources. Honorius himself recognised the position in 411 by advising the British towns to look to their own defence. In Romanised parts of Wales, this meant that the civic authorities, as in the other provinces, tried to maintain the structure. Neither they nor the Imperial authorities expected the emergency to last for ever.

CHAPTER FOUR

'Dark Age' Wales

LIFE AFTER THE ROMANS

Although the so-called Dark Ages are by no means as obscure as they were once supposed to be, and certainly no more warlike than the centuries before, it is difficult to trace a continuous thread of developments in Wales. There were few towns of any size and there are signs that Caerwent, perhaps the largest, was burned during the first half of the fifth century, probably by raiders coming up from the coast. With no major urban centres to provide rallying points, it is likely that the old underlying tribal structure came back into its own. To the east, for those who felt inclined, there were rich pickings to be had from raiding the villas and farms whose owners had fled to the cities. Much the same happened in south Wales, where archaeologists have traced how the villa at Llantwit Major fell into decline. The lives of many thousands were in flux. Some Romanised communities probably remained intact. Other inhabitants continued to live in their round houses, rear their cattle, till their little fields, and maintain a lifestyle that went back for centuries before the Romans had come. All needed to ensure their own protection. The bearing of weapons, forbidden by the colonial government, became a necessity. Military deserters, runaway slaves, homeless people roamed in the countryside, camping out in abandoned sites.

But the centuries of Roman Empire could not fail to leave their mark on Wales, though it was less profound than the impact on England. The forts, the roads, the town walls remained for a long time, crumbling slowly, quarried for their re-usable blocks, their origins gradually becoming a matter of legend rather than memory. Latin had been a daily language for many people whose work or position brought them in contact with the army, or who were town-dwellers. Apart from its liturgical and scholarly applications, it gradually fell out of use, but left many loan words behind in the old Brittonic language of the people. That language itself was changing, imperceptibly in any one generation, but gradually taking the form that would be recognisable as Welsh. The process of this has been charted in a scholarly work by Kenneth Jackson, who traces a series of stages of sound changes and grammatical modifications through the fifth and sixth centuries.

In the former provinces of south Britain to the east, the Brittonic-speaking inhabitants had more to fear than deserters and beggars. Lowland Britain, with its fields and forests, was an inviting place to the land-hungry tribes of the

THE LATIN INFLUENCE ON WELSH

As a result of the Roman occupation, the ancestral form of modern Welsh took in many Latin loan words, most of which have come through into modern Welsh. Such words show what the Romans had that the Welsh tribes did not; and the areas in which the two sides came into contact. Military engineering terms like *ffos*, trench, *pont*, bridge, *castell*, castle, form one area. Writing is another, with *llyfr*, book, *llythyr*, letter, and *ysgrif*, script, among others. The Romans' superiority in architecture and building is shown by the borrowing of such words as *ffenestr*, window, *ystafell*, chamber, and *colofn*, pillar. Many domestic items, such as *cyllell*, knife, *ffiol*, bowl, *cannwl*, candle, come from Latin. *Cadair*, throne, is another borrowing, but, unlike the Gaels, the Welsh did not use the Latin *rex* for king, retaining instead the traditional *brenin*. As Sir John Lloyd pointed out in 1911, although popular speech may employ words like *pobl*, people, and *estron*, foreigner, the language of Welsh law, harking back to an older tradition, has very few Latin terms other than *tyst*, witness. Latin also gave the Welsh a number of first names, at least one of which remains current today, Emrys, from Ambrosius.

North European coast. Frisians, Jutes, Angles and Saxons all knew that there was unprotected territory for the taking. It did not remain unprotected for long, as the Britons organised themselves for defence, but they were exposed on all fronts. From the north the Picts came down, by sea. From the west the Scots came, pressing in from north and south of the Welsh landmass. From east and south came the Germanic invaders. These were the most dangerous in the long run. The Picts and Scots came to raid and retreat; the Anglo-Saxons came to settle. The beleaguered Britons formed a federation; as the Gauls had done under Vercingetorix and the Caledonians under Calgacus, so they united behind a leader who might win the war for them. Known only by his title, Vortigern (Gwrtheyrn) or 'great lord', he strove to become master of the situation. His origins are unknown, though one legend ascribes them to the Welsh borders. As with any leader facing separate groups of enemies, he tried to use one foe against the other. The Anglo-Saxon raiders were still relatively few in number; it would have been a bold prophet who foresaw that in a few generations they would have been rulers of almost all of south Britain. Vortigern made some kind of treaty with them: according to the story related by Gildas, he invited their leaders, Hengist and Horsa, to make a treaty bewailed by subsequent generations. Despite this latter recognition of a fatal step, modern historians have recognised the British resistance as something unique at the time – 'an initiative unparalleled in the empire' according to Professor Sheppard Frere.

A SPIRITUAL BATTLEGROUND

Although the western empire finally collapsed in 476, a supra-national institution based in Rome remained in being, in the form of the Christian church.

During the tumultuous events of the early fifth century, the Christian church was vexed by a serious internal problem of its own. This was the heretical view put forward by the British-born lawyer and theologian, Pelagius. His place of birth may have been Ireland, but he settled for a time in south Wales; much of his adult life, from around 380, was spent in Rome. From there he fled to Carthage when Rome was sacked in 410. Pelagius' preaching denied that original sin existed. In his view, the state of sin was not inherited from Adam, but was attained when people copied Adam in disobeying the divine commands. Pelagius was influenced by the number of people who, through belief in original sin, considered themselves already damned and consequently felt no incentive to reform. For the leaders of orthodoxy, led by his contemporary St Augustine, this was a most dangerous heresy, denying the very possibility of redemption. But large numbers of influential churchmen agreed with Pelagius, especially in the east. His views were also widely supported in Britain. He died in 420, and in 431 his teachings were finally condemned in a general council that was held at Ephesus.

It was to preach against, and root out, Pelagianism that the Gaulish bishop, Germanus (Garmon), was sent to Britain in 429. In a great open meeting held at Verulamium (St Albans), the Pelagians were routed in debate. Germanus, who had formerly been a Roman officer of high rank, is then said to have led an army of newly baptised Christians to fight a force of invading Picts allied with Saxons. With 'Alleluia' as their war cry, the Britons were victorious. The battle was fought in a mountainous district, sometimes taken to be north Wales, though what the Picts and Saxons were doing there is not clear: the Peak District of England might be a more probable area. What is clear is that by the mid-fifth century, Christianity, though still chiefly a religion of the small urban centres, was beginning to spread out into the more sparsely populated countryside; and that its dynamic was not seriously affected by the cutting off of links with the Imperial administration.

GIANTS AND HEROES

Germanus was the subject of a biography soon after his death. The accounts we have of figures such as Vortigern do not come from their own time, but somewhat later. Any contemporary documents have disappeared, but they would have been few in number. Although druids had used writing, it was only to a limited degree, and it was only with the development of scriptoria, or writing-rooms, in the monasteries that the keeping of records became a regular thing. Around 540 the monk, Gildas, whose district is not known, though it was either in Wales or south-west Scotland, compiled a work called *De Excidio et Conquestu Britanniae* ('On the Fall and Conquest of Britain').

GILDAS

The author of *The Fall and Conquest of Britain* was one of the Men of the North, born (according to a biographer who lived some centuries later) in Arecluta, the lower Clyde area, around AD 500. He was well educated both in Christian doctrine and in Latin rhetoric and literature; the same biographical source says he was taught by St Illtud, who kept a school for promising and well-born boys. Gildas became a monk, and from his own work he clearly was an impassioned believer in the virtues of Celtic monasticism. His account is not a history, but a reformist tract aimed at the rulers of the British. In Gildas's view, the disasters of the Anglo-Saxon invasions can be laid at the door of the wickedness and sinfulness of the British people and their kings, five of whom he mentions by name, including Maelgwyn Gwynedd. The historical information of his work is incidental, and used only to point his moral. Writing in the time of relative peace which followed the British victory of Mount Badon, his is a prophetic warning, that sinfulness will result in a further catalogue of downfall and calamity.

Apart from its historical importance, though many historians have cursed him for what he might have put in but did not, Gildas's 'Letter' as he refers to it, is interesting as it seems to be a purely individual effort. He was not a bishop or abbot, and had no formal position of power. A burning desire to say what he had to say seems to have driven him on. He is the last spokesman – in polished Latin – of the Romano-British world, disappearing fast in his day. The pagan Anglo-Saxons, the barbarian Picts and Scots, are equally scorned. He harks back with sad pride to the exploits of Ambrosius (Emrys Wledig). There can be no doubt that Gildas pursued his theme in sermons and other letters and writings which have not been preserved. Although he was an unwelcome figure in Wales, his influence in other parts of the 'Celtic fringe' appears to have been strong, notably in Ireland and in Brittany, where he died, around 565.

Gildas's text is not a history but a moral tract, complaining bitterly of the standards of his time, especially those of kings and in particular those of Maelcon or Maelgwn Gwynedd, King of Anglesey. History comes into it since he recounts the story of the Saxon invasions, and blames the foreigners' success on the sinfulness of the British. Isolated as it is, there is no way of being certain whether Gildas's was a lone voice or whether his diatribe is a typical product of the age.

Gildas does not name Vortigern, though he refers to him, but some evocative names crop up for the first time in his text, including that of Ambrosius Aurelianus (*Emrys Wledig*). Nothing is said of Arthur, who with Ambrosius would play a large part in later Welsh and British mythology. Their origins, deeds and status are lost in obscurity, and their actual existence has often been challenged. But it is evident that the British had leaders, and reasonable to suppose that Vortigern was succeeded by other leaders or over-kings. The advance of the Anglo-Saxon kingdoms was not a sudden one, but happened over a lengthy period, more than a century, punctuated by periods of calm and stability. Both Arthur and Ambrose have been claimed for Wales, partly on account of the Welsh etymology of their names. Arthur may stem from *arth* ('bear') and *gwr*

MAELGWYN GWYNEDD

Because he is specially singled out for criticism in the writing of Gildas, we know more about this sixth-century figure than about most early regional kings. Also known as Maelgwyn Hir, he was clearly taller than the average. He had a distinguished father in Cadwallon, who conquered the Irish who had settled in north Wales. Although he ruled Anglesey, his main stronghold seems to have been Degannwy (the name a memory of the Decantae tribe). Gildas describes him as generous in charitable giving as well as profuse in sin, and he is also mentioned in a number of biographies of saints, for both these reasons. One of Maelgwyn's misdeeds was to maintain a troop of bards at his court. Whilst they no doubt sang the king's praises, the bards at this time also preserved a great deal of verse from pre-Christian times, which earned them the enmity (duly repaid) of the evangelists. It seems that Maelgwyn had a taste for older traditions. He had strong connections with the Cumbric peoples of the north, and may even, through a form of royal marriage, have been the father of the celebrated Bridei, King of the Picts, who received St Columba at his court near Inverness. Legend also links him with the bard, Taliesin, in a contest in which Taliesin releases his master, Elphin, held in prison at Maelgwyn's orders. Maelgwyn died of 'the yellow plague', in or around the year 547.

('hero'); and he is associated with the Great Bear constellation. *Arddhu* ('very black') has also been suggested. Emrys Wledig is described by Gildas as 'last of the Romans', though modern historians think there may have been two Emryses; the younger one perhaps commander of the British forces against the Saxons in the battle of Mons Badonicus, 'the Badonian hill', which happened in the late fifth or early sixth century at a location now unknown. This British victory stabilised the boundaries between Britons and Saxons for half a century or more. During such periods as this it is likely that there were diplomatic and trading contacts between the British kingdoms and the new kingdoms of the Germanic speakers, with such conventions as the exchange of royal brides being observed.

The incomers remained restless and expansionist. In 577 they won an important strategic battle at Dyrham, near Bath, which enabled them to gain territory as far as the Bristol Channel. The Britons of Wales and of south-west England were now cut off from each other by land. The victory also enabled the Saxons to push northwards up the valley of the Severn.

TRIBES, DYNASTIES AND KINGDOMS

Events among the Welsh tribes through the fifth and sixth centuries have to be inferred since the sources are so few. By the end of the period, the tribes or federations recorded in Roman times no longer exist, or continue under a new identity. The likelihood is that the removal of Imperial rule and the cessation of the marketing, trading and industrial economy that accompanied it, encouraged a break-up into smaller social units which could be self-sufficient in food produce and which possessed, or rebuilt, a hill-fort for its own security. From here it could defend its territory, and perhaps from such early beginnings come the land divisions of medieval Wales, the *cantrefi* ('hundreds'). Such a patchwork, especially in the aftermath of monolithic rule, would not be a stable one. Deaths of leaders, the emergence of ambitious strong men or 'warlords', alliances and attacks would all make for a shifting pattern, but with a trend towards larger groupings. It was still a largely pagan society, retaining most of the characteristics of 'Celtic' social life already described. From this basis, dynasties developed – royal lineages which extended their power by intermarriage, by warfare and by alliance, and by the peaceful absorption of smaller tribal groups for their own protection.

Throughout this period, raids and attempts at colonisation from Ireland continued. The long exposed promontories to north and south were especially vulnerable. In the latter part of the fourth century an Irish tribe, the Deisi, established themselves in what is now Pembrokeshire. A strong Irish presence existed as far inland as Brecon, where the name recalls the fifth or sixth century Irish chief Brychan and his eponymous kingdom of Brycheiniog (Brecknock). Stones carved in the Irish manner, using the Irish Ogam alphabet, are found in this area, in the north-west and south-west. Indeed, Wales might have become a Scotland before ever the Scots set up their colony of Dàl Riada far to the north in Pictland, but it seems that the Irish invasions to the north were stemmed.

CANTREFS AND COMMOTES

*C*antref means 'a hundred houses', or perhaps 'a hundred hamlets', and is the oldest known subdivision of Welsh territory. The main divisions defined the land occupied by particular tribes, the *gwlad*, or later land ruled by a particular chief; thus the *gwlad* ruled by Morgan in the tenth century came to be Glamorgan. It was probably the hierarchical structure of the tribe that encouraged the formation of the *cantref*, as an area under the authority of a sub-chief. The regularity of size implied by the name was probably less so in reality, though it may have had a military purpose, supposing that each *cantref* could furnish approximately the same number of armed men to the warband. Within his *cantref*, the sub-chief exercised considerable power, through an assembly of the *uchelwyr*, or leading men, of the district. The *cantref* court was used to decide on disputes among the free tribesmen: mostly land and boundary matters. In the course of the eleventh century, the *cantref* came to be seen as too large to cope with the volume of legal business, and the commote or *cymyd*, was created, with several commotes replacing each *cantref*. In Mon, for example, there were three *cantrefs*, of Aberffraw, Cemais and Rhosyr, each subdivided into six commotes. Each commote had its court, organised on similar lines to that of the *cantref*. When, under English rule, Wales was 'shired' in the thirteenth and sixteenth centuries, the county boundaries generally followed the ancient boundaries of *gwlad* and *cantref*.

*A stone bearing Ogam
inscriptions*

The credit for this has been attributed to a migration by a large section of the Votadini or Gododdin tribe, from the country just north of Hadrian's Wall – this region, Lothian, was already under pressure from the Angles based at Bamburgh. The leader of this migration, Cunedda, was the grandson of Padarn Pesrut, and was also claimed to be the ancestor of Maelgwn Gwynedd. By tradition, it was Cunedda and his warriors who thrust the Irish back from north Wales. The story is probably a mixture of truth and legend. There is nothing inherently unlikely in the migration: something similar happened several hundred years later when the Cumbric dynasty of Strathclyde collapsed. But the account of Cunedda's eight sons, each of whom established a royal lineage in different parts of Wales, is a typical myth, comparable to that of Cruithne and his seven sons, supposed founders of seven Pictish kingdoms. Irish settlements, especially in the south, remained for many generations, however, and were only gradually absorbed into the developing Welsh kingdoms.

The rise of these kingdoms is shrouded in obscurity, which the accounts of later chroniclers do not greatly illuminate. As the dynasties grew in power and rivalry, their own propaganda tried to make them as grand and ancient as possible. Magnus Maximus plays a part in many of these genealogies, indeed John Davies says that: 'In the history or the mythology of the beginnings of the kingdoms of Wales, Magnus is a ubiquitous lurker … perhaps it is not over-fanciful to consider 383 as the year of the conception of the Welsh nation and to accept Magnus Maximus as the father of that nation' (pp. 53–4). The conception of a nation, no matter how many daughters Magnus wedded to chieftains, is a large undertaking. It is impossible to say how much of a sense of nationhood was present among the tribes of Wales at that time. The Teutonic invasions had not begun, and there was still a community of Brittonic-speaking peoples from the southern bounds of the Scottish Highlands to Cornwall.

By the middle of the sixth century, a number of kingdoms can be identified. Gwynedd, comprising Anglesey and part of the mainland across the Menai Strait, with its king, Maelgwn, was already a significant power. In the south-west the name of the Demetae remained current for a long time in what was to become the kingdom of Dyfed: Gildas refers to his contemporary Gwrthefyr as 'ruler of the Demetae'. On the north coast, the name of the Deceangli was preserved in the often-disputed territory of Tegeingl, bordering the River Dee. On the eastern edge small kingdoms arose in the land of the Cornovii, eventually to coalesce in the kingdom of Powys. In the south-east, another set of kingdoms arose in the one-time territory of the Silures: Brycheiniog, Glywysing and Erging (a name long preserved in English as Archenfield). The divisions between these little states was not hard and fast; Erging, based on the Romano-British Ariconium, would become part of England from the late eleventh century. Glywysing split into Morgannwg, Gwynllwg, and Upper and Lower Gwent. The destiny of a kingdom depended on the strength of its people, on the vigour and ability of its king, and, not least, on the chance of whether he had sons or daughters, brothers or sisters, to maintain his own family line.

Early in the seventh century, the energetic and ambitious Northumbrian king, Aethelfrith, began the expansion which for two generations was to make Northumbria the most powerful kingdom in Britain. He defeated the forces of the Scots and Strathclyde Britons at a site known as Degsastan, somewhere on the Scottish border, in 603. Twelve years later he won a crushing victory, somewhere near Chester, over the Britons who occupied the areas of Lancashire, Cheshire and Powys. Here occurred the notorious massacre of the monks of Bangor. Said to number 1,200, they had come, like the old druids of Anglesey in Agricola's time, to exhort their warriors to victory; and they suffered the same fate in defeat. Aethelfrith was killed in battle in East Anglia in 616, but his successor Edwin continued the Northumbrian expansion, wiping out the British kingdom of Elmet, in west and north Yorkshire, and establishing Northumbrian rule from coast to coast. He also invaded Gwynedd and took possession of Anglesey. The King of Gwynedd, Cadwallon ap Cadfan, is said to have taken refuge on the island of Priestholm and then fled to Ireland. On the Northumbrian army's withdrawal, Cadwallon returned to Gwynedd, and made a crucial alliance with Penda, a leading figure among the pagan Mercians who had settled the English midlands. In 632 the combined forces of Cadwallon and Penda defeated the Northumbrians, at Hatfield Chase, near Doncaster, and Edwin was killed. Cadwallon's intention was to devastate Northumbria so thoroughly that it would no longer be a threat to the Britons. Aethelfrith's kingdom had reverted to its old constituent parts of Bernicia and Deira; in a further battle in 633 Cadwallon defeated the southern Northumbrians of Deira, and, apparently by trickery also killed Eanfrith, King of Bernicia. Cadwallon seemed on the brink of achieving the great British restoration, when at the end of 634 he was defeated and killed in battle against an army led by Eanfrith's brother Oswald. This fight, near Rowley Burn, south of Hexham, re-established the power of Northumbria, and also marked the start of the rise of Mercia, where Penda had become king in 632. Instead of a British ascendancy, once again the British kingdoms were hemmed in.

SAINTS, MONKS AND BARDS

In Wales, the Dark Ages were also the age of the saints. Christianity spread across the country. A number of factors contributed to this. The kingdoms of Wales did not lose touch with developments on the continent of Europe. The western seaways remained an open route, and were as important as they had always been as a conduit of culture and ideas. Ireland had been converted to Christianity during the fifth century by a number of notable missionaries from Cumbric Britain, of whom St Patrick was to become the best known. Following the establishment of monasteries there, Ireland in turn became a source of missionary effort. There are many evidences of this in Wales, not least those saints descended from Brychan and associated with places in the centre and south. The cult of Brigid or Brid was early brought to Wales in the form of St Ffraid. Then again, memories of the Roman Empire died slowly in Wales, and the prestige of Christianity as the religion of Constantine the Great was a valuable asset. When northern Europe, and much of the territory of south Britain, was overrun by pagans, Christianity was one of the means by which the Britons could show their difference to the invaders. Above all, perhaps, there was a steady supply of dedicated and intrepid men prepared to bring the gospel message to every part of the old tribal lands. Pious, austere, inspired, they set personal examples of unworldliness, asceticism and charity. It was of their church that the French historian Ernest Renan wrote: 'Few forms of Christianity have offered an ideal of Christian perfection as pure as the Celtic church of the sixth, seventh and eighth centuries. Nowhere, perhaps, has God been better worshipped in spirit' (*Etudes d'Histoire Réligieuse*).

Because of its isolation, the Christian church in Wales, as in Ireland and Scotland, took a distinctive form. Its origins lay in the tiny self-seeding cells of Christians in Romano-British communities. Before the collapse of Rome, bishops had gone from Britain to attend conclaves in Europe. Whilst over much of Europe, the Christian church was stifled, here on the edge it flourished. Naturally enough, with no outside influences to shape it, it took a form that aligned it with the structure of society. Just as the druids had played an important part in the life of the tribe, so did the bishop begin to play an important part in the life of the kingdom. Bishops were often also abbots, and tended to be men of high social rank. Spiritual responsibilities and ecclesiastical contacts were combined with the role of royal advisers and diplomats. With a corps of monks trained in writing and decorating parchment scripts, the abbeys became repositories of historical records.

A consequence of this was a sundering of the bards and the bardic tradition. In pre-Christian days, bards and druids had complementary and often overlapping functions. The orders in which they were ranked indicated a unity of structure. A strong poetic tradition developed within the Christian church, and since panegyric and praise had been important aspects of the poetic repertoire, these transferred naturally to the writing of hymns. But a strong pagan and secular tradition also remained among the bards. In the pre-Christian community, their skill with words was closely allied to magic, and the power of satire and cursing was something personal and integral to their role as bards. They were loath to give this privileged role up to the priests of the new order. There was rivalry between bards and priests. Maelgwn Gwynedd, the king reviled by Gildas for his tepid attitude to religion, may have had Taliesin as his chief bard; and Taliesin was renowned for insisting on the prophetic, magus-like role of the bard:

> These are Taliesin's rimes,
> These shall live to distant times,
> And the bard's prophetic rage
> Animate a future age.

Taliesin came from the Men of the North, the Brittonic-speaking lands north of Hadrian's Wall, and though much magical and mythical material has accreted round his character and deeds, a core of some dozen songs has always been ascribed to him, and throughout Welsh history he remains the great exemplar of the bardic spirit. The bards continued to be a strong element of society, with a ritual and ceremonial of their own, and leading bards were highly placed, as well as highly esteemed. In 1784 Edward Jones wrote in *An Historical Account of the Welsh Bards*:

> *The Bard of the palace, who was in rank the eighth officer of the Prince's household, received at his appointment a harp and an ivory chess-board from the Prince, and a gold ring from the Princess. On the same occasion he presented a gold ring to the judge of the palace. At the Prince's table on the three great festivals of Christmas, Easter and Whitsuntide, he sat next to the master of the palace, and publicly received from that officer the harp upon which he performed. When he went with other Bards on his Clera or musical peregrination, he was entitled to a double fee. He was obliged, at the Queen's*

desire, to sing to his harp three pieces of poetry, but in a low voice, that the court might not be diverted from their avocations. He accompanied the army when it marched into an enemy's country; and while it was preparing for battle, or dividing the spoils, he performed an ancient song, called 'Unbennaeth Prydaia', the 'Monarchy of Britain'.

The bards not only maintained their style, but occasionally became too demanding in their requests for rewards and benefits, all expressed in careful metre and amidst the most flowery compliments (and sometimes thinly veiled threats) to the potential giver. In later times Gruffudd ap Cynan would pass a law to restrain what the bards might ask for from a patron.

THE CHURCH IN WALES

But there was no questioning the increasing power and influence of the Welsh church. In each of the strongest centres of kingship, an important monastery also arose. Long before formal dioceses were set up, these served the kingdom and grew rich on the donations from king and people: Bangor in Gwynedd, St Davids in Dyfed, Llandaf in Glamorgan, Llanelwy, later St Asaph, in Denbigh.

The alignment of church with kingdom meant that the Welsh church was in effect a federation of churches, each with its own head. A single doctrine was preached and preserved, but there was no hierarchy above the abbot-bishops. They knew of, and paid respect to, the Bishop of Rome, but did not consider him to be the head of their church. When in 597 Pope Gregory the Great sent Augustine as the first Roman bishop in England, the clergy of Wales responded somewhat stiffly to the initiative. In the *History of the English Church and People*, Bede records two meetings between the Bishop of Canterbury and a group of bishops from 'the nearest British province' which certainly meant, or included, Wales, since at the second meeting some are recorded as coming from Bancorna-burg (Bangor). There were numerous differences to be resolved, but the Welsh bishops, arriving later than Augustine, took offence at his remaining seated to greet them, and refused to accept the three points he put to them: '... to keep Easter at the correct time; to administer the Sacrament of Baptism according to the rites of the holy, Roman and apostolic church; and to join with us in preaching the word of God to the English.' The Welsh church would be the last of the Celtic churches to fall into line with Roman practice in the matter of fixing the date of Easter, and in the way the clergy were tonsured. This earned them the ire of Bede, writing from an English monastery in the eighth century, but given that the church was in effect the tribe at prayer, and that the Welsh kings looked askance at the advancing boundaries of Anglo-Saxon kingdoms, whether Christian or pagan, they had little incentive to fall into line. They were

Llandaf Cathedral, Glamorgan, in Victorian times

also proudly aware of a long tradition of maintaining the faith at a time when Canterbury and York were centres of pagan sacrifice.

Among writers of the post-Reformation era, this independence of the Welsh church was sometimes seized upon as evidence of a sort of precocious Protestantism, but of course it was nothing of the kind. The Celtic churches practised the same basic rites as Rome, and considered themselves fully part of the whole Catholic church, as their long history of missionary endeavour into Europe makes clear.

It is somewhat surprising that the religion of peace and goodwill, of resigning the things of this earth, should have found such apparently ready acceptance among a people who saw warfare as heroic, who relished conspicuous display, and who had no sense of sin. The process is charted in Sian Victory's *The Celtic Church in Wales*. Helped by the relatively vague form of Celtic religious belief, and the localised nature of so many spirits, at holy wells, river confluences, tarns, favourably exposed fields and so on, the missionaries managed to embroider much of the folk tradition into their own message. The church did not succeed in ending warfare in Wales, any more than it did anywhere else. Nor did it stop the cult of head-collecting. A hint of the syncretism – the combination of aspects of different cults – practised not only in the early years but later too, can be seen in the famous triple head sculpture in Llandaf Cathedral.

Many of the missionaries themselves became closely identified with a single region, district, or even parish. It is to this that Wales owes its many hundreds of Llan-names, the great majority denoting a church founded by, or dedicated to, a particular saintly person. The saint who has emerged with greatest distinction is of course St David, whose church at remote Menevia has become Wales's greatest cathedral. Many churches dedicated to him throughout the south testify to his work. But others were also active. Padarn, bearer of a name with some resonance in tribal history, established the church at Llanbadarn Fawr and linked up with the Irish or Irish-descended missionaries coming out of Brycheiniog. A great Roman villa took on a new identity when St Illtud established his church by its site: it is still known as Llantwit Major. Further west and into the hills, St Teilo founded the church at Llandeilo Fawr. In the north one of the chief moving spirits was St Beuno; his centre was at Clynnog Fawr but he or his followers penetrated right into Anglesey and along the north-east coastal strip. There is much hagiography from later centuries about the work of the founders, and regrettably little contemporary material. Even the seventh-century *Life of St Samson*, still preserved, though it confirms some names such as that of Illtud, has almost nothing in the way of historical detail. Authors of the lives of saints were not concerned to record history; their aim was to magnify the spiritual impact of their subject and consequently there are more miracles than facts to be found in these texts. The procedure of the evangelists was usually to establish a monastery, a little ecclesiastical settlement with a church, dwelling huts, and the necessary farm sheds. From this centre, trained monks could go out and establish churches as daughter foundations.

Although monks from Iona were the first to bring Christianity to the Angles of Northumbria, and others, like St Fursey, to East Anglia, the Anglo-Saxon kingdoms, as they became converted, tended to follow the rule of Canterbury. As papal authority grew stronger, Roman-trained clerics like St Wilfred came back to England determined to ensure that their church followed that of Rome in all respects. At a synod held in Whitby in 664, the respective cases of the Celtic and Roman churches were debated. Wilfred's polished oratory won the day. Mocking the pretensions of the Celtic church, a remote and small body, to be right and for everyone else to be wrong, he convinced the Northumbrian King, and from then on the church in Northumbria followed Canterbury. Wilfred, incidentally, is the first recorded exponent of the unpleasant sense of superiority with which the Anglo-Saxons chose to regard the Celtic peoples. Gradually the Celtic churches fell into line with European practice, though the process took several generations. The churchmen of Wales were the last to give way, more than a hundred years later, in 768.

STRUGGLES AND ALLIANCES

It is a striking aspect of Wales in the Dark Ages that the kingdoms west and north of the River Severn appear to have had more close and regular contact with the far-off tribal kingdoms of southern Scotland, than with the other Brittonic-speaking kingdoms to the east. Memories of *Gwr y Gogledd*, 'the Men of the North', ring out in Welsh legend and ancient history. There were two of these kingdoms: on the east side, occupying present-day Lothian, was Manaw Gododdin, descended from the old Roman-friendly Votadini tribe, from where Cunedda and his people may have come to Gwynedd. In the south-west, and stretching far south into the client-kingdom of Rheged (present-day Galloway and Cumbria), was Strathclyde, with its capital at Dumbarton on the Clyde estuary. Perhaps the old adage, that the nearest neighbours are not the best friends, had something to do with these long-range links, which were reinforced by royal marriages. On the ill-defined eastern bounds, the rich alluvial farmland once occupied by the Cornovii, and controlled from the former Roman fort at Wroxeter, may have been disputed between kings in Powys and rulers of tribal kingdoms to the east, causing friction. Easy communication with Strathclyde was also possible by sea. Strathclyde was the stronger and more secure of the Brittonic kingdoms north of Hadrian's Wall. Manaw Gododdin was under threat from the expansionist aims of the Angles, based at their fort of Bamburgh.

That threat, and the response to it, is preserved in the earliest piece of literature in the language that was to become Welsh, *Y Gododdin*, a poetic lament of 1,480 lines traditionally ascribed to the sixth-century bard Aneirin, who himself features in its verses. It brings a heroic age vividly to life, describing how Mynyddog Mwynfawr, 'the wealthy' King of the Gododdin, summons a corps of some 300 mail-clad and mounted heroes to his fortress, Din Eidyn, traditionally identified with the rock of Edinburgh Castle. For a year they feast and train, then set off to do battle with the Anglians at a place called Catraeth, 'cataract', possibly present-day Catterick. The expedition is a complete disaster; despite heroic fighting, the champions are slain with only one or two able to escape, including, so he tells us, the bard himself. The implication of the elegies over the fallen is clear: better to die fighting than in bed. The historical truth, and the relative importance, of the raid are now impossible to ascertain. *Y Gododdin* is a thoroughly pagan poem and there may have been a hidden purpose behind its making, to extol the virtues of the 'old ways' in a changing era. Although Professor Kenneth Jackson jestingly called it 'the oldest Scottish poem', its place and significance in the Welsh tradition are incontestable.

By 640, the Votadini had been overrun by the Angles, and the invaders' kingdom stretched now to the Firth of Forth. Especially in the south, the Welsh tribes had problems of their own to face. Following the victory at Dyrham in 577, the Anglo-Saxons pushed south-westwards into the Brittonic area of Somerset, and also began to exert pressure on the land route into south Wales. The details of campaigns fought in the early decades of the seventh century are unclear, but the traditional account of a great victory in Gwent over the invaders in 620 or 630 is probably correct, since they failed to establish themselves beyond the Wye. In the north, however, as we have seen, the Northumbrian Anglians occupied the country from sea to sea, cutting off the land route from Wales into Strathclyde.

OFFA'S DYKE

The Welsh kingdoms were isolated. Through the eighth century, the struggle for survival was enough to preoccupy the people. Anglo-Saxon power was being consolidated to the east. The now powerful kingdom of Mercia, with its subkingdoms, was spreading in the English west midlands. An Anglian people, the Magonsaetan, moved into the area of north Herefordshire and south Shropshire. Some early English place names, now in Wales, show that they had attempted to settle to the west, and had been later driven, or negotiated, out. By the mid-eighth century, Mercia was the most powerful state in England under its king, Offa, who styled himself *Rex Anglorum*, 'King of the English'. Ruthless in the acquisition and keeping of power, Offa was also something of a realist.

The Welsh *Annals* record plenty of fighting between Mercians and the Welsh kingdoms in the earlier part of his reign. In 760 there was a battle fought at Hereford, already by then established as a border fortress. In 778 Offa made heavy raids into Dyfed, and another invasion is recorded in 784.

In the later part of his lengthy reign, probably the 790s, Offa caused the long earthwork to be built that ever since has borne his name both in English and Welsh: Clawdd Offa, 'Offa's Dyke'. This vast and expensive undertaking was begun at a time of peace between Mercia and the Welsh kingdoms, and must have been built with a measure of agreement between both sides as to its line. In *Anglo-Saxon England*, Sir Frank Stenton notes that: '. . . the course chosen for the frontier north of the Wye seems to have meant the abandonment of English territory to the Britons.' He cites the Radnor place name of Burlingjobb (Old English, Berchelincope) as an example. Nevertheless, it remains true that: 'Over more than seventy miles of broken and sometimes mountainous country its visible remains rarely fail to command the land towards the west, against whose inhabitants it marked the English frontier' (p. 212–14). There was to be no doubt as whose wall it was; and if its intention was chiefly to make a political frontier, it was still laid out with an eye to its military uses. The line of Offa's frontier runs from the coast at Chepstow north to the coast at Prestatyn. Its northernmost sections are largely vanished, but long stretches of the central section can be clearly followed as they rise and fall over hill-slopes and down into valleys. In the then thickly wooded stretch through northern Herefordshire, the wall was built only intermittently across valleys and clear spaces; then for a time the River Wye formed the boundary, to a point four miles south of Monmouth: on the far side was the old kingdom of Erging, now assuming its English name of Archenfield but still a home of independent Brittonic-speakers.

The effect of Offa's Dyke was to create a great Brittonic enclave. Elsewhere, the Anglo-Saxons would push their conquests forward, through Devon and into Cornwall; through the Pennines, gradually eliminating the last of the Brittonic-speaking kingdoms east of the Dyke. In Wales, the nature of the countryside, the number of the inhabitants, and their ferocity in war were such as to make conquest too great a task. The construction of Offa's Dyke will certainly have

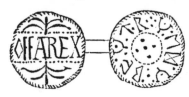

A silver penny of Offa, King of Mercia

been accompanied by treaties and undertakings binding the hillmen to stay on their side and not to conduct cattle raids across the new border. In 796 Offa again invaded Dyfed, which suggests that the temptations for some of the Welsh were too great, and intermittent warfare went on into the ninth century. No longer could the Welsh kingdoms consider themselves as part of an interrelated set of peoples occupying almost the whole of the British landmass. The realisation of this probably fostered the development of the name Cymry, 'comrades', which came to be the Welsh people's own name for themselves. However great their internal arguments and dissensions, they were aware of an essential unity. To the Anglo-Saxons, they were the Wallas, 'foreigners', a name which leads directly to present-day Welsh.

CHAPTER FIVE

The Early Middle Ages

KINGS OF GWYNEDD

This sense of being a kindred may have assisted the process by which princes were able to extend their rule over neighbouring kingdoms. The most striking example in the ninth century was Rhodri Mawr, 'the Great'. Earlier in the century Merfyn Frych, 'freckled', King of Gwynedd from around 820, also acquired the kingship of Powys, by marrying Nest, sister of Cyngen, with whom a line of kings of Powys died out. Merfyn's son Rhodri inherited the kingship of Gwynedd from Merfyn in 844, and that of Powys through his mother, Nest, due to the failure of the male line, in 855. He too made a profitable marriage, with Angharad, whose father was King of Ceredigion. In 871 he also became King of Seisyllwg, a kingdom stretching from Ceredigion to the Gower, making him the master of more than half of Wales. If Rhodri gained his kingships by diplomatic marriage and genealogical good fortune, he had often to fight hard to keep them. Despite the wide extent of his domains, it was only the kingship of Gwynedd that he could pass on to his own heir when he died fighting the Norsemen in 878. He was not in a position to consolidate his family's rule across several distinct kingdoms, as his contemporary Kenneth MacAlpin, King of Scots, succeeded in doing with Dàl Riada and Pictland in the 840s.

   In the time of Merfyn and Rhodri there is some evidence of wider contacts between their courts and other royal centres, notably that of Charles the Bald, King of the Franks. Merfyn had come from the Men of the North to marry a princess of Gwynedd and become its king; he could trace his pedigree back to Coel Hen, most prestigious of the ancient kings of Strathclyde. It was probably at Rhodri's court that the traditions of the Men of the North were first written down. There was an intellectual life there: a party of visiting Irishmen was subjected to a test of their cultural knowledge before being admitted to the intimacy of the king and his attendants.

CHALLENGES BY SEA AND LAND

By 789, a new element entered the political scene of north-west Europe, one that would have a profound effect. In that year the first Viking raids on the coast of Britain were recorded. The first Vikings came simply to plunder. Rich monasteries situated on or near the seacoast were soft targets. Warlike as the island-dwellers were, the bloodthirsty barbarity of the raiders caused shock and horror. The narrow long-boats had no space to transport slaves; the Norsemen left the bodies of men, women and children among the smoking remains of their wattle houses. Very soon, it became clear that they were also colonising places on the western seaboard. They occupied the Hebrides and forced their way in to the Scots' kingdom of Dàl Riada, pushing the Scots east into an eventual unification with the Picts. One of their largest settlements was at Dublin, just across one of the short sea routes from north Wales. Slave-raids began. The shoreline of Wales offered plenty of opportunity, but the Norsemen were less successful at settling here. Any settlements were small and did not become beachheads for a larger occupation. Their attempts to overrun Anglesey were frustrated by Rhodri Mawr, who defeated a Danish force on the island in 856, and it is likely that he also had to repulse Viking invasions coming in through Dyfed.

Offa's Mercian empire remained dynamic for a time under his successors. But Mercia was not destined to last. The new power arising in England was Wessex, the land of the West Saxons. In 829, Mercia became a sub-kingdom of Wessex. Seven years before, in a last gasp, the Mercians had taken control of Powys. It seems that Rhodri Mawr won it back, but the West Saxons maintained the pressure over the next decades. In 877, Rhodri was killed fighting there, with his son Gwriad. The establishment of Danish kingdoms on the eastern side of England opened new opportunities for Welsh diplomacy: Britons, Saxons and Danes could form two-against-one alliances, as Cadwallon had done with the Mercians against the Northumbrians. Rhodri Mawr's successor in Powys and Gwynedd, Anawrad, made treaties with the York-based Danes. Concerned by this reinforcement of the House of Rhodri, smaller Welsh states cultivated a relationship with Wessex, which from 871, under King Alfred, was engaged in the long struggle to push back the Danes that would continue into the next reign. Later, Anawrad also entered into alliance with Alfred.

NENNIUS

The name of Nennius, or Niniaw, has been associated for more than a millennium with the text known as the *Historia Brittonum* ('History of the Britons'). Modern scholars regard him not as its author – if it had a single author – but as a kind of editor, copying and rewriting more ancient works. Nennius lived in the early ninth century, at a time when classical learning was in decline; his Latin is much less assured, if also less ornate, than that of Gildas. His aim was to set out a history of the British struggle against the Anglo-Saxons, and among the resources he had were a life of St Germanus, a list of the 'cities' of Britain, and copies of the royal genealogies of six Anglo-Saxon kingdoms, as well as the chronicles of Latin writers including Jerome, and Isidore of Seville. The *Historia* is one of the earliest works to refer to Arthur, describing him as a military leader and recording his twelve victories.

HYWEL DDA AND THE WELSH LAWS

The pattern of combined kingships lapsed with Rhodri's sons but resumed vigorously with the next generation. His grandson, Hywel ap Cadell, ruler of Seisyllwg, extended his kingship over Dyfed and Brycheiniog and formed them into a new kingdom, Deheubarth. In 942 Hywel acquired also Gwynedd and Powys, on the death of Idwal ab Anawrad ap Rhodri. After his death he was known as Hywel Dda, 'the Good'. Although economic life clearly developed under his rule – he established a coinage in Wales for the first time, using the facilities of the mint at Chester – the sobriquet was probably earned by the codi-fication of the laws of Wales, which are traditionally ascribed to his kingship. Amid the extremely tenuous information which we have on Welsh kings at this time, it is refreshing to find one who, leader in warfare as he must have been, also had time and inclination to give his attention to the good conduct of soci-ety. The laws of Wales, though known as *cyfraith Hywel*, were not created afresh in the tenth century; they represent a tradition of justice and the settlement of disputes that reaches back many centuries. As such, they represent the society in which they evolved, and concern themselves with the issues which arise in the sort of tribal society we have seen developing.

The population was divided into three main classes, at the top being the free tribesmen, the *bonheddwyr* or *bréyr*, who held ownership of the land and its stock, then the subject people, the *taeogion*, who were part of the overall kindred or *cenedl*, but whose rights were restricted. At the bottom, and with no rights under the law, was the slave population, known as *caethion*. Another distinct group was the *alltud*, composed of foreign incomers. A distinctive feature of the laws, and a clear indication of their tribal origins, was that in the case of a misdemeanour by an individual, his whole immediate kin-group was held responsible for paying the fine, normally in cows. The proportion of payment was determined by the status of people within the group, and the sharing of the proceeds was carried out in the same way. Land tenure was at the basis of society, which was almost wholly agricultural, and unsurprisingly much of the laws are concerned with defining and protecting land ownership. Compared to the vast amount of present-day regulation, the range was limited. Since the warrior culture above all needed to express pride and prowess, a certain rivalry and touchiness among members of the *bonheddwyr* was inevitable. This could lead to murder, family blood-feuds, and long-remem-bered resentments. It was to moderate, if not stamp out, such vendettas, that the law of *galanas* was introduced; the word itself means 'blood-feud', and it provided a scale of payments to be made for the murder of a person, depending on his status.

The earliest surviving manuscripts containing the laws date to almost three centuries after Hywel Dda, and numerous copies in Latin and Welsh survive from the thirteenth and fourteenth centuries. These are of interest as they show that the laws were capable of evolution and adaptation as time went on and circumstances changed. Archaic laws, even if no longer in force, remained in the books, along with new clauses and new laws, presenting a spectrum of the changing position over the centuries. Interpretation of Hywel's laws was the task of a professional corps of lawmen, whose knowledge was probably orally maintained rather than written down.

As we have seen, faced with the consolidation of the larger kingdoms, the leaders of smaller Welsh kingdoms sought to make alliances with the growing power of Wessex. Under Hywel Dda, this process took a long step forward. Despite his ruling vast tracts of Wales, he associated himself closely with the kingdom of Wessex, under both Alfred and Athelstan. His codification of the laws may have come from this association. From this time also comes the concept of English overlordship in Wales. Hywel made a number of visits to the court of Wessex and his name is found as a signatory – first among Welsh princes – on seven royal charters, as a *subregulus*, 'lesser minor king' and later as a *regulus*. This policy, however, kept Hywel's territories free from invasion and the resulting long period of peace no doubt helped to identify him as 'the Good'. Not all his subjects approved: the anonymous writer of the poem *Armes Prydein*, composed probably about 930, complains about the upstart English, and urges that the men of Wales should combine with those of Ireland – including the Dublin-based Vikings – and Strathclyde to drive them out.

On Hywel's death in 950, his son Owain became King of Deheubarth, while Gwynedd-Powys was ruled by his cousin, Meurig ab Idwal ab Anawrad. In the south-east, the kingdom of Morgannwg (Glamorgan) had come into being under a line of kings which also stemmed from Rhodri Mawr through his daughter Nest who had married Owain, King of Gwent and Glamorgan. Though smaller than the others, Morgannwg possessed a higher proportion of good farmland.

THE PATTERN OF KINGDOMS

At this time in Scotland, a powerful ruling family, the MacAlpins, was engaged in consolidating its grip on power. The kingdom of Strathclyde, sorely battered by Scots, Vikings and Anglo-Saxons, though it retained a separate identity until 1034, had since 889 been ruled not by a king stemming from the royal lineage of the Men of the North, but by a member of the Scottish MacAlpin family. In that year, when the kingship of Strathclyde finally ended, many of the Strathclyde nobility, with their retinues and portable goods, trekked or sailed south to Wales, where they settled mostly on the north-eastern and eastern border. This migration must have brought a further cultural contribution to Welsh tradition and legend. Meanwhile in Strathclyde, though the old Cumbric speech of the region would remain in isolated pockets for many years to come, Gaelic speakers flooded in, Gaelic place names replaced many older ones, and Gaelic laws supplanted those of old Strathclyde.

In the old 'Celtic' countries, there was a definite trend in the later ninth and early tenth century towards larger political units. It was most obvious in Scotland, which by 1034 had become a united kingdom. In Ireland, where the archaic tribal structure was least changed, there were provincial over-kings; and for a brief period between 1002 and 1014, Brian Bóruma established something like a unified kingdom. Wales in the later ninth century had three kingdoms, whose rulers had some degree of family relationship. It had a strong sense of identity, and a clearly defined frontier. There was the code of laws and the Welsh church – it might have been expected that Wales too would progress towards unification.

In the years after Hywel Dda's death, a number of factors combined to inhibit such progress. Perhaps the most important was tradition, particularly the traditional procedure by which a new king was installed. In Wales, as elsewhere in the 'Celtic' lands, the king's first-born son was not the automatic successor. The king was still a war-leader: he had to be a man of maturity and ability, or at least ruthlessness. In the royal kindred, all men were eligible to be king who could trace their descent from a great-great-grandfather who had been a king. This normally provided a number of candidates, with consequent opportunities for rivalry. Perhaps, among the lawgivers and senior counsellors of the *bonheddwyr*, there was resistance to reducing this competition to a single throne. Evidently, in the hundred-plus years between Hywel Dda and Gruffudd ap Llewelyn, no single king was able to impose himself over all the kingdoms. During this period, Wales, after a long time of relative security, began to be attacked again by the Vikings. These onslaughts were a mixture of plundering raids in the old style, and of vigorous attempts at colonisation. Dublin was an important trading station and the Vikings, with their far-spread connections to the Baltic, into Russia, and as far as Constantinople, were looking to set up trading stations at locations such as Cardiff and Haverfordwest. A substantial Norse community established itself in southern Dyfed. But further north, the Viking kingdom of the Hebrides, with its capital on the Isle of Man, was essentially a collection of piratical and marauding bands. A number of significant coastal locations from north to south acquired Scandinavian place names, like Swansea, 'Sven's seaplace', Fishguard, 'fish yard', Anglesey, 'island of the strait', Skomer, 'split island', but, in the words of Sir John Lloyd: 'all traces of the Northmen disappear as one leaves high-water mark and strikes inland' (I, p. 321). Warfare to east and west had a destabilising effect. Raiding into Mercia, a Welsh party killed an abbot, and a retaliatory raid in 916 reached as far as Brycheiniog and kidnapped the queen – presumably the wife of a local chieftain or *subregulus*. In 918, Cyfeiliog, a bishop in the south-east, was kidnapped by a Viking band and ransomed by Edward the Elder, King of Wessex. This perhaps indicates how far English kings were involving themselves with events in Wales. Whilst they sought undertakings from Scottish kings to be their 'man', to forbear from attack and join in defence, they did not actively interfere. In Wales, however, Athelstan went as far as to impose a tax in 929, something done only to a subject people. Another factor may be size. Wales is a small country, much smaller than Ireland or Scotland, and lay adjacent to the rich English province of Mercia, while Ireland was an island, and Scotland was separated from England by hills and mosses. Wales was accessible, and always a threat. It was understandable that in their pursuit of power and security, English kings should seek to negate that threat, and do everything to prevent a unified kingship of the Welsh.

GRUFFUDD AP LLEWELYN

In the century after Hywel Dda, a number of kings appeared from obscurity to seize or assume power. One of these was Llewelyn ap Seisill, who married Angharad, great-grand-daughter of Hywel Dda, and became King of Gwynedd in 1018. Llewelyn's son, Gruffudd, was a man with the necessary qualities to impose himself on his contemporaries. In succession, between 1039 and 1057, he seized the kingships of Gwynedd, Powys, Deheubarth and Glamorgan. Unlike Rhodri Mawr, Gruffudd achieved his position by force. By battle, murder and intrigue, he cut his way to supreme power. From 1057 until his death in 1063, he was King of Wales. Those seven years were dramatic ones, and they have left their mark upon the Welsh imagination. Gruffudd had never been prepared to be constrained within the frontier of Offa's Dyke. As early as 1039 he had won a battle at Rhyd-y-Groes, near Welshpool, against Leofric, Earl of Mercia. In 1055, allied with Leofric's disaffected son, Aelfgar, he destroyed Hereford and extended Welsh control over a wide swathe of countryside that took in most of the fertile Herefordshire basin as well as a long stretch of borderland to the north. Harold Godwinson, Earl of Wessex and later to be, briefly, King of England in 1066, was the broker of some kind of compromise settlement at this time, but it did not last. In 1062 Harold mounted a campaign by land and sea to bring Gruffudd down. Caught by surprise at his *llys*, or palace, at Rhuddlan, Gruffudd escaped by sea, taking the last resort of every hunted Welsh ruler, and retreated into Snowdonia, where he was killed in 1063. Two sources, the *Brut y Tywysogyon* and the *Ulster Chronicle*, say he was killed by Welshmen: his own men according to the *Brut*;

'THE HISTORY OF THE PRINCES' AND THE 'ANNALS OF CAMBRIA'

*B*rut y Tywysogion and *Annales Cambriae* are the main parts of the sparse set of ancient documents which record Welsh history in early medieval times. As the titles suggest, the 'History of the Princes' is in Welsh, and the 'Annals' in Latin. Texts of the 'History' are preserved in three Welsh versions, made in the thirteenth century from a now-lost Latin original. It records events between the years 680 and 1282; whilst entries for the earlier centuries are brief, often no more than a sentence, those for the eleventh century onwards are much more detailed, though still covering the same type of events. These are battles, royal accessions and deaths, and the appointments and deaths of bishops and abbots; interspersed with occasional terse notes of plagues, eclipses, earthquakes and exceptionally hot summers and cold winters. The 'Annals' date from around 1100; briefer than the 'History of the Princes', they cover events from 447 to 954, and so the two records frequently give the same information. The existing versions are copies of an original which itself was probably compiled from several different sources. With Nennius' *Historia Brittonum*, the 'Annals' provide the only mentions of Arthur prior to Geoffrey of Monmouth. Two entries refer to his part in the battle of Mount Badon (516) and the battle of Camlan, in which he was killed (537).

and by Cynan ap Iago according to the *Ulster Chronicle*. Iago ab Idwal, of the House of Gwynedd, had been one of Gruffudd's many victims on his way to the top.

Gruffudd ap Llewelyn was the last of his brief line to rule. The warlike qualities which had sustained his rise were also responsible for his fall. Some historians regard him favourably – David Walker in *Medieval Wales* refers to him as 'the outstanding Welsh ruler of the eleventh century' (p. 18). But his kingdom, built on bloodshed, had no staying power, and he left no legacy beyond the memory that Wales had, for a time, been a nation under a single king. Yet, if that had happened once, could it not happen again? Not if English policy had anything to do with it. Following the downfall of Gruffudd ap Llewelyn, Harold made sure that Wales reverted to being a set of separate kingdoms. Gwent and Gwynwllg returned to being a distinct kingdom, while the ousted Cadwgan ap Meurig resumed rule of the rest of Glamorgan. Bleddyn and Rhiwallon, half-brothers of Gruffudd ap Llewelyn, became the kings of Gwynedd and Powys respectively, and Maredudd ab Owain, a descendant of Hywel Dda, became ruler of Deheubarth. Long before Machiavelli spelled it out as a precept for sovereigns, 'divide and rule' was a fact of policy, in England as elsewhere.

CHAPTER SIX

The Normans in Wales

NORMAN ENTRENCHMENT

This was the situation in Wales when the Anglo-Saxons met their great catastrophe in 1066. The Welsh kings could only be spectators of events in England, or at best indulge in some raiding, at a time when English earldoms were in a state of flux, or intrigue with the old Anglo-Saxon nobility against the invaders. The conquest of England offered some opportunity, but consolidation of the Norman victory at Hastings happened with remarkable speed and efficiency. Four years later, William I was securely in control of all England except Cumbria, which remained a Scottish domain until 1092. Harold's dispensation in Wales did not hold for long. Gruffudd ap Llewelyn's sons rose up against their uncles in 1070, only to die fighting, along with Rhiwallon. Constant struggling for non-vacant kingships weakened the country. In 1072 Caradog ap Gruffudd, King of Gwynwllg, defeated and slew Maredudd ab Owain of Deheubarth, and two years later he also seized Glamorgan, sending Cadwgan into exile once again. Maredudd's brother Rhys attacked and killed Bleddyn in 1075, and was in turn killed two years later by Caradog ap Gruffudd. The remorseless rise of the latter came to an end in the battle of Mynydd Carn in 1081, when he was killed, along with Trahaearn ap Caradog, who had succeeded Bleddyn as King of Gwynedd.

William I's policy towards Wales soon became clear. His dispensation was a drastic and original one, destined to have a massive effect on future Welsh history. He created a series of lordships all along the length of the border, installing in each a tough Norman baron. The holdings of these 'Marcher' lords were different to those of other barons, in that their westward boundaries were left undefined. In Hereford, William fitzOsbern was installed as Earl of Hereford, with substantial powers, and in turn established Norman knights as his vassals in strong points, such as Ralph de Tosny at Clifford Castle and Walter de Lacy at Weobley. Further north, Shrewsbury was entrusted to Roger Montgomery and the earldom of Chester to Hugh the Fat, Viscount of Avranches. Adept colonisers, the Normans had worked out a method of securing themselves in hostile countryside which they practised with little change all the way from the Welsh Marches to Sicily. Its basis was the castle, a strong point, built hurriedly of wood at first, but replaced as soon as possible by a stone structure. Built on top of a motte or artificial hill, it was impregnable to any military arts possessed by the Welsh tribes. The castle was the great and prime symbol, proclaiming its owner's domination. But with the castle came also the town and the market place. The larger castles especially, with their bigger population, needed to be fed, and their inhabitants traded for food. In time, around the access to the castle, a tiny town would develop, a trading centre under the lord of the castle's protection, with a charter to define its rights and his share of the proceeds. The cosmopolitan lords of the castles, and their women, with cousins in Normandy or Palestine, wanted luxury goods that the Welsh kings had never aspired to. While much of these came in by sea, or across England, Welshmen too found it profitable to be importers and merchants. But any hunger for luxuries came far short of the Normans' hunger for land. By the time fitzOsbern died in 1071, he had consolidated his position and begun the great stone castle of Chepstow, or Strigoil, on the Welsh side of the River Wye, intentionally as a base from which to launch invasions into Gwent. By 1086, a further castle was going up at Caerleon, and the Welsh kingdom of Gwent was no more. In the central Marches, Roger of Montgomery, Earl of Shrewsbury, also moved into territory which was indisputably Welsh. The old mound, Hen Domen, at Montgomery shows the site of the first castle there.

By 1073 they had gone far beyond that, penetrating into Ceredigion, building a castle on the site of Dyn Geraint, and threatening to push southwards into

Chepstow Castle

Dyfed. Largely through the efforts of his cousin, Robert de Tilleul, also known as Robert of Rhuddlan since it was there he set up his base, Hugh the Fat also extended Norman control along the northern coastline. By 1086 Rhuddlan was a trading centre with special privileges, its profits shared between the Lord of Rhuddlan and his feudal superior in Chester. The Domesday Book, the great record of land tenure in the Norman kingdom, shows Robert as paying £40 for north Wales. He was possessor of Gwynned; its Welsh king, Gruffud ap Cynan, spent twelve years as a prisoner of the Earl of Chester. On escaping, he was reduced to making small-scale raids into his erstwhile kingdom. Despite their castles, the Normans were not completely inviolate. In one of the raids mounted by Gruffudd, Robert was killed, and Gruffudd reinstated himself.

Norman incursions into south Wales beyond Gwent were checked by Rhys ap Tewdwr, who not only established himself as a strong Prince of Deheubarth – by this time the old form of king, or *brenin*, was being discarded – but maintained cordial personal relations with William the Conqueror himself. William made a visit to St Davids in 1081, essentially a display of overlordship, though Welsh sources sought to present it as a pilgrimage to their greatest shrine. Rhys ap Tewdwr, like Robert of Rhuddlan, paid the English King £40 for the right to rule his princedom. But the peace only lasted for William I's lifetime. In the reign of his son, William Rufus, a new generation of Normans was encouraged to extend dominion into Wales. Rhys ap Tewdwr was killed in 1093, fighting in a vain attempt to keep the Normans out of Brycheiniog. Bernard of Neufmarché built a castle at Aberhonddu where he also founded the priory church, now Brecon Cathedral; soon his knights had their castles at strategic points such as Tretower, Crickhowell, Hay and Bronllys. Another old Welsh kingdom vanished, to be replaced by a Norman lordship. Glamorgan too was invaded. Robert fitzHamo, who had a large landholding in Gloucestershire, was encouraged by William Rufus to occupy Glamorgan. He established a beachhead with a castle at Cardiff, but his and his successors' progress in extending control throughout the old kingdom was slow, and the uplands of Morgannwg remained under Welsh control. Following the death of Rhys ap Tewdwr, the Normans from their base in Ceredigion pressed south as far as Pembroke, where the castle was begun by Arnulf of Montgomery in 1093; another expedition led by William fitzBaldwin set up a lordship based on a castle at Rhyd y Gors, near Carmarthen.

From the original granting of frontier lordships, the Normans with typical insouciance had progressed rapidly towards domination of much of the best land of Wales. The native princes, more or less reluctantly acknowledging the overlordship of the English king, found that they received neither protection nor consideration in the face of these inroads. But the Normans were relatively few in number, and their lines of communication were stretched very thinly.

Between 1094 and 1098 a number of efforts were made to drive them out, but with little result, except in Gwynedd, where Gruffudd ap Cynan would rule for many years. The Norman castle of Rhyd y Gors was abandoned for several years. But even when a Welsh army defeated them in battle, as happened at Aber Llech in Brycheiniog, the invaders still had their castles to fall back on. A revealing contrast is found in Glamorgan, between the Norman keep at Cardiff, a state-of-the-art piece of military architecture, and the earthwork ramparts constructed by the Welsh leaders in the mountains, essentially the same kind of fortification that their Iron Age ancestors had built, hundreds of years before.

WALES UNDER HENRY I

King Henry I of England appears to have considered Wales as simply part of his own domains. Far more than William I and William II, or any later king until Edward I, he made his own dispositions there during his long reign between 1100 and 1135. Faced with rebellion from the Mortimers, he deprived Hugh of Shrewsbury and Arnulf of Pembroke of their earldoms; instead, royal officials were put in, answerable directly to the king. Henry introduced Flemish settlers, skilled workers in the cloth industry, to Pembroke, and these spread later to the Welsh-controlled Cydweli and Ceredigion. Control of the numerous Welsh

GEOFFREY OF MONMOUTH

Not a lot is known about his life: 'of Monmouth' is how he referred to himself. Born some time before 1100, he lived until 1155. He was a churchman, based for a considerable part of his life in Oxford. In 1152 he was made Bishop of St Asaph, but died two or three years later. He has been described as 'the inventor of British history', being the first writer to attempt to combine the known elements into a coherent narrative. Unfortunately, 'invention' also applies to most of Geoffrey's content. He wrote the *Historia Regum Britanniae* ('History of the Kings of Britain'); also a Life of Merlin in Latin verse. He claimed to have had the use of a 'very ancient book written in the British [Welsh] language' in writing his history, but this is not taken seriously. What Geoffrey did was to write the history of Celtic Britain from its supposed foundation by Trojans led by Brutus, through ninety-nine kings to Cadwaladr, son of Cadwallon, who died in 689. Geoffrey gives a major role to a figure who would otherwise scarcely rate a footnote in history, King Arthur, the great hero of Britain, with his wizard-counsellor Merlin. His book marks the start of a torrent of Arthurian literature, and gives medieval and modern European literature one of its greatest themes. Despite some scepticism even at the time the first copies were circulated (his contemporary Giraldus Cambrensis being one unbeliever), it was not until the sixteenth century that the facts of Geoffrey's version were seriously questioned, and even two hundred years later he still influenced wishful thinkers. Writing in an age when fake pedigrees and imaginary episodes 'reinforcing' truth were common, he may have been deliberately seeking to glorify the Welsh tradition, at a time when Norman rule was being imposed.

enclaves between the Norman territories of south Glamorgan and Pembroke was assured by the building of a royal castle at Carmarthen. At this time the two most powerful Welsh princes were Gruffudd ap Cynan of Gwynedd, and Cadwgan ap Bleddyn in Powys. Benefiting from the relative weakness of the earldom of Chester, where the Earl of Chester was a minor, Gruffudd maintained something of the old style of Welsh kingship. Cadwgan was too friendly with Earl Robert of Shrewsbury for Henry's liking, and when Robert was sent in disgrace back to France, Henry replaced Cadwgan with his brother, Iorwerth, in Powys, and gave Ceredigion to Cadwgan. But he also is said to have told a Norman magnate, Gilbert de Clare: 'Now I will give you the land of Cadwgan ap Bleddyn. Go and take possession of it.' It was an old Norman formula, on the lines of 'might is right'. If de Clare could impose himself on all or any of Ceredigion, he was welcome to have it. Henry had also pledged other territories to Iorwerth, but defaulted. No Welsh prince was to be allowed too much power. De Clare rose to the challenge, taking over the castle at Cardigan, building another at Aberystwyth and a number of subsidiary keeps for his feudal dependants. As David Walker notes in *Medieval Wales*, soon only one of the ten commotes of Ceredigion did not have a Norman castle, with a Norman castellan busy turning the old Welsh district into his own lordship. Gruffudd ap Cynan was more successful in developing an independent stance. By 1137 he had achieved a tight grip on an enlarged Gwynedd which included three of the four *cantrefi* of the Middle Country, or Perfeddwlad, the region between the Conwy and the Dee; and in that same year, in defiance of the de Clare castles, he took Ceredigion. His son, Owain ap Gruffudd, known as Owain Gwynedd, completed the dispersal of the Normans from Ceredigion in the following year.

Aberystwyth Castle in Victorian times

During this reign, the Marcher lordships established the curious identity, part-English, part-Welsh, part-independent, which would characterise them in future centuries. On their western and northern edges was Wales; to the east was England and in between was a string of domains, some large, some quite small, whose rulers were subjects of the English king, but who applied their own laws, and who were free of most of the constraints placed by the kingship on the nobles. They could build fortifications as they pleased, raise their own warbands, and make war as they thought fit – in one direction only, of course. Historians have often been exercised to explain the remarkable powers of the Marcher lords. The situation was not paralleled on the Scottish border, where at this time the frontier was in active dispute between Scottish and English kings. Some historians have likened the Marcher lordships to petty kingdoms and suggested that a Welsh royal tradition was invoked in their organisation. This seems quite probable: the Marcher lords were always happy to quote Welsh precedents when it suited their case. It may simply be, though, though that they owe their existence to Norman pragmatism: they were seen as an expedient way of keeping the warlike Welsh in check. As the forms of English common law developed, and as justice began to be centred in the royal courts rather than be left in the hands of barons, the Welsh Marches were regarded as a special case and left outside these dispensations. Two Waleses emerged: 'Inner' and 'Outer' Wales; the former largely based on Gwynedd and Ceredigion, and still under Welsh rule; the latter taking in much of Powys, all the old south-eastern kingdoms, Glamorgan, and Dyfed, and largely governed by Norman colonists. Even within a Norman domain, there might be differences. If it contained large areas of higher ground, these were usually left to the Welsh inhabitants as 'Welshries', where Norman-style agriculture could not be practised. Under a local sub-chief, such Welsh communities continued to live in the old style, whilst the full rigour of the feudal system was introduced on the lower ground.

THE CHARACTER OF NORMAN RULE

Like their Viking ancestors, the Normans were a commercial people. In the districts where their power was established, they set up markets, organised trading links with other places, and introduced the use of coinage. Their demands for agricultural and land produce of all kinds extended to by-products such as leather, encouraging a strong agricultural economy in areas like Pembroke, Glamorgan and Brecon. Agricultural life was based on the manor, with open fields tilled each year in rotation, and a hierarchy of landworkers arranged in strict feudal order, each owing service to his superior, and with the lord of the manor at the head. He too would be required to supply a share of produce to his earl, and be ready to give military service.

In the complex psychological make-up of the Normans, piety was present, as well as cruelty. By the early twelfth century, abbeys and priories, endowed with generous grants of land, were being built. Basingwerk Abbey, on the Dee estuary, built on a site fortified by the Mercians, was founded by Ranulf, Earl of Chester, in 1131. Llanthony Priory, in a valley of the Black Mountain, was set up by the de Lacys in 1108. Ewenni Priory in Glamorgan was set up on the site of an old Welsh church by Maurice de Londres, the local baron, in about 1141. St Dogmaels Abbey, a mile west of Cardigan, was founded around 1113 by Robert fitzMartin, Lord of Cemais. Each of these was inhabited by a different order of monks, Cistercian, Augustinian, Benedictine respectively.

There were numerous others, with Benedictine houses in the majority, usually established as daughter-foundations of monasteries in Europe. They remained part of the structure of Norman Wales, inhabited by Norman monks, giving their counsel and hospitality to the Norman lords as they travelled through the countryside.

THE TRANSFORMATION OF THE CHURCH

St Dogmaels was founded on the site of the Celtic monastery, or *clas*, of Llandudoch. It seems likely that by this time the Welsh church was in a poor way of organisation and morale. The warfare between kingdoms, their breaking-up and re-forming, constantly split up the pattern of bishoprics. At the time of the Norman invasions, the number of bishops was very small, perhaps only two, those of St Davids (Deheubarth) and Bangor (Gwynedd). It was an era of ecclesiastical and monastic reform throughout Europe, spurred on by the urgings of Pope Gregory VII. The *clasau* of Wales, like the comparable *ceile dei* monasteries of Ireland and Scotland, had a very distinctive organisation. Their monks could marry, could own property, and pass on their positions by heredity. The monasteries themselves were simple affairs. The church (and every other building) was most likely constructed from timber framing filled with wattle and daub. To the Normans, who already were masters of the grandly impressive new Romanesque style of building in stone, they were laughably primitive.

In the space of a few decades, the public face of religion was transformed. New bishops were appointed. St Davids Cathedral and Bangor Cathedral were rebuilt in stone.

A new cathedral was built at Llandaf. This site had a long, though legendary, tradition as the religious centre of Glamorgan. The reinvigorated see of Canterbury, with its Norman archbishop, did not lose the opportunity to make sure that new bishops in Wales paid homage to it. The Welsh church became a sub-province of greater Christendom, brought into line in matters of liturgy, rule of life, canon law, and organisation. Many of the *clasau* converted themselves, or were converted into houses of the new orders, often the Augustinian; many others simply ceased to exist, except perhaps as local churches. The old spiritual tradition had perhaps lost its purity and ascetic edge: the age of saints was long gone. But the lives of the saints, their asceticism and simple devotion, were by no means forgotten. It took the Welsh some time to adjust to the new style of religion, identified as it was with the land-grabbing incomers. But in time they warmed to the austere virtue of the Cistercian Order, which seemed to hark back to the spirit of the old Celtic church. When the Lord Rhys established his rule in Ceredigion in 1165, he took over patronage of the newly founded abbey at Strata Florida. It was resited, rebuilt, enlarged, and gifted with great tracts of

The ruins of Strata Florida Abbey (Ystrad Fflur) in Victorian times

rolling green hillsides. Welsh lords and princes would come here in their old age, to prepare for death and burial. If Strata Florida became the prime Welsh abbey, it was still only one of many Cistercian abbeys endowed by Welsh lords.

As each new abbey was established, it tended to send forth monks to start a new daughter house. Thus Strata Florida had been founded from Whitland; and itself sent a colony to Aberconwy in 1186. Strata Marcella, founded with princely support in Powys in 1170, established a daughter-house at Valle Crucis, on a site full of historical resonance, near Llangollen (1201). A few hundred metres away is the Pillar of Eiliseg, set up in the ninth century to commemorate the glories of the royal line of Powys. Male monasticism was always more popular in Wales than female monasticism. Even by 1300, there were only three nunneries in the country, at Llanllyr in Ceredigion, Llanllugan in Cedewain, and at Usk.

Although their belief in the spiritual dimension of life and death was sincere, the Normans also knew the value of an organised church as part of the fabric of an orderly society. They established a fourth bishopric, that of St Asaph, in 1143. Like Llandaf, it was a site of ancient sanctity, identified (though only in unprovable legend) with St Kentigern, or Mungo, the sixth-century Cumbric

GIRALDUS CAMBRENSIS

Gerald de Barri or 'Gerald the Welshman' as he was proud to call himself, was born around 1146, to a Norman father, William of Barri, Lord of Manorbier, and a half-Welsh mother, Angharad, granddaughter of the matriarchal Nest, whose father was Rhys ap Tewdwr. His uncle was Bishop of St Davids and he too was educated, in Gloucester and Paris, for a church career. Made Archdeacon of Brecon when still a young man, he never achieved his aim of becoming Bishop of St Davids, despite having been nominated by the cathedral chapter in both 1175 and 1198; and having made the most strenuous efforts in defence of his claim on the second occasion, including three visits to Rome. Gerald's aim was to establish Wales as a separate province of the church and thus he was opposed both by English royal policy and by the implacable opposition of Canterbury. Between 1184 and 1194 he was a royal adviser both on Wales and Ireland; he was a member of the entourage of the future King John in Ireland in 1184; and he escorted Baldwin, Archbishop of Canterbury, round Wales in 1188. Above all, he was an author, writing in Latin with an inveterate interest about himself, his countrymen, their condition and habits, and reporting and interpreting what he saw on his travels. His two books on Ireland are patronising to the native Irish; his *Journey Through Wales* and *Description of Wales* are much more favourable to the people and their traditions. In later life Gerald retired to Lincoln, having resigned his archdeaconry to his nephew. Somewhat embittered in his last years, especially by the failure of the chapter of St Davids to nominate him for the again-vacant bishopric in 1214, he became more polemical and self-justificatory in his writings, including his *Autobiography* and the anti-Plantagenet *On the Instruction of Princes*. His battle for St Davids has made him a Welsh patriot, and his two Welsh 'travel books' give an absorbing, highly readable and historically invaluable account of twelfth-century Wales.

saint who later worked to convert the Britons of Strathclyde. In the twelfth century the Rhuddlan region was constantly being overrun by Welsh and Anglo-Norman forces, and the founders may have hoped to stabilise matters there; it is unlikely this aim was achieved.

THE WELSH FIGHT BACK

In both Ireland and Scotland, it is notable that with time the incoming Normans (and with them Bretons and Flemings) became increasingly 'gaelicised'. They adopted the language and culture of the society in which they found themselves, although they also brought many changes. In Wales, it seems the Normans and the Flemings of the south-west, were less inclined to take on a native colouring. This may be partly because most of them were in large enclaves like Pembroke and Glamorgan, and parts of the north-east, where they were cut off from the Welsh inhabitants. They were also much closer geographically to their cousins in England, particularly those in the Marcher lordships, and this helped to maintain a clear sense of identity. Another fact helped to confirm them in their Normanness: the Welsh continued to fight them.

Between 1135, when Henry I died and the chaotic reign of Stephen began, and 1154, the accession year of Henry II, the Welsh princes set about regaining their historic ground. Owain Gwynedd added the easternmost *cantref* of the Perfeddwlad, Tegeingl, to his kingdom of Gwynedd. Large parts of the kingdom of Deheubarth were reclaimed by Owain and his brothers, the sons of Gruffudd ap Rhys ap Tewdwr, and they also became masters of Ceredigion. The Lord of Powys, Madog ap Maredudd, captured Oswestry and other lordships of the March. For a time, with no central authority in England, the Marcher lords felt a new insecurity.

THE REIGN OF HENRY II

Many of these Welsh gains were reversed in the reign of Henry II, when the mailed fist and the will-power to wield it returned to English government. In 1157, Henry II invaded Gwynedd. Owain Gwynedd, already at odds with his brother Cadwaladr and with Madog of Powys among others (whom Henry scooped into alliance), was subjected to attack by land and sea. He made a strictly tactical submission, and as soon as the invading forces had withdrawn, returned to an independent style. The old stand-off between Gwynedd and Powys resumed. Ever on the lookout for English weakness or distraction, the Welsh soon became aware of the internal problems faced by Henry II as a result of his long quarrel with the Archbishop of Canterbury, Thomas Beckett, who was finally murdered by Henry's agents in 1170. Henry mounted another invasion in 1165, and Owain Gwynedd – styling himself *princeps Wallensium*, 'chief of the Welsh' – put himself at the head of a federation of Welsh leaders. Appalling weather in the Berwyn Mountains prevented any meeting of armies, and Henry withdrew in angry frustration. Possessed of a number of young Welsh hostages, he had them mutilated by blinding, an act of spite which was long remembered among the Welsh. The royal castle at Rhuddlan was razed and Owain, who had lost Tegeingl, regained it. But with Owain's death in 1170, Gwynedd ceased to be an active centre of resistance, collapsing into civil war among the sons of Owain and existing as little more than a set of petty states for the next generation.

In the south, intense pressure on Dyfed and other Norman lordships was kept up by the four sons of Gruffudd, who had taken control of Ceredigion, Emlyn and Cantref Bychan. By 1155, only one remained, Rhys ap Gruffudd, Prince of a reinvigorated Deheubarth. His career falls into two great phases, the first as enemy of Henry II, who forced him out of Ceredigion and Cantref Bychan. Rhys did not accept this lightly, and warfare continued. It was due to intense Welsh pressure on Norman holdings in the south-west that the Norman colonisation of Ireland began. In 1169 Robert fitzStephen, former castellan of Cardigan, was allowed by Rhys to lead a force to Leinster, where the ousted King Dermot was seeking help to regain his throne. The following year, another force accompanied Richard, Earl of Pembroke, known as Strongbow, to Ireland. There were Welsh and half-Welsh in this expedition, as well as Normans. Dermot died, and, in a process hardly unfamiliar to anyone who knew the Normans, Strongbow

---

GIRALDUS CAMBRENSIS ON THE WELSH AND ENGLISH

. . . if they [the Welsh] had only one prince, and that a good one; this nation, situated in so powerful, strong and inaccessible a country, could hardly ever be completely overcome. If, therefore, they would be inseparable, they would become insuperable . . . especially as the English fight for power, the Welsh for liberty; the one to procure gain, the other to avoid loss; the English hirelings for money, the Welsh patriots for their country . . . Hence during the military expedition which King Henry II made in our days against South Wales, an old Welshman at Pencadair, who had faithfully adhered to him, being desired to give his opinion about the royal army, and whether he thought that the rebels would make resistance, and what would be the final event of this war, replied, 'This nation, O King, may now, as in former times, be harassed, and in a great measure weakened and destroyed by your and other powers, and it will often prevail by its laudable exertions; but it can never be totally subdued through the wrath of man, unless the wrath of God shall concur. Nor do I think, that any other nation than this of Wales, or any other language, whatever may hereafter come to pass, shall, in the day of severe examination before the Supreme Judge, answer for this corner of the earth.

Description of Wales, final chapter

---

became King of Leinster. These Irish adventures took place without the permission or approval of Henry II, who had no intention of seeing an independent Norman state arise in Ireland. To secure his position in Wales, he appointed the warlike Rhys ap Gruffudd as his Justiciar in the south, in 1172. Rhys was more than a warlord; diplomacy and marriage had also helped extend his domains, making him overlord of Gwrtheyrnion, Maelienydd, Elfael and great tracts of Glamorgan, Gwent and Brycheiniog, where Welsh chieftaincies still controlled all the high ground. For twenty-five years peace was maintained in the south.

The most difficult thing for a Welsh prince to achieve was an orderly succession. The brawling of his sons cancelled out all that Owain Gwynedd had achieved. The Lord Rhys had worked hard to establish marriage alliances across the south and mid-Wales, with Norman as well as Welsh families. The result was a network of mutual suspicion as much as alliance. When he died in 1197, out of credit with the King of England, Deheubarth ceased to be a power.

CHAPTER SEVEN

The Princes

PRECARIOUS PRINCEDOMS

Rhys ap Gruffudd, known also as the Lord Rhys, and Prince of Deheubarth, made Cardigan his chief base, occupying the stone castle constructed by the Normans. Rhys is sometimes referred to as *proprietarius princeps Sudwallie*, 'proprietary Prince of South Wales'. *Princeps* was already an ancient word in the vocabulary of power; Emperor Augustus had used it, in the sense of 'principal citizen', serving to tone down the Imperial reality of his position, and for centuries it had been equated with supreme power. By this time it was already acquiring the sense of a ruler of lesser status than a king. Whether he called himself king, prince, or even King Henry's Justiciar, there was no maintaining Welsh courtly tradition without maintaining Welsh culture. It was an era of high bardic accomplishment, and Rhys is recorded as having held a great *eisteddfod* in 1176:

> *At Christmas, in the year 1176, Rhys, Prince of South Wales, gave a magnif-icent entertainment with deeds of arms and other shows in his new castle of Cardigan or Aberteifi, to a great number of illustrious natives and foreigners; notice of which has been given a year and a day before by proclamations throughout all Britain and Ireland. The musical bards of North Wales and South Wales, who had been expressly invited to the festival and a poetical contest, were seated in chairs with much ceremony in the middle of the great hall of the castle. Animated with their usual emulation, the presence of their noble audience, and expectation of the rich rewards promised to the victors, they pursued to a great length their generous strife, which terminated with honour to both parties, the pre-eminence in Poetry being judged to the poeti-cal Bards of North Wales; and in music to the domestic musical Bards of Prince Rhys.*
>
> (Edward Jones, *An Historical Account of the Welsh Bards*)

Rhys's primacy among the Welsh rulers was helped by the splitting of Powys at this time into two parts, where the descendants of Madog ruled only the north, the Dee Valley from Edeirnion to Maelor, which came to be known as Powys Fadog. The southern part, Powys Wenwynwyn, started from the grant of a single district, Cyfeilioig, to Owain and Meurig, nephews of Madog.

PRINCE MADOG AND AMERICA

In the reign of Elizabeth I, at a time when England was contesting Spanish claims to the Americas, a curious legend gained currency. It told of Madog, a son of Owain Gwynedd, who in the late twelfth century sailed on an expedition westwards past Ireland, finding a previously unknown land. He returned to Wales to tell of his discovery, then left again to repeat his voyage. He was never heard of again. The story, usefully, establishes a Welsh discovery of America – to be exploited by Tudor England – three hundred years before Columbus. In the 1790s, tales began to circulate about the Mandans, an Indian tribe, said to be white like Europeans, and who spoke a language that seemed to closely resemble Welsh. The legend gained enough credence for a young Methodist, John Evans, from Waenfawr in Snowdonia, to journey up the Missouri river until he met with the Mandan Indians. Unfortunately, the Mandan language did not resemble Welsh and the Indians had no story of ancestors from across the ocean. Evans's maps were however to be of great value to Lewis and Clark in their first crossing of the American continent in 1804.

Under Owain's expert manipulation, this area, much enlarged, was passed to his son Gwenwynwyn on Owain's death in 1197. From then there were two Powyses.

In Gwynedd, Dafydd ap Owain ruled somewhat uneasily, under constant threat of challenge from within his own family, though sustained by the favour of Henry II, to whom he swore allegiance in 1177. Three years earlier he had married Henry's illegitimate half-sister, Emma. The balance of power in Wales probably suited Henry well; with a prince in the north and one in the south, each having sworn allegiance, he might feel that Wales was a problem-free zone. But his dispositions did not last. Both in Gwynedd and in Deheubarth, quarrels within the ruling family made the princedoms unstable. The Lord Rhys faced rebellion by his son, Maelgwn, in 1194, and was imprisoned briefly; in 1195 two other sons conspired against him, bringing the old lord into military action to defeat them. Rhys went on to ravage the domains of the Marcher lord, William de Braose, whose daughter was married to his son, Gruffydd. The Lord Rhys died in 1197 and was buried in St Davids Cathedral. Sir John Lloyd wrote of him: 'His name will live in Welsh history as that of the greatest of the princes of Deheubarth, whose long and persistent struggle against the Anglo-Norman power was the chief means of keeping alive in south Wales the idea of Welsh nationality and independence' (II, p. 583). His son, Gruffydd, was the nominated successor, but Gruffydd's brother, Maelgwn, from his own base in Ceredigion, made alliance with Gwenwynwyn of southern Powys, and Gruffydd was captured and imprisoned. On his death in 1201, his son, Rhys Ieuanc, was able to claim only a small part of the old kingdom, Cantref Mawr, between the Tywi and the Teifi. King John of England, who had acceded to the throne on the death of Richard I in 1199, favoured Rhys Ieuanc's uncle, Maelgwn, bestowing

Ceredigion and Emlyn on him. Maelgwn resigned Cardigan Castle to John. 'Lackland' John he might have been in England, but in Wales he was the master, through his marriage, of the great fertile domain of Glamorgan, and felt himself to be experienced in the ways of the Welsh.

LLYWELYN AB IORWERTH

By 1194, the tottery rule in Gwynedd of Dafydd ap Owain was brought to an end by his nephew, Llywelyn ab Iorwerth Drwyndwn, who assembled an army and defeated Dafydd in a battle near the Conwy estuary. When his cousin Gruffudd died in 1200, he became sole ruler of Gwynedd. A royal wife was found for him, in the person of King John's illegitimate daughter, Joan, in 1205.

In his southern part of old Powys, Gwenwynwyn was a powerful and restless figure. Aspiring to princedom himself, he set out to fight the incursions being made by a new generation of Marcher families, the de Braoses and the Mortimers. In 1198, he was heavily defeated near Painscastle. When King John fell out with William de Braose in 1208, Gwenwynwyn attempted to take over what de Braose had wrested from Welsh lordships, but this was not part of John's plan. The dynamic was seized by Llywelyn ab Iorwerth, who took possession of Powys Wenwynwyn, and also of northern Ceredigion. This turn of events, threatening to bring about a new Greater Gwynedd, did not suit John, who brought a royal army against Llywelyn in 1211 and forced him to yield. Llywelyn's rule was restricted to the lands west of the Conwy. Llywelyn's surrender was inspired in part by the lack of Welsh support for him; this was to change within a year, as it became apparent that John was building a new fortress at Aberystwyth and had no intention of being a remote and relatively benign, undemanding overlord.

King John at this time had his troubles elsewhere; and the insurgent Welsh, reunited behind Llywelyn, had the unusual pleasure of finding themselves with grand international allies. Pope Innocent III blessed their cause, and King Philip Augustus of France sent an emissary to Llywelyn, whose reply is still preserved in the national Archives of France. What had begun as little more than a jockeying for position among Welsh lordships was suddenly part of a European strategy in which the Welsh had little direct interest. But Llywelyn well understood what was going on in England between King John and his barons, and his capture of Shrewsbury in May 1215 was a deliberate act on behalf of the barons, which helped precipitate the ceremony at Runnymede a month later, when King John sealed the compact of the 'Magna Carta' between himself and the nobles. There is little reference to Wales in that celebrated document, apart from the clause which stated that neither Welsh nor English should remain in possession of lands unjustly seized; and that in Inner Wales the right to landownership should be under the Law of Wales, while in Marchia Wallie, 'Wales of the March', it should be under the Law of the March.

Within Wales, Llywelyn's campaign went on. Two major castles, Carmarthen and Cardigan, fell to the Welsh. In effect he was master of most of the territory. In 1216, after some form of revolt by Gwenwynwyn, he seized Powys Wenwynwyn. Using the feudal instruments provided by the Normans, he received the homage of most of the Welsh rulers. At the time of John's death in 1216, his power was at its height. A reluctant English government acknowledged this reality in the Treaty of Worcester of 1218, accepting Llywelyn's pre-eminent position in Wales.

This was never more than a holding position as far as the advisers of the new king, the boy Henry III, were concerned. The basic maxim with reference to Wales had not changed, and English policy was to force Llywelyn back within the boundaries of Gwynedd. In 1223 the castles of Carmarthen and Cardigan were snatched back by William, Earl of Pembroke, on behalf of Henry III. Hubert de Burgh, Justiciar of England, sought to build a new castle at Montgomery. Llywelyn defeated him at Ceri in 1228, and in 1231 led an army to Brecon, which he destroyed by fire, then continued down into the plain of Glamorgan and similarly destroyed Neath. In the Peace of Middle, concluded in 1234, Llywelyn was again confirmed as first among the leaders of the Welsh. He took a new title, Prince of Aberffraw and Lord of Snowdonia. Whilst both these styles related to the north, they had never been used before, and shed a unique lustre on their bearer.

LLYWELYN'S LEGACY

There must have been many who saw the dream of the Principality of Wales again promising to take form. Llywelyn, after decades of rule, was established as pre-eminent among the rulers of Wales, enjoying the homage and support of virtually all the others. He had obtained from the Pope the right to leave the throne of Gwynedd not to Gruffudd, his eldest son (by a Welsh mother) but to Dafydd, his son by Henry's sister, Joan. Dafydd in turn married Isabella, daughter of William de Braose; the most important of a series of marriages linking the ruling house of Gwynedd to this upstart Norman family from the Marches. In a curious episode, Llywelyn had William de Braose hanged in 1230 for seducing Joan, though their marriage survived.

Llywelyn died on 11 April 1240, with his power and authority intact. In a long career, he had combined military resourcefulness and strength with an ability to make and maintain diplomatic solutions, and had earned the sobriquet, 'the Great' which later historians bestowed. An abiding friendship with

Ranulf, Earl of Chester, was the key to peace on his eastern flank; his daughter Helen was married to Ranulf's heir, his nephew, John; but the marriage was childless and the earldom in due course reverted to the Crown. Within Wales he was able to contain the rivalries of other rulers, not least the restless Gwenwynwyn, and to prevent them making alliances with outside forces. His use of the trappings of Norman feudalism, and the numerous marriages of his dependants to Norman husbands or wives have been criticised as showing too great a leaning away from Welsh tradition. His court has sometimes been seen as a 'Normanised' one. In many respects it probably was, whilst remaining an essentially Welsh one in language, literary and musical tradition. Llywelyn appears to have been a pragmatic ruler, able to read the signs of the times, and able to use instruments that would otherwise be used against him. In his time, the law increasingly became the prince's law rather than the 'Laws of the Welsh'.

Dafydd ap Llywelyn was not permitted to receive the homage of Welsh rulers as his father had done; this was to be reserved for the King of England. His elder half-brother, Gruffudd, was sent as a hostage to the Tower of London (he fell to his death trying to escape on St David's Day, 1244). In that year Dafydd renewed his father's alliances with the lordships of the south, and Henry III invaded Gwynedd. Dafydd wrote to the Pope, offering to hold his principality as a direct papal vassalage, thus cutting out the English overlordship; he referred to it as the 'Principality of Wales'. But in early 1245, the Pope rejected the suggestion. English representation at the Lateran Court was strong and determined, and English gold spoke louder than Welsh aspirations.

THE RISE OF LLYWELYN II

Dafydd died childless in 1246, while English armies occupied his lands. At the time of his pledging allegiance to Henry III, the English king had inserted a clause that, if Dafydd had no heir, his kingdom would fall to Henry. In the event, Henry did not pursue this option; Gwynedd – again to the west of the Conwy – was ruled by Dafydd's nephews Owain and Llywelyn ap Gruffudd, under very strict terms. In 1252 a third brother, Dafydd, joined the ruling group. Their power was heavily limited, and real power was held by Henry's tax collectors. In 1255 Llywelyn, grandson of Llywelyn the Great, took action for himself. He had his brothers arrested and imprisoned, seized control of Gwynedd uwch Conwy, and, in the following year, also of the Perfeddwlad, or 'middle country' east of the Conwy. With the people rising in his support, he swiftly extended his authority as far south as Glamorgan, and as far west as Ceredigion and Ystrad Tywi. In the battle of Y Cymerau, near Llandeilo, a royal army was defeated. Henry III led an ineffective invasion of Gwynedd, whose failure brought the Lord of Powys Fadog, Gruffudd ap Madog, on to

Llywelyn's side. Writing as Prince of Wales, Llywelyn called for aid from Scotland.

Between 1258 and 1262, Llywelyn II consolidated his position within Wales. His chief aim was to have his position accepted by England. But despite annually renewed truces, an agreement was not reached. Henry III's attention was distracted by the baronial revolt led by Simon de Montfort. In 1262 Llywelyn invaded the Marcher lordship of Maelienydd, and in the following year invaded the lands of Brecon and Abergavenny. Although he suffered a military defeat of the slopes of the Blorenge, he appears to have gained the support of most of the inhabitants. Finally he entered into alliance with de Montfort in 1264, just before the latter became for a time the controller of events in England. In June 1265, at Pipton, near Glasbury on Wye, Simon de Montfort, on behalf of the English Crown, solemnly recognised Llywelyn as Prince of Wales and as overlord of the *magnates Walliae*, 'great men of Wales'. The Principality of Wales was held as a vassalage of the King of England, and Llywelyn was to pay the Crown 30,000 marks over a ten-year period.

Six weeks later, de Montfort was dead on the battlefield of Evesham, his document a dead letter. But Llywelyn still had all his gains. It took another two years until the Treaty of Montgomery, made with Henry III, largely through the good offices of the Papal Legate, Ottobuono, confirmed his position as Prince of Wales and gave him the right to receive homage from all the Welsh lords except Maredudd ap Rhys of Dryslwyn, who had never swerved in loyalty to Henry III (Llywelyn acquired this right for a separate payment in 1270). He retained the Marcher lordships which he had taken, or was given the right to prove his claim. The payment this time was 25,000 marks. The Treaty awarded more than anyone might have expected England to concede. But it was far from being an acknowledgement of Welsh independence. It was framed as a personal grant from Henry as Llywelyn's sovereign, giving him his lands and title.

LOYALTY AND NATIONHOOD

This was an era in which the concept of a *patria*, or 'fatherland', was scarcely recognised. Ownership and loyalty was vested in individuals. It was perfectly possible for the head of one family to be the holder of estates in three different countries and to be answerable to a different overlord for each one. His prime duty (and self-interest) lay with his largest estate, but such a man would have regarded a question as to his nationality as quite bizarre. How far the Welsh saw themselves as inhabitants of a *patria*, and how far this affected their thoughts of political independence, is impossible to tell. They enjoyed a long-established cultural independence, speaking a language which they used in law and business, as well as in history and song. They had a long historical tradition, recently heavily embroidered by Geoffrey of Monmouth in his *Historia Regum Britanniae*, 'History of the Kings of Britain', but shining all the more brightly for that. Part of that tradition was that a Welsh hero would arise to drive the Saxons back into the sea. Since then the Saxons had been supplanted by the Normans. How important was it to a member of the *bonheddwr*, in his old rambling low house in the uplands of Ceredigion or Glamorgan, with his flocks and his fields, whether he was ruled and taxed by a French-speaking military aristocrat or by a Welsh-speaking descendant of Rhodri Mawr and the House of Aberffraw? His Welshness was secure within his culture, and did not necessarily need to be expressed in a political way. Perhaps he would prefer the one who left him most alone, to be a petty king himself amongst his own immediate kin group and its dependants.

Yet it is clear that there was a desire to see the Principality of Wales firmly established. In the minds of many Welsh people it must have seemed as if this wish had been answered at last. Apart from the castleries of Carmarthen and Cardigan, and the strip of Marcher territory along the south coast from Gwent to Dyfed, virtually the whole country was under Llywelyn's authority.

Here a vexed question arose: what was the basis of that authority, other than cold steel? Llywelyn II was not the senior living member of the House of Aberffraw. He was a younger brother, who had defied his elder brothers. He was the son of the unfortunate Gruffudd whose legitimacy had been tainted by the papal decree conferring the heirship of Gwynedd on Dafydd ap Llywelyn. He had other younger brothers, who might claim a share of what he had won. He had neither wife nor child of his own. Some of those who paid him homage, like Gruffudd ap Gwenwynwyn, did so with obvious reluctance. Their loyalty could not be counted on.

EDWARD I ASSERTS HIS AUTHORITY

Confirmed as Prince, Llywelyn II kept his attention focused on the most vulnerable area of his domain, the south-east. Glamorgan was the lordship of Gilbert de Clare, a magnate of vast wealth and pride who did not take kindly to the Prince of Wales probing his northern bounds. Llywelyn's aim may have simply been to obtain the homage of the semi-independent Welsh upland lordships, as he was entitled to do. De Clare responded by constructing Caerffili Castle, a strongpoint of massive dimensions, and by setting out to stamp out any vestiges of local rule in the Glamorgan uplands. The main Marcher lords of the south, Bohun around Hereford and Mortimer around Ludlow, were making furious efforts to retrieve the lands that Llywelyn had seized. In 1274, his brother Dafydd and Gruffudd ap Gwenwynwyn seem to have combined in a plot against Llywelyn's life. The plot failed and both fled to England. Dafydd was

Caerffili (Caerphilly) Castle

Llywelyn's heir, perhaps anticipating his inheritance; his failed coup concentrated Llywelyn's mind on thoughts of marriage. The bride was to be Eleanor de Montfort, daughter of Simon, and a proxy wedding ceremony took place. But the new King of England, Edward I, disapproved. Eleanor's ship from France was intercepted, and she was held in captivity at Windsor.

Llywelyn's relations with Edward I got off to a bad start, and did not improve. Both sides were able to point to grievances. England was holding his wife captive, was harbouring the Prince's would-be assassins, Dafydd and Gruffudd, and was doing nothing to support his rights under the Treaty of Montgomery against the Marcher lords. Llywelyn was behind with his payments of the 25,000 marks. He did not attend Edward's coronation and by April 1276 had ignored five summons to perform homage to the new king. Both courts became engaged in a 'you first' dispute, with Llywelyn unwilling to pay homage until his grievances were attended to; and Edward unwilling to do anything until Llywelyn's homage had been received. Edward's position was made clearer in a letter to the Pope. He claimed that the Treaty of Montgomery was null and void, since by Welsh tradition, Llywelyn had no more rights than his three brothers. If Dafydd ap Gruffudd was the architect of this idea, it certainly found a suitable site in the mind of Edward.

In three letters, Llywelyn set out his case to Edward and proposed that the King of France should act as arbitrator. Edward I was not the sort of person to accept arbitration of any sort in what he regarded as a dispute with a recalcitrant vassal. In November 1276 Llywelyn was proclaimed a rebel. The Marcher lords had already been given full backing in their claims against the Prince. And in the spring of 1277, Edward in person entered Wales at the head of an army of 15,000 foot soldiers and 800 knights. Not since the days when Agricola had come to slaughter the Ordovices had any expedition come on such a scale and with such punitive intentions. In the face of such massive force, resistance was futile. Rhys ap Maredudd, ruler of Dryslwyn, speedily deserted his allegiance to Llywelyn. Powys Fadog surrendered, and Dinas Bran, its great stronghold, was destroyed by fire. Anglesey was captured and the grain harvest fell to the English. Rhys Fychan, ruler of north Ceredigion, fled into Gwynedd. But Llywelyn had no option but to surrender, which he did at Aberconwy on 9 November 1277. Once again, the ruler of Gwynedd was confined to the west of the Conwy. The title of Prince of Wales was left, an empty blazon, with Rhys Fychan of Ceredigion and four lords of Powys Fadog to pay it homage. East of the Conwy, the treacherous brothers got their tracts of land – Rhufoniog and Dyffryn Clwyd to Dafydd, Llyn to Owain, while Edward took the rest.

The methodical and careful Plantagenet took further steps to ensure that no opportunities were left for Llywelyn to obtain the kind of leverage that might start a new rise to power. He seized northern Ceredigion and built a large new castle at Aberystwyth. Further castles were built or rebuilt at Rhuddlan, Flint and Builth. Royal control was extended in the south through a county system, with a royal justice appointed. Meanwhile, Llywelyn was allowed to complete his marriage, in Worcester Cathedral, in October 1278, having paid homage to Edward for his lands and title in December 1277.

THE WELSH REVOLT

Under the two Llywelyns, the Welsh had groaned at the imposition of taxes, and some at least had thought fondly of a remote suzerainty based in London, which would leave them to their own devices. Under the regime of Edward I's administrators, justiciars and tax collectors, they soon learned what was expected of a subject people – obedience, swift payment, and silence. If Edward's own actions normally fell within the letter of feudal law, as he understood it, many of his officials were happy to get away with as much as possible.

The uprising appears to have taken the occupying forces by surprise. It originated not in west Gwynedd, where Llywelyn appears to have behaved with complete propriety, but in the *cantrefs* of Rhufoniog and Dyffrynn Clwyd, where Dafydd ap Gruffudd had had ample opportunity to see how cold and meagre was the English reward for his earlier disloyalty. On Palm Sunday (21 March) 1282 it began with an attack led by him on Hawarden Castle. A few days later it had spread across the country. Llywelyn was left in a painful quandary. He was the natural leader and beneficiary of the revolt. But Dafydd had begun it – was he going to jump on to a bandwagon started by so treacherous a brother? It seems he refrained from giving it his full support for several weeks, during which time his wife Eleanor died giving birth to their daughter, Gwenllian, on June 19. At first all went favourably for the Welsh. By late in the year they had won victories over English armies near Dinefwr and at the Menai Strait, had won several castles including Aberystwyth and Builth, and had lost no ground. Then, in a minor skirmish on the bank of the River Irfon on 11 December 1282, Llywelyn, Prince of Wales, was killed by an English soldier who did not even know who he was.

When the body was recognised, Llywelyn's head was cut off and sent to Edward I. His death did not mean the end of the revolt, but the heart was out of it. Dafydd, who had after all started it without asking Llywelyn's leave or blessing, continued the fight, but there was no Prince of Wales to lend hope, justification, and legitimacy to the venture. The bards saw the meaning of it and expressed it in their different ways with the same bleak message as this of Gruffudd ab yr Ynad Coch – their world was coming to an end:

> *Och hyd atat ti, Dduw, na ddaw mor dros dir!*
> *Pa beth y'n gedir i ohiriaw?*

> 'O God, that the sea might engulf the land –
> Why are we left to long-drawn weariness?'

WELSH SOCIETY IN THE THIRTEENTH CENTURY

In the ninety years covered by the two Llywelyns, Wales enjoyed its nearest state to nationhood. Its fortunes soared, plummeted, soared again, collapsed – but for long periods of relative stability, it was almost as if it truly was a nation, with its ruler, its institutions, its long-established pattern of doing things. So much was already in place, by way of law and custom, of language and ancient lore, that it seemed such a little step still to take. But not for the first or the last time in the history of humanity, in Wales as elsewhere, the aspirations of the many were cast away on the greed of a very few. The Welsh, with their ingrained respect for genealogy and noble ancestry, were bound to their aristocratic leaders. Llywelyn I and Llywelyn II were worthy of the trust and responsibility which went with these roles. Most of their fellow-nobles could not see beyond their own backyards and placed their own self-interest firmly at the top of their priorities.

For the Welsh people, the thirteenth century was mostly a time of progress.

The overwhelming preoccupation of the inhabitants was still with agriculture, and stock-rearing in particular. But there is evidence that more money was in circulation. Trade was not simply a matter of barter. Some members, at least, of the *bonheddwyr* were paying their dues to their prince not in kind but in cash, or a combination of the two. The princes needed money to purchase goods and skills. They built castles at great expense. Monopoly control of lead and gold mining helped to boost their incomes, but especially at times of war, the need for money must regularly have outrun the supply. Within Gwynedd, the prince had his own system for the collection of taxes and dues. In the other lordships, his officers had to contend with the local lord's view of his own requirements and of the ability of his people to pay.

The population appears to have grown rapidly at this time. This itself is an indication of relative peace and prosperity, and agricultural output will have risen to match. New ground would be taken in for tillage. The forms of trade are quite hard to track down, but undoubtedly trading took place on a wide scale, if not to a very high economic level. However self-sufficient the medieval household or community was in foodstuffs, it needed salt, while other spices were highly desirable to add taste and variety to a limited diet. Richer households had other requirements including luxury goods, and everything had to be paid for.

Wales was well off in certain primary products, including cattle, hides and horns. A substantial flannel-producing industry grew up in the river valleys – the English term is from *gwlanen*, 'woollen article'. Not all exports were low price and high bulk. The breeding of hunting dogs was another speciality, and Welsh hunting dogs were highly prized. The natural trading partner for Wales was of course its great neighbour, England. Land routes led conveniently into the English lowlands. The great port of Bristol was a short sail from south Wales, and Bristol was a gateway to France and Spain. This was fine in times of peace. But in times of war or hostility, England was in a position to close the doors on Welsh trade, stopping the import not only of luxury items but also of essentials, like corn, salt and iron.

With a strong sense of national identity and strong princes as national leaders, it was an era that fostered Welsh culture. In the words of Edward Jones:

WELSH RABBITS

Rabbits were brought to England by the Normans in the twelfth century, and by the thirteenth they were common in Wales. Originally they were farmed, in warrens, and were an important part of the winter diet, apart from the wrapping of many a 'Baby Bunting' in their fur. In 1387–88, over 3,000 rabbits were trapped on the islands of Skomer, Skokholm and Middleholm.

'The Poets of these memorable times added energy to a nervous language, and the Musicians called forth from the harp its loudest and grandest tones, to re-animate the ancient struggle of their brave countrymen for freedom and the possession of their parent soil.'

Among the celebrated bards of the age were a Lord of Powys, Owain Cyfeiliog, Llywarch, Einion ap Gwalchmai, Gwalchmai ap Meilir, and Gruffudd ap yr Ynad Coch.

THE CHURCH IN THE TIME OF THE PRINCES

A fresh framework of support for the princes of Wales came from the new foundations of the Welsh church. If the earlier monastic foundations of the new order had been planted by Normans and Marcher lords, the later set were much more the creation of the Welsh leaders. Even such Norman foundations as Whitland (1140) – the first Cistercian monastery of Wales – and Strata Florida (1164) came under Welsh influence with the growth of the kingdom of Deheubarth, and in the later twelfth century they were followed by a stream of new foundations, including Strata Marcella, Cwmhir, Aberconwy, and Valle Crucis. The monks and lay-brothers who occupied these places were Welsh, not Norman, renewing a tradition of Welsh churchmen whose learning and piety were infused with patriotism. They maintained the tradition of historical record-keeping found in the *Brut y Tywysogyon*. From such institutions the princes had a supply of educated clerks who could write in diplomatic Latin and make use of the church's international network of contacts on behalf of their secular master. There is some evidence that despite the substantial English diplomatic presence at the Vatican there was sympathy there for the Welsh cause.

The Welsh church, with its four bishoprics, was of little direct support to the princes. Its organisation had been set up by Normans, under English royal dispensation, tied firmly into the see of Canterbury. The Scottish church at this time was a powerful ally in the cause of national independence, which it associated firmly with its own independent status, but the position in Wales was quite different. Only in Bangor was the bishop likely to be appointed under the aegis of a Welsh prince, and even there it was a struggle to enforce a Welsh nominee's appointment. In St Davids, Llandaf and St Asaph, the bishop was likely to be an appointee who owed his elevation – and future prospects – to the English king or an English magnate like the Lord of Glamorgan or the Earl of Chester. The bishops had their own preoccupations. They were very poorly funded; even the richest, St Davids, had only a fraction of the wealth of the greater English cathedrals. Their poverty was accentuated by the fact that many churches situated in their dioceses were actually granted to abbeys and priories

St Davids Cathedral in Victorian times

in England, drawing away yet more of what little income there was. Yet, in the words of Sir John Lloyd: 'The laws of Hywel the Good, dating from a time when the bishop often o'ertopped the local chieftain in dignity and power, conceded much in the way of ecclesiastical immunity which Llywelyn, here following in the footsteps of his grandfather, was unwilling to allow' (p. 744). The impecunious bishops of Wales were not minded to lose any of their few privileges and perquisites. Anian, Bishop of St Asaph, sometimes known as Anian Saes, or Saxon, accused Llywelyn in 1273 of hostility to the church, and especially to the monks. This was a serious accusation against a ruler who needed to cultivate papal favour. But seven abbots ranged themselves against the contumacious Anian and protested strongly to the Pope at what they saw as an unjust attempt to blacken Llywelyn's character.

By their very nature, the Cistercians were withdrawn from contact with the people. But Llywelyn II encouraged the spread of the Franciscan and Dominican preaching orders, who actively sought to reach the public and built large churches as preaching-halls. By the late thirteenth century, the few towns of Wales had at least one friary church; Cardiff had two. Augustinian canons based at Penmon on Anglesey served its two little towns, Llanfaes (Welsh) and Beaumaris (English); they also had houses at Carmarthen and Haverfordwest.

CHAPTER EIGHT

England's Province

THE IRON HAND OF EDWARD I

Although Llywelyn was dead, his demise triumphantly reported by Edward I to the Pope, the struggle in Wales went on. There is a curious resemblance to the situation in Scotland some ten years later. There, with no king, the leader of the resistance (though no claimant to even a prince's diadem), William Wallace, was trapped and brutally executed by the English. The country was held down by an army of occupation. Annexation to England, in some form or other, seemed to be Edward's plan. Yet in Scotland the tenuous elements of a sovereign state held together and were able to be used by the man who eventually proclaimed himself king, Robert Bruce. These elements, the hereditary roles of steward and constable, the appointed role of chancellor, were enough to convey legitimacy and give national status to an individual's claim – Scotland escaped from Edward's iron clutch. But Wales had no steward, no constable. Within each principality, each major lordship, lay the knowledge and the structure that secured its own succession and maintained its own traditions. But these were nothing to do with the princedom of Wales. It was a weakness of Wales, with so many aspects of nationhood, that each prince had to invent himself.

The closest aspirant to that currently somewhat dubious and exposed role was Dafydd ap Gruffudd. Edward I remained in Gwynedd to see his campaign through to its conclusion. The easy Welsh victories of 1282 did not recur in 1283. Edward's army crossed safely from Anglesey to the mainland, established control of the coast and began to drive inland. Llywelyn's chief castle of Dolwyddelan fell in January. Dafydd, having taken refuge in Snowdonia, moved south towards Cader Idris. For a time he settled in the castle of Castell-y-Bere. It was plain that the revolt had utterly failed. On 25 April, having left the castle, he was handed over by Welshmen to the English forces. He was taken to Shrewsbury, tried, and condemned as a traitorous vassal. He was executed in October 1283. The penalty, hanging, drawing and quartering, was a gruesome medieval ritual designed to prolong the victim's agony for as long as possible.

Dafydd's sons, Owain and Llywelyn, were destined to be prisoners for the rest of their lives; Llywelyn II's daughter Gwenllian was sent to an English convent at Sempringham. There were to be no hereditary princes of the line of Llywelyn. Edward made other dispensations as well. By this time, after almost a century of activity, the Welsh lordships were dotted with castles, some of which had been

Caernarfon Castle

destroyed and rebuilt, or refortified for greater strength. For Edward I, who had resolved that Wales would no longer be a problem, the answer was more castles still. Some of his new castles, like those at Flint and Rhuddlan, replaced earlier structures with their state-of-the-art military architecture. Others rose on sites previously unfortified, like the riverside at Conwy, at Beaumaris on the other side of the Menai Strait, and at Harlech and Caernarfon. Edward's chief architect and engineer was from Savoy – James de St Georges d'Esperanche – and building managers came from his own domains in Gascony to assist with the works. The new castles, combining fortress and trading borough within their walls, were intended to be impregnable, and to make any kind of insurrection in Gwynedd unthinkable.

THE STATUTE OF RHUDDLAN

The two most apparent aspects of his new order of things, castles and law, show the cast of Edward I's mind. By 19 March 1284 he was ready to issue the Statute of Rhuddlan, by which his Welsh subjects would know how they were to be governed. There was no suggestion of Welsh independence; the statute treated

Wales as annexed territory. With a few special exceptions, Wales was to pass under English law. The English system of shires, each with its sheriff and coroner as royal officials, was extended to Wales. The shires of Flint, Anglesey, Caernarfon, Meirionydd, Cardigan and Carmarthen date from here. Up until now, the law in Wales had been the old collection known as the Laws of Hywel Dda, though recodified and amended on numerous occasions under such princes as the Lord Rhys. It remained the law of a community, with many old-fashioned or obsolete aspects, but one of its strengths had always been a degree of adaptability which preserved its usefulness. There was a still a corps of educated Welsh professional lawmen to interpret it, and, particularly in the twelfth century, much of it had been written down. Under the Lord Rhys, who was also King's Justiciar for the south, there may have been a combined manuscript with virtually the whole corpus of law in it. The Statute of Rhuddlan did away with all that. Justice was to be as in England, a department of the Crown, with royally appointed judges to rule on both civil and criminal cases. At the head of this process would be a justiciar for Wales. English law at this time was relatively modern. In the course of the twelfth century much work had been done to make it more just and more closely adapted to the needs of society. There were few situations with which it could not cope, and for greater ease, the law professionals wrote down models of procedure, known as 'writs of course', which set out the process of reaching judgement in cases such as land and inheritance disputes. Through regular circuits by the judges, the law was brought to the people.

This was the system now to be introduced in Wales. The Statute of Rhuddlan provided a number of specimen writs deemed to be particularly relevant to Wales. In these, the basis of English law was emended to take account of traditional Welsh practice. In England by now, primogeniture was standard, with an eldest son inheriting from the father. In Wales, where primogeniture – as in other old 'Celtic' societies – had never been regarded as possessing special rights, the rights of co-heirs and heirs in differing degrees of kinship were allowed for. 'Partible', or divisible, inheritance was specifically allowed for. One old Welsh practice, that of allowing a share of inheritance to a bastard offspring, was forbidden by the English under the new code. But widows were to benefit from an extension of the English law relating to dower land, allowing them to retain up to a third of their husband's estate for their own lifetimes. One archaic but still current fact of Welsh legal life was preserved, in that fines for default could be paid for in cows as well as in cash. This betrays the still highly restricted use of coinage in Wales.

The Statute of Rhuddlan had been carefully considered and worked out. It was not a punitive law system and it incorporated some of the most progressive thinking of the age. But it was an imposed system. There was a colonialist thought process behind it, which combined the notion of 'this is good for you', with that of 'this is what you are getting'. At a stroke, an alien system replaced one that, however archaic, had satisfied the needs of Welsh society for many generations. If the Laws of Hywel Dda were one of the great supports of Welshness, then a great support was now removed. Soon, also, the Welsh were to find that the letter of Edward's law was often fairer than the spirit in which it was applied by his officials. There was ample opportunity to bend and twist the law. And the language of the new law was not Welsh, but Norman French, placing the Welsh speakers at a distinct disadvantage. Occasionally the justiciar might be a professional, but most often the role fell to an English magnate, usually a Marcher lord. Barons such as Roger Mortimer of Chirk, and Edmund fitzAlan, Earl of Arundel and Lord of Bromfield and Yale, in turn exercised the royal authority across the whole of Gwynedd as well as ruling their own Marcher lordships on the old model of the Law of the Marches.

TWO REBELLIONS

Castles, laws, taxes, all backed up by a demanding royal bureaucracy, were seen as enough to keep the conquered province in check. But there were to be two uprisings before the thirteenth century was over. The first came in June 1287, when Rhys ab Maredudd, of Dryslwyn, rebelled. Maredudd, though briefly in league with Llywelyn II, had been mostly a loyal supporter of Edward I and had been accordingly rewarded, notably after the events of 1282–83. But the rewards had not come up to expectation, and Rhys had been humiliated by the king for failing to take possession of his lands by proper feudal procedure. His rebellion was small-scale, and Dryslwyn was captured in September. Rhys retreated to Ceredigion, holding out against Edward in the castle of Emlyn until it fell in January 1288. After that he was on the run as an outlaw, but survived until 1292, when he was betrayed by his own people in the commote of Mallaen. He was executed at York. Rhys seems to have been expressing his own disgruntlement. His revolt struck no fire elsewhere, while bringing harshly punitive measures against his own people.

A more ambitious uprising was led in September 1294 by Madog ap Llywelyn, self-styled Prince of Wales. A descendant of Owain Gwynedd, he was a distant cousin of Llywelyn ap Gruffudd. His family had maintained a claim to rule Meirionydd, but both the Llywelyns had forced them out. Madog had managed to put together an alliance of Welsh chiefs, largely from the south. His main associates were Morgan ap Maredudd, son of the Lord of Caerleon, Maelgwn ap Rhys Fychan, a landholder of northern Ceredigion, and one Cynan from Brycheiniog. They may have reckoned on Edward I being preoccupied by events in Scotland, England and France, especially the last, where he was deeply involved in war in Gascony. Edward's constant military activity meant heavy taxes, and in 1294 he also withdrew large numbers of men from the Welsh castle garrisons to bolster his army in France. On 30 September, the day his levies were mustered at Shrewsbury, the revolt began, with attacks made on Aberystwyth, Builth, Castell-y-Bere, Denbigh, Cricieth, Harlech, Caernarfon and Morlais. Madog himself broke through the defences of Caernarfon, where the defending castellan was killed. With his troops already mustered, Edward began a massive response. His loyal barons and castellans were ordered to pacify their own districts. Armies were mustered at Chester, Montgomery and Gloucester. There was a setback when Edward himself, attempting a swift march on Bangor from Conwy, lost his baggage train to a surprise attack, and sat out an uncomfortable winter in Conwy Castle. But the army at Montgomery caught up with Madog on 5 March 1295, and routed him at Maes Madog in a night attack. With the whole of Wales an English armed camp, Madog surrendered in June. His fate is unknown. The seriousness of his revolt is hard to assess, but its co-ordinated nature clearly caused alarm, as did his ability to virtually destroy the castle at Caernarfon, where a major rebuild was needed.

A COUNTRY OF CASTLES

Madog's was to be the last uprising in Wales for nearly a hundred years. For that period, the country was largely at peace, though England was not. Welsh troops continued to be used on a large scale to further Edward's campaign in France and Scotland. It was the destructive fire of Welsh bowmen that sealed his victory over Wallace at Falkirk in 1298. With peace came the opportunity for economic life to develop. Edward I's monster castles, with their associated *bastides*, or fortified towns, generated demands for services and trades just as the Roman camps had done more than a thousand years before. Welsh lords had also been quick to see the financial benefits of supporting a market, and of suppressing rival centres.

In the time of Llywelyn II, one of the reasons for dissension between himself and Gruffudd ap Gwenwynwyn had been the his desire to set up a castle at Dolforwyn in the Severn Valley, with an associated borough town at Abermule. This may have been a deliberate attempt to create a strategically sited central 'capital', but it was fiercely opposed by the Mortimers of Montgomery and by Gruffudd ap Gwenwynwyn who had his own castle and trading centre at Welshpool.

The populations of these little castle-towns were quite mixed. Incomers might be English, Flemish, Irish or French. Troops on a royal payroll attracted the attention of all sorts of hawkers, pedlars, fortune-tellers and con-men and

Powis Castle, Welshpool

women of various sorts, quite apart from the more settled trade of tavern-keepers, tailors, shoemakers and metalworkers. The castellan had to be certain, especially in the early days when memories of uprisings were recent, that his residents were loyal and reliable. That meant non-Welsh. Yet it was also necessary to allow in the Welsh from round about in order for the town to function as a marketplace. David Walker notes that: 'Even where burgage tenure might prove difficult, Welsh people were moving into, and settling in, boroughs throughout north Wales. An upwardly mobile element was clearly discernible in the fourteenth century... ' (p. 160). Certain towns were however almost wholly Welsh, like Llanfaes on Anglesey, which at this time, with Welshpool, was the largest borough under Welsh control. Llanfaes was burned in Madog's revolt, and its site was used as the workmen's camp for the new English castle-town of Beaumaris. Most of its activity was resited on the west side of Anglesey, where Newborough was established and given a royal charter. Small as they were, the towns were densely populated, and property keenly sought after. Many houses were let and sublet several times. Burgesses had rights but also duties, especially relating to defence. These duties stemmed from ownership, and a sub-tenant might be free of such responsibility.

PRINCES OF WALES AFTER EDWARD I

In 1301 Edward I set the seal on his Welsh policy by investing his son as Prince of Wales. By a mixture of luck and adroit management, the boy had actually been born in the castle at Caernarfon, seventeen years before. The ceremony of investiture took place not in Wales but in Lincoln. It was not a mere title; the Prince was to receive the income generated by the Principality, a substantial £4,000 a year in contemporary money, and was to act as its feudal lord. In 1307 he acceded to the throne as Edward II, and among the few who mourned him at the end of his unfortunate kingship were the Welsh. This regard seems to have been prompted by nostalgia as much as anything else; though Edward II made sympathetic noises towards Welsh complaints on more than one occasion, he had little power or opportunity to do things on their behalf. During his reign there was a revolt in Glamorgan in 1316, when Llywelyn Bren rose against the repressive regime of royal functionaries like Payne de Turberville of Coety, a notorious opponent to all things Welsh. The revolt ended with Llywelyn's execution in Cardiff in 1317, and a collective fine of £2,330 was imposed on the recalcitrant Welsh. The southern March was dominated by Hugh Despenser, Edward II's leading supporter in the increasingly bitter struggle between the king and the reformist barons and a conscientious land-grabber. The northern March, and most of the Principality, was at the mercy of Roger Mortimer of Chirk, who exercised justice at Caernarfon and Carmarthen for most of the time between 1308 and 1322. Under Gruffudd Llwyd, there was a Welsh uprising in 1322, which may have been on behalf of Edward II against his barons, among whom were aligned virtually all the lords of the March. This resulted in a dramatic reduction, for a time, of Mortimer influence. Edward held a parliament at York which included forty-eight Welsh members, but his ascendancy was brief. In 1323 Roger Mortimer of Wigmore escaped from prison and fled to Paris. There he became the lover of Edward's Queen, Isabella. In September 1326 Roger and Isabella invaded England, and Edward retreated into Wales, where he was caught in the wilds of the Rhondda on 16 December. Hugh Despenser and his father, of the same name, were executed. A Welsh attempt to rescue Edward II from Berkeley Castle failed, and the king was assassinated there in September 1327.

Mortimer was now supreme in Wales. He made himself Justiciar of Wales, took the title of Earl of March, and his possessions extended from Denbigh to his old base at Wigmore and west to Pembroke. But he fell from power in 1330, was hanged, and the Mortimer lands were forfeited until 1354. In 1343 a new Prince of Wales was invested, in the person of Edward, the Black Prince, eldest son of King Edward III. In his time a serious effort was made to combine the Principality and the March; as Prince of Wales, Edward believed he was due the homage of the Marcher lords for their territories. This was not permitted by Edward III, and when, following the Black Prince's death, his son Richard of Bordeaux in turn became Prince of Wales, it was made clear that the March owed its loyalty to the Crown of England and not to the Prince of Wales.

It is notable by now that whilst occasional Welsh names irrupt into the narrative, like Rhys ap Gruffudd who tried to rescue Edward II from Berkeley Castle, the political basis of Welsh life was essentially being worked out among English magnates, with their chief power bases in the March.

LIFE – AND DEATH – IN THE
FOURTEENTH CENTURY

The native Welsh existed at a variety of levels, from a state bordering on luxurious living to the most abject penury. Official surveys, or 'extents', dating from this time, and covering large areas, help to give an impression of the way people lived. Their chief purpose was to assess tax values. In large tracts of Gwynedd, Powys and Deheubarth, the Welsh were virtually the only population. Chieftains and local leaders who maintained good relations with the nearest castle, and who managed their land well, could pay their taxes and live well. The typical Welsh family was one of free status, with its own house and its own piece of land, which would include a share of the *hafod*, or upland pasture. At this time a large number of people still remained in a condition of serfdom. Deprived of freedom, they were simply part of the value of their lord's estate. They were bought and sold, and if they ran away, were retrieved and punished. The degree of serfdom varied, and it was probably most common in pockets, like Holywell, where there were hereditary tasks, in this case lead-mining. The majority of families belonged, or saw themselves as belonging, to the ranks of the *bonheddwyr*, though there was a wide range of income and status, between those who were near-peasants and those who were near-gentry. The great majority lived in the countryside, with perhaps only 2 per cent grouped in the boroughs. In many cases their lifestyle had changed little since the times of Giraldus Cambrensis, Hywel Dda or even earlier. But by 1300 a number of distinctive changes were taking place, at a different pace in different parts of the country. There was a steady drift towards a monetary economy, with English coinage (there was no mint in Wales). There was a growing appreciation of the fact that Wales, like it or not, was part of a larger political unit with consequent opportunities for the ambitious. At one level this meant a constant demand for Welsh foot soldiers, especially longbowmen. At a higher social level, it encouraged the leaders of Welsh society to adopt English sympathies and English ways – including the use of the English language. These families, the *uchelwyr*, or gentry, embarked on a slow drift towards English ways. But at this time they were still very much the mainstays of Welsh tradition, including the bardic tradition. The bards had not forgotten their prophetic past: 'It was the bards who, above all, preserved these traditions. They transmitted them to the sons of the *uchelwyr*, of whom they were the teachers, and, travelling from noble household to household, they kept the old hopes alive as they retold the ancient prophecies around the blazing hearth or the banqueting board on long dark winter evenings' (Glanmor Williams, *Owain Glyndwr*, p. 7).

Around the time of 1300, the population of Wales reached a peak, perhaps around 300,000 people, which it would not touch again for a long time. The fourteenth century, despite its relative peace, was a time of frequent bad weather, poor harvests – three disastrous ones in a row between 1315 and 1317 – and above all, bubonic plague. The Black Death struck in 1348–50 and wiped out perhaps a third of the population. This was the greatest single disaster ever to afflict the people of Wales. The poet Ieuan Gethin wrote, in the spring of 1349:

> *We see death coming into our midst like black smoke, a plague which cuts off the young, a rootless phantom which has no mercy for fair countenance. Woe is me of the shilling in the armpit; it is seething, terrible, wherever it may come, a head that gives pain and causes a loud cry, a burden carried under the arms, a painful angry knob, a white lump. It is of the form of an apple, like the head of an onion, a small boil that spares no one. Great is its seething, like a burning cinder, a grievous thing of an ashy colour … the early ornaments of black death, cinders of the peelings of the cockle weed, a mixed multitude, a black plague like halfpence, like berries. It is a grievous thing that they should be on a fair skin.*

The social effects of the epidemic were widespread. In the lowlands, the loss of so many lives accelerated the decline of the old Norman manorial system. In *The Black Death*, Philip Ziegler notes that: 'The garden of the manor, with no one to tend it, was more and more often let out as pasture. The dovecote and fish stew were allowed to fall into disuse and often never reactivated. The lords of the manor renounced the farming of the manorial demesne and began to let it out at the best rent they could get. The principle of bondage thence forward played a far less significant part in the social structure of the manor. The system, in short, broke down because of the shortage of labour and the improved bargaining position of the villein' (p. 168).

Further plague attacks, less horrific but still taking a heavy toll, recurred at twelve- to fifteen-year intervals. Economic life stalled, as demand for produce fell. Less land was tilled, less money circulated. The people at the bottom of the system, labourers and serfs, suffered greatly. Many took to a wandering life, and

107

bands of rootless, homeless, often desperate beggars added to the hazards of life in the vicinity of the towns. It was not a universally bad time, however. There were good years, and even stretches of good years. There were always things to be celebrated. It was a time of superb poetry in Welsh, the old tradition refreshed and renewed. The greatest of all Welsh lyric poets, Dafydd ap Gwilym, was at work between around 1340 and 1370. Although there was no Welsh court, such as that of Llywelyn the Great, to act as the centre for a bardic tradition, the poets took the opportunity for a more intimate, personal and less highly formalised expression, which often shows a strong feeling for their own countryside.

CHAPTER NINE

The Last Prince

UNDER THE ENGLISH YOKE

Throughout the fourteenth century, in bad times and in good, it was impossible for the Welsh to ignore the fact that they lived as a subject people in their own land. The Principality was the fief of an English prince, whose officers managed and taxed it for his benefit, and their own. Far and near, the castles rose, symbols of this domination. Within the protective embrace of the castles, English merchants jealously guarded their trading privileges. When trade worsened, they succumbed to the latent paranoia of isolated communities, blaming the clannish and foreign-tongued Welsh. The soldiers who came and went had done well out of the French wars in the days of Crecy (1346) and Poitiers (1356), but later in the century, things were going far less well. As the Hundred Years War went on, England would be, bit by bit, forced out, back to the Channel coast. Disputes between Welsh and English became more frequent, and sharper. It was noticeable that fewer Welshmen were appointed to positions of authority, even secondary authority, during the reign of Richard II. The Welsh church had become a home for English bishops. Of sixteen bishops appointed in the four dioceses between 1372 and 1400, fifteen were Englishmen. (The exception, John Trefor of St Asaph, perhaps proved the English point by associating himself with Glyndwr's revolt.) For people who cared about the Welsh tradition, the outlook was not promising. In law and religion, the country was run as a department of England. There was no Welsh metropolitan see to give unity to the church. There was no university where the youth of Wales might be educated. Economic life was firmly in the grasp of a foreign community. Among the *uchelwyr*, even the most favourably disposed towards the English regime could see that things were not as they had been. The regime itself was jumpy. In the 1370s there had been the alarming episode of Owain Lawgoch, 'Red Hand'. A martial descendant of the princes of Gwynedd, he had, like many of his countrymen, gone abroad to make his fortune by his sword. As a commander for the King of France he had won considerable renown. Success, fame, and the unstinted praise of Welsh bards prompted him to proclaim himself Prince of Wales. With French support, he promised to return and lead his people to a restored independence. The threat of Owain Lawgoch was terminated by the knife of a Scot, a secret assassin employed by the English government, in 1378.

By the end of the century, unrest was simmering in Wales. Events in England were also at a critical point. The unsettled reign of Richard II had seen tremendous upheavals among the grandees of the Welsh Marches. Richard had dispossessed three great men in 1397: the Duke of Gloucester, the Earl of Arundel and the Earl of Warwick. The first two had been executed. In 1398 Roger Mortimer, Earl of March, had died. Early in 1399 John of Gaunt, Duke of Lancaster, died. It was this death that precipitated matters; Henry of Lancaster, John of Gaunt's son, was already in exile and was refused permission to return. Taking advantage of Richard's expedition to Ireland against the revolt of Art McMurrough, Henry landed in north-east England. A campaign to regain his rights very soon took on the appearance of a march to the throne. Returning in haste, Richard II marched across Wales from Milford to Flint, but, bereft of support, was captured and deposed. Henry of Lancaster was installed as Henry IV. By the end of January 1400, Richard was dead.

THE RISE OF OWAIN GLYNDWR

Like that other luckless king, Edward II, Richard II had had a strong personal following in Wales. Henry IV lost no time in making his own teenage son Prince of Wales and in levying a tax on the Principality. He also gave control of north Wales to Harry Percy, or Hotspur, whose family had long lived on the Scottish border and who knew nothing about Wales. For the Welsh gentry, these were arbitrary actions and resented as such. They had no expectations of any improvement in their position from Henry. One of their number was Owain Glyndwr, already embroiled in a dispute with his powerful neighbour, Lord Grey of Ruthin, a Marcher lord and close confidant of the new king. Owain's complaint, laid before parliament in 1399, was that Grey had illegally seized an area of common land which bordered their territories. No action was taken in support of Owain's grievance.

Up to this time, Owain's career had been exemplary, as much a picture of the fully absorbed and adjusted upper-class Welshman as any English administrator could have hoped for. He was in his forties, lived on his estates, was married to a daughter of a prominent Anglo-Welsh family, the Hanmers, and had a large family of his own. He had been educated in London, at the Inns of Court. He had seen military service in the English army in Scotland, and participated in a naval campaign under the Earl of Arundel, who appears to have been a patron of his, at least until some years prior to his fall in 1397. But, despite his service, in an age when chivalric distinctions were taken seriously, he never received a knighthood. He had a wide circle of relatives among the *uchelwyr*, including the prominent Tudur family in Anglesey. In a nation keen on genealogies and pedigrees, he was well-descended on both sides. His father, Gruffudd Fychan, traced

FROM A POEM IN PRAISE OF SYCHARTH, THE HOME OF OWAIN GLYNDWR

Upon four wooden columns proud
Mounteth his mansion to the cloud;
Each column's thick and firmly based,
And upon each a loft is plac'd;
In these four lofts, which coupled stand,
Repose at night the minstrel band;
Four lofts they were in pristine state,
But now partitioned form they eight.
Tiled is the roof, on each house top
Rise smoke-ejecting chimneys up.
All of one form there are nine halls
Each with nine wardrobes in its walls.
With linen white as well supplied
As fairest shops of fam'd Cheapside.

Iolo Goch (*c*.1320–98), translated by George Borrow

his ancestry back to Madog ap Gruffudd, a prince of northern Powys, who died in 1236. His mother, Elen, daughter of Owain ap Thomas Llywelyn, was descended from the royal house of Deheubarth and through her Owain inherited land in Ceredigion as well as the patrimonial territories of Glyndyfyrdwy and Cynllaith. Ever since the division of Powys, the lords of that area, caught between the hammer of the Marcher lords and the anvil of Gwynedd, had kept a relatively low profile in Welsh affairs, without the resources to strike an independent attitude. Although the mountainous district of Glyndyfyrdwy gave him the name Glyndwr, 'Glen of Waters', it was the more fertile Cynllaith that generated his income, and his home was situated here, at Sycharth. Sycharth was not a castle but a house of timber, set on top of a mound. Though praised by poets, it was not a large house, but well-appointed and comfortable for its time.

The role of the bards in prompting Glyndwr to action has often been assessed. He was a patron of two celebrated poets, Iolo Goch and Gruffudd Llwyd, both of whom were masters of incitatory verse, reminding the Welsh of ancient glories and still-unfulfilled prophecies. It is likely that they simply exacerbated resentments, but their songs undoubtedly helped to create a climate of unrest and dissatisfaction.

REVOLT AND REPRESSION

On 16 September 1400, in his mountain retreat at Glyndyfyrdwy, Owain Glyndwr was proclaimed Prince of Wales by a small group which included Hywel

Cyffin, Dean of St Asaph, and the prophetic bard, Crach Ffinnant. Two days later they raided and plundered Ruthin, and attacks were made on other towns, as far away as Welshpool. The rising was speedily stopped by an English force hastily raised by Hugh Burnell, Sheriff of Shropshire, but Glyndwr's cousins, Rhys and Gwilym ap Tudur, began a revolt in Anglesey. Henry IV led an English

Owain Glyndwr

army through north Wales as far as Caernarfon, then returned south of the Snowdonia massif to Shrewsbury. It was a show of force, with no battle, but Glyndwr's estates were confiscated. In a similar situation, Edward I had shown a degree of magnanimity, but Henry, his hand forced by a panicky and anti-Welsh parliament, made no effort to respond to the many grievances of the Welsh. Instead a set of repressive acts made matters worse. Welshmen were forbidden to own property or hold office in the English boroughs of Wales and the towns of the Marches. No Englishman in Wales was to be tried by any other than English justices. Strict rules banning public gatherings were introduced. Showing an awareness of the inflammatory role of the bards, it was ordered that they and other 'vagabonds' should be restrained. Further fines were levied on the Welsh community.

In the spring of 1401, Welsh attacks erupted like bush fires. The Tudur brothers captured Conwy Castle. On two occasions the Welsh were defeated, by Hotspur on the slopes of Cader Idris, and by John Charlton, Lord of Powys. Glyndwr moved his campaign southwards, winning a victory at Mynydd Hyddgen in the Pumlumon area, and taking the war into Carmarthenshire, where his mother's ancestry helped win him the loyalty of the men of the south, and he had a valuable ally in Henry Dwn, Lord of Cydweli. He also sent out diplomatic messages to France, Scotland and Ireland, though any hope of a grand alliance soon faded.

Through 1401 and into 1402, he consolidated his position, and in April 1402 he captured his enemy, Lord Grey of Ruthin. Keeping up the pressure on the Marches, Owain invaded the lordship of Maeliennydd (Radnor) and won a significant victory at Bryn Glas, near Pilleth. Edmund Mortimer, another great Marcher lord, was taken prisoner, and, with Grey, was held against a rich ransom.

Three royal armies were deployed against him, from Shrewsbury under Henry IV, from Chester under Henry the 'other' Prince of Wales; and from Hereford under the Earl of Stafford. Aided by unseasonably bad weather, Glyndwr successfully avoided the pitched battle sought by the English, and picked them off in guerrilla raids. Anti-Welsh agitation in England grew ever more strident. In 1402 the English were forbidden to trade with the Welsh.

INTERNATIONAL ALLIANCES

The house of Lancaster was not secure on the throne. Henry IV's claim was not the most legally convincing. Glyndwr was drawn deeply into diplomatic scheming which, he hoped, would secure his own position in Wales as well as a new dispensation in England. A central role in this was played by the Mortimer family. Glyndwr's erstwhile prisoner was married to his daughter Catherine and became his ally. Mortimer's nephew, the young Edmund Mortimer, Earl of March, descended from the second son of Edward III, was seen by many as a more legitimate king than Henry IV, descended from the third son. Mortimer's sister was married to Henry Hotspur. An alliance of great potential, between Owain, Mortimer and Hotspur, threatened Henry IV. Driven to action, he forced Hotspur to battle at Shrewsbury, in the summer of 1403, where the Percy was defeated and killed. But Glyndwr remained master of most of Wales. In the spring of 1404 the two royal castles of Harlech and Aberystwyth fell into his hands. He called a parliament at Machynlleth – this may have been partly to demonstrate the popular acceptance of his rule, though tax-gathering is more likely.

It is clear that in his council, led by the cleric Gruffudd Young who became his chancellor, Glyndwr was seriously laying the foundations for a state of Wales. The institutions of state which had been so notably lacking were to be set up. On 14 July 1404, a formal alliance against Henry IV was concluded with King Charles VI of France, and a French fleet made a few token raids on the English coast. Another diplomatic initiative, the Tripartite Indenture, was sworn between Owain, Mortimer and the Earl of Northumberland on 28 February 1405. This document, anticipating the demise of Henry IV and the accession of young Edmund Mortimer, divided England into three parts

Harlech Castle in Victorian times

among the signatories. Owain was not only to be Prince of Wales but lord of a great tract extending over the Marches and into the English midlands.

Much would have to be done before such a dramatic solution was reached, including the military defeat of the house of Lancaster. In early 1405, however, it was the forces of Owain that suffered two sharp defeats, one from Prince Henry near Grosmont, the other from Lord Grey of Codnor at Pwll Melyn, near Usk; in this fight Owain's brother Tudur was killed and his eldest son, Gruffudd, taken prisoner. Owain's hopes remained high, pinned on a French invasion. In August 1405 he convened a further parliament at Harlech. Four representatives from each commote under his rule attended this gathering, and agreed to supply men and money to help him accomplish his strategy. That same month the French landed at Milford, with the results described in the introductory chapter.

THE TIDE TURNS

With the Welsh army back in Wales, Henry IV proceeded to muster a large army to pursue it. Once again the weather was on Owain's side. There was no major battle, but the Welsh were able to seize the English baggage train as their army retreated. By early 1406 the French contingent had returned home. The Welsh were on their own again, with little to show for the much-anticipated joint invasion of England. Owain still had diplomatic cards to play, however. The Great Schism had rocked the church since 1378, with rival papacies at Rome and Avignon. England, with the Welsh bishoprics also, had supported Pope Urban VI in Rome; France and Scotland inevitably took the other side and supported Clement VII in Avignon. By 1406, the Pope in Avignon was Benedict XIII. Anxious for support wherever it could be found, and with Charles VI as middleman, Owain and Benedict entered into negotiation. The Welsh proposal was that St Davids should become the metropolis of an archdiocese completely independent of Canterbury. Its sphere would not be restricted to Wales, but would incorporate the dioceses of Exeter, Bath, Hereford, Worcester, Coventry and Lichfield. Within Wales, ecclesiastical appointees would require to understand the Welsh language. Benedict was also asked to approve the foundation of two universities, one in the north and one in the south. This ambitious scheme, known as the 'Pennal Policy' would have confirmed Wales not only as an independent but as a modern state. Indeed it is remarkable how little looking back there was to older traditions of Wales. Owain was not seeking to turn the clock back; and this openness to contemporary ideas, one of his strengths, also shows how unparochial his attitudes were. It had the misfortune to be framed, however, just as Owain's fortunes began to decline.

In April 1406 Owain was defeated in battle and the Earl of Northumberland lost a further battle in July, against an army raised in Cheshire and Shropshire, led by John Charlton of Powys. Pushing in from the Marches, the English began to regain ground, especially in the south. But Anglesey also yielded. Henry IV's position grew steadily stronger, while Prince Henry's reputation for generalship rose sharply. The English brought in siege artillery to bombard the castles still held by Glyndwr, and their economic campaign was also beginning to wear down the Welsh. By this time the country had been at war for five years; much of it had been laid waste and there had been many deaths. A sense of discouragement was setting in. By 1407 Owain had lost great tracts of country, but still controlled Harlech and Aberystwyth and much of the west. He might still have been able to regroup his resources, but he was losing allies. The Earl of Northumberland was killed in February 1408 and the Tripartite Indenture became a lost dream. In the course of 1408, Harlech and Aberystwyth fell; Prince Owain's wife, daughters and granddaughters were captured and taken to the Tower of London. He himself no longer had a fixed base. But he was not on the run, as he had been in 1402; he still had support and armed men at his command. His last major effort was a raid into Shropshire in 1410 – a disaster in which he lost three men who had long been associated with him, Rhys Ddu, Philip Scudamore and Rhys ap Tudur. But still he could not be captured and still he proved himself a force to be taken seriously. In 1412 he captured an old enemy, the pro-Lancastrian Dafydd Gam. He outlived Henry IV, and in 1415 refused the offer of a pardon from Henry V. After 1415 he is not heard of, and is believed to have lived in seclusion, unmolested, with his daughter Alice (all his daughters married Englishmen) who lived in the Golden Valley east of Abergavenny with her husband, John Scudamore.

Glyndwr's remarkable career would have been impossible without solid and enduring support from the people of Wales. Not all this support may have been voluntary; all military leaders had to resort to tough tactics in order to compel men to join them. But there is contemporary evidence of Welsh farmworkers returning from their seasonal labours in English fields to join Glyndwr's army, just as Welsh students left Oxford and other universities to lend support. The ordinary people had less obvious gains to look forward to than did the *uchelwyr*, or the intellectual class. In part they were following an old tradition of following their lord. In all parts of the country, the old Welsh leaders still had their *plaid*, or following of armed supporters, which could be called out in support of local feuds and rivalries as well as other causes. But there is no reason to doubt their shared commitment to a national cause.

CHAPTER TEN

Towards Union

THE AFTERMATH OF THE REBELLION

The Wales that might have been was lost. It must be asked whether, even at its least grandiose, the state envisioned by Prince Owain would ever have been allowed to exist. The English had, after all, invested heavily in their western colony. When free of disturbance and strife, it was estimated to be worth £60,000 a year to the royal coffers. That was a huge sum of money. There was an element of pride and 'face' as well; the Principality had been made an appanage of the English Crown Prince, and not to be yielded. The Wales that had existed before Glyndwr's revolt returned. But now, in addition, all the hostile legislation of those years was still in place.

Henry V had issued a general pardon, and, with the fading away of Glyndwr, peace returned. None of Owain's sons survived to prolong the dynasty in the male line. The gentry gradually settled back into their accustomed roles, but many feuds and recriminations, both within and between families, were to follow. In castle and borough, the old ways resumed. The country was in a poor way. Few buildings of any size had been unscathed. Farmland had been left to return to the wild, animals slaughtered, towns partially destroyed. Many farms simply lay empty. Trade was at a low ebb. In many a marketplace, like that of Llanrwst, as Sir John Wynn observed, the grass grew green for a long time after the fighting was over. As Glanmor Williams records: 'A century later, in 1536–9, when the great antiquary, John Leland, was touring Wales, he recorded ruin after ruin said to have been "defaced in Henry the Fourth's days by Owen Glendower"'(p. 57).

During the second and third decades of the fifteenth century, the slow process of rebuilding and renewal continued. Those landowners who, through supporting the winning side or by an adroit change of loyalty, still had purchasing power, were able to enlarge their estates by buying from discredited neighbours. The country gentry who were to dominate Welsh life for the next centuries were beginning to take over. But the March remained divided into the great estates of English aristocrats. It was a still-depressed and embittered Wales which was drawn into a new English dynastic adventure, as the Marcher lords embarked on the sporadic campaigns of the Wars of the Roses between 1455 and 1485. Welsh involvement was inevitable, since lords on both sides owned territory in the March. In the early stages, the Yorkists held most of the northern

March, formerly the Mortimer estates, and also Glamorgan and Abergavenny. Jasper Tudor, Earl of Pembroke, supported Lancaster; William Herbert, who replaced him, was a Yorkist. Both sides offered opportunities for Welsh mercenary soldiers, and many Welshmen died in battles outside Wales, such as that of Northampton (1460) and Tewkesbury (1471). But within the Principality, the rivalry of different barons and royal officials, and the lack of central authority, inevitably created a climate of social disorder. The process of law set out in the Statute of Rhuddlan was disrupted by conflicting loyalties and the presence of strong-arm gangs who acknowledged no justice but their own. The March especially became an area of lawlessness, penetrated from both sides by outlaws and bandits. In 1443 the Marcher lords had convened a meeting to discuss the situation, but no action could be agreed on. In fact the March was beginning to outlive its usefulness to the Crown of England, but no Marcher lord was about to give up the privileged state that had existed for almost four hundred years.

ASCENDANCY OF THE HOUSE OF TUDOR

It was during this disturbed time that the House of Tudor began its meteoric rise. Back in the thirteenth century, around 1215, one Ednyfed Fychan had become the *distain*, or seneschal, chief officer of Llywelyn the Great. He married a daughter of the Lord Rhys, and owned land in several parts of Wales. But he, and his descendants, are chiefly associated with Anglesey, where they remained one of the leading families on the island. One of those descendants married the sister of Elen, mother of Owain Glyndwr, and his sons Rhys and Gwilym ap Tudur were, as we have seen, deeply involved in the uprisings of 1400 and after. They suffered accordingly, and for a time their estates were forfeited. A scion of the house, Owen Tudor, went to London where good luck or family connections procured him a post in the royal household of Henry V. He became Clerk of the Wardrobe to Queen Catherine of Valois. Henry died in 1422 and Owen retained his role with the Queen Dowager. Around 1428, they secretly married, and the widowed Queen bore Owen Tudor four children. She died in 1437. Somewhat surprisingly, and perhaps because they had no English royal blood, Henry VI accepted the children of his mother's second marriage and Owen Tudor became a loyal servant of the house of Lancaster. He was executed in the market-place of Hereford after the Lancastrian defeat at Mortimer's Cross in 1461. But by then one son, Edmund, was Earl of Richmond, and another, Jasper, Earl of Pembroke. Edmund married Margaret Beaufort, daughter of the Duke of Somerset, who was descended from John of Gaunt. Edmund died in 1456; his posthumous son, Henry Tudor, was born in 1457. The link to John of Gaunt gave him royal blood.

Pembroke, where the baby had been taken, fell to the Yorkists in 1461, and the young Henry Tudor grew up at Raglan in the care of the Yorkist-sympathis-ing Lord Herbert, until Herbert's execution in 1469 after the battle of Edgecote. After a bloody sequence of events in 1471, with Edward IV's Yorkist victories at Barnet and Tewkesbury followed by the murder of Henry VI, the boy Earl of Richmond emerged as the Lancastrian claimant to the throne. For his safety, his uncle, Jasper, removed him to Brittany, where he remained for twelve years. There was a botched effort to claim the English Crown in 1483, with the back-ing of the powerful Duke of Buckingham. Buckingham's campaign misfired and he was executed. After a further two years at the court of France, and profiting from the disillusionment and division among Yorkist sympathisers following Richard III's seizure of power, Henry led a Lancastrian invasion spearheaded by 2,000 French soldiers, landing at Dale in Milford Haven on 7 August 1485. A number of prominent Welsh sympathisers were waiting, including Rhys ap Thomas, who led one set of forces through Brecon, Builth, and Newtown to Welshpool, while Henry with another army took a route via Cardigan, Aberyst-wyth and Machynlleth, meeting up again at Welshpool for the march into England. Many Welshmen joined them, and further reinforcements from the north-west met them at Welshpool. On 22 August Henry's army met that of Richard III at Bosworth. By the end of that day Richard was dead, and Henry was King Henry VII of England, the first Tudor monarch.

This was a consummation of events that not even the most prophetically endowed bard had foreseen, though the bards were understandably jubilant, and Henry Tudor for them became the 'son of prophecy'. In the veins of Henry VII ran a rich cocktail of blood, but the Welsh element was undeniable, and he

Henry Tudor (Henry VII of England)

bore the surname of the Clerk of the Wardrobe. Wales was his boyhood background. The Welsh could only view it favourably. The Anglesey Tudors themselves had recovered from the disaster of Owain's downfall. Gwilym ap Gruffudd, a squire who had married into the family, had early separated himself from Glyndwr's cause, and was granted the lands forfeited by his in-laws. Once again they were a powerful family in the Welsh scheme of things.

HENRY VII'S WELSH REFORMS

Those who saw the events of 1485 as a Welsh conquest of England were to be disappointed. Henry VII celebrated his Welsh connections in a variety of ways. The Welsh dragon was one of his armorial supporters, along with the Beaufort hound, and was also featured on the royal standard. It was with an eye on Welsh tradition that he chose the name of Arthur for his eldest son. Before his invasion, he had proclaimed his intention of restoring the people of Wales to their 'erst liberties, delivering them of such miserable servitudes as they have piteously long stand in'. Now those who had supported him were well rewarded: apart from receiving the English dukedom of Bedford, his uncle, Jasper, was made Justiciar of South Wales and added the lordship of Glamorgan to the earldom of Pembroke. Rhys ap Thomas was given charge of Carmarthen and Cardigan castles, and was steward of the lordships of Brecknock and Builth. Many positions were given to Welshmen, which had been seen as Englishmen's preserve for generations.

But, though many Welshmen now flocked up to London, as Scots would do in their turn in 1603, Henry VII was far too astute to prejudice his kingship of England by making it appear that the Welsh had taken over. It was not long since the whole English government propaganda machine had been concentrated on showing the Welsh as vicious, scoundrelly and deceitful, and considerable prejudice still existed on both sides. Apart from his very small inner circle, in which Jasper Tudor was prominent, he employed professional English administrators who owed their careers and preferment directly to him.

Within the Principality and the Marches, there was need for action. In 1489, the three-year-old Arthur was named Prince of Wales, and was also given a number of Marcher lordships then in the possession of the Crown. A Council in the Marches of Wales was established to administer the Prince's estates, with its headquarters at Ludlow Castle in Shropshire. Although it was not formally constituted until shortly before Arthur's early death in 1502, it was active during the 1490s, and its keenness to maximise the Prince's income was responsible for a brief revolt in Meirionydd in 1498. Concern to regularise the finances was matched by the need to impose the rule of law throughout the March. Often with the connivance of the Marcher lords, or their agents, criminals and wrongdoers had been able to evade arrest simply by crossing into a separate jurisdiction. In 1504, Henry VII compelled the Marcher lords to give up this practice. He also acted to remove some of the most restrictive anti-Welsh legislation of previous reigns. This made it possible for Welshmen to buy and own land, including manors, castles and burgage plots; and to hold official posts including those of sheriff and justice of the peace.

The trend of Henry's reforms, which were significant though piecemeal in their implementation, was to remove the distinction between the English and Welsh inhabitants of Wales. There is little doubt that they were pressed on him by members of the *uchelwyr*. An important change at this time was made in inheritance law. The old Welsh practice of partible inheritance – division of the estate among the sons – which had been enshrined in the Statute of Rhuddlan, was now abolished in favour of the English system of primogeniture. There were protests from the English colonies, which saw their old privileges given away to the despised Welsh, but the trend of events was against them. They were at their strongest when the Welsh were insurgent. But Wales, with its Welsh king, even if he was far away in London, was among the most peaceful parts of Henry VII's realm.

THE HOUSE OF TUDOR AND THE MARCHER LORDSHIPS

In 1439 William Gruffudd had submitted a petition to the parliament 'to be made English'. His aim was to be allowed to buy and hold land in Wales according to English law, and 'enjoy all other liberties as other loyal Englishmen'. His pragmatic request points up the anomalous position of Wales and its inhabitants. Wales was not part of the realm of England, and the Welsh people were not part of the English people. The Principality of Wales, under Llywelyn II, was a vassal state of England, but nevertheless a separate state. Since Edward I's conquest, the Principality had been under English rule, and its legal and administrative organisation was largely English in style. But this had happened in an *ad hoc* way. In some ways, the status of the March was even more anomalous. Although the ruling families rose and fell, the essential nature of these domains had not changed greatly since the twelfth century. The Welsh revolts and the Wars of the Roses had encouraged a spirit of rough independence. Within their holdings, the Marcher lords were free of all constraint other than those of basic homage and fealty to the English king. In the royal estates, bailiffs and stewards were largely their own masters. An armed escort was vital to their pride and often their survival. To their tenants and dependants they offered their own interpretations of March Law, exacting fines, penalties, and 'free gifts'. Every three to five years, they were supposed to hold the Sessions in Eyre, or Great

Sessions, to deal with important cases and issues of both civil and criminal law. The practice of remitting the Great Sessions, and replacing the income from fines which they generated, by a sort of annual tax on the tenants, had become common in the south especially. This was better news for the criminal than for the law-abiding tenant. On numerous occasions, Henry VII urged the Marcher lords to take their legal responsibilities seriously.

Many of the lordships were administered by Crown officials, but there were still great family holdings. Chief among these in the early 1500s were those of the Stanleys in the north, of the Earl of Arundel around Oswestry, of the Greys who had inherited Powys by marriage from the Charltons, of the Duke of Buckingham in Brecknock and Gwent, and of the Somersets in Gower and around Raglan and Tretower. A whole string of lordships in the south-west had fallen under the control of the Bishop of St Davids. Often, a lord's domains formed a scatter of isolated estates, difficult to administer effectively.

The ordinances and instructions sent out by Henry VII's government make it clear that the king was finding it more and more necessary to interfere in the running of the Marcher lordships. His eighteen-year-old son, who succeeded him in 1509 as Henry VIII, was no less ready. Naturally suspicious of any too-great member of the aristocracy, the king kept a watchful eye on the Duke of Buckingham, who was eventually executed in 1521. The excuse was that he had applied for permission to be accompanied into south Wales by a bodyguard of three or four hundred men. Buckingham may well have considered this necessary for his safety, as there was considerable unrest on his estates, from which he was trying to raise as much income as possible. Henry VIII had none of the personal links with Wales that his father had had (though he did make Anne Boleyn Marchioness of Pembroke in her own right), and Buckingham's part in the Tudor victory was by now ancient history. Another family which had done well out of Henry VII's accession was struck down under Henry VIII. Rhys ap Gruffudd, the grandson of Sir Rhys ap Thomas, was accused in 1529 of plotting to replace King Henry by King James V of Scotland, and to make himself the Prince of Wales. He was executed in 1531.

HENRY VIII AND THE ACTS OF UNION

Henry VIII was not a man who shrank from grasping nettles. His concern, and that of his minister, Thomas Cromwell, for good order in Wales stemmed in part from his reformation of religion. The Welsh coast lay open to Ireland and any troubles there were likely to result in Irish refugees arriving. As Henry's break with the papacy became more and more irreparable, there was fear of invasion by a Catholic army. From 1534 the Council in the Marches of Wales was dominated by a strong man, appointed as Lord President by Henry, to do a strong job. This was Rowland Lee, Bishop of Lichfield, whose correspondence with Thomas Cromwell, Henry's chief secretary, sheds a great deal of light on the administration of justice at this time. Lee was not a typical bishop; even one of Cromwell's own agents described him as 'an enemy to all godly learning'. He was in no doubt about the perils of the task, writing to Cromwell: 'Although the thieves have hanged me by imagination, yet I trust to be even with them shortly in very deed.' Part of Lee's energetic action was to arrange for the drafting of a number of new statutes relating to criminal law, and extending their practice in the Marcher lordships as well as in the Principality. Lee moved to suppress the pressurising of juries, the illegal movement of criminals and of animals, and the abuse of legal procedures by lords and officials. Bringing weapons to court was forbidden, and certain weapons were made illegal. Such ancient and profitable practices of landlords as *cymorth* – originally a form of mutual aid among tenants but long since a forced contribution to landlords – and *arddel* – protection extended by a landholder to persons wanted elsewhere for crimes – were now banned. Even the ancient custom of *galanas*, or blood-money, was still widely maintained in the Marches.

To assist in the process of justice, justices of the peace, on the English model, were appointed to the Welsh shires in 1535, though almost all from a lower economic base than the anuual income of £20 set in England. Few Welsh squires were so rich. Lee also had considerable doubts as to the Welsh squires' will to obey the law. The 'Reformation Parliament' of 1536 also passed a statute providing for 'Laws and Justice to be ministered in Wales' on the same basis as in England. Thomas Cromwell and his civil servants had finally tried to define how Wales and England stood to each other. His aim was that: 'Wales shall be, stand and continue for ever from henceforth incorporated, united and annexed to and with this his Realm of England.' This somewhat glossed over the previous status of the Marcher lordships, but their fate was made clear: they were to be dissolved. As 'no Parcel of any other shires where the Laws and due correction is used and had', and as areas of disorder, they were to be 'united, annexed and joined to divers of the shires of England, and divers of the … said Country or Dominion of Wales'. Five new shires were established in Wales, comprising former Marcher lordships: Denbigh, Montgomery, Radnor, Brecknock and Monmouth. Other lordships were joined to English or Welsh counties; that of Mawddwy, one of the most lawless, was attached to Meirionydd. Whilst new chanceries and exchequers for the new counties were set up at Denbigh and Brecknock, Monmouthshire was attached to England for legal purposes, though by now, of course, the laws were the same. As compensation for loss of functions and revenue, the lords of the March were to receive half the goods and forfeitures of convicted felons. The Welsh shires and shire towns (that of Meirionydd excepted) were to send

THE BANDITS OF MAWDDWY

After the wars of the Houses of York and Lancaster, multitudes of felons and outlaws inhabited this country, and established in these parts, for a great length of time, from those unhappy days a race of profligates, who continued to rob, burn and murder, in large bands, in defiance of the civil power, and would steal and drive whole herds of cattle, in mid-day from one county to another with the utmost impunity. To put a stop to their ravages, a commission was granted to John Wynn ap Meredydd, of Gwedir, and to Lewis Owen, in order to settle the peace of the country, and to punish all offenders against its government. In pursuance of their orders they raised a body of stout men, and on a Christmas-eve seized above four-score outlaws and felons, on whom they held a jail delivery, and punished them according to their deserts. Among them were the two sons of a woman who very earnestly applied to Owen for the pardon of one: he refused; when the mother in a rage told him (baring her neck): *These yellow breasts have given suck to those who shall wash their hands in your blood.* Revenge was determined by the surviving villains. They watched their opportunity when he was passing through these parts to Montgomery assizes, to waylay him in the thick woods of Mowddwy, at a place now called, from the deed, Llidiart y Barwn; where they had cut down several long trees, to cross the road and impede the passage. They then discharged on him a shower of arrows; one of which sticking in his face, he took it out, and broke. After this they attacked him with bills and javelins, and left him slain, with above thirty wounds.

Thomas Tennant, *Tours in Wales*

representatives to the English parliament, one from each shire except for Monmouth, which provided two.

It was prescribed that the language of justice and administration in Wales should be English, and no one who did not speak that language could exercise any official post. 'No person or persons that use the Welsh speech or language shall have or enjoy manor, office or fees within the realm of England, Wales or other of the King's dominions upon pain of forfeiting the same offices or fees unless he or they use and exercise the speech or language of English' (Act of 1536). As the majority of the Welsh gentry spoke both languages, and, when at all educated, also Latin, this probably created few exclusions, though it set an important precedent for the future. At this time, the great bulk of the Welsh population spoke only Welsh; it would have been impossible for even the most upper-class and Anglic-oriented Welsh persons not to have a command of the native language, even if they avoided it in the private rooms of their new houses. The English government clearly disapproved of Welsh: 'Because that the people of the same Dominion have and do daily use a Speech nothing like, nor consonant to the natural Mother Tongue used within this Realm, some rude and ignorant people have made Distinction and Diversity between the King's Subjects of this Realm and his Subjects of the said Dominion and Principality of Wales, whereby great Discord, Variance, Debate, Division, Murmur and Sedition hath grown between his said Subjects …' This was a severe observation on the Welsh language and its part in maintaining a separate Welsh identity, but it does not appear to have resulted in specific measures against the use of Welsh, unlike Henry VIII's Irish policy of 1537, which actively demanded that all Irishmen 'to the utmost of their power, cunning and knowledge, shall use and speake commonly the English Tongue and Language.'

Part of the prescriptions of the Act of 1536 was a three-year period in which alterations could be made in the light of experience. This period proved too brief, given the scale of change that the act brought about, and it was extended by a further three years. In 1540, sheriffs' appointments were all renewed or replaced, to last for one year only; and four itinerant justices were appointed to the four judicial areas centred on Caernarfon, Carmarthen, Denbigh and Brecknock. Among other piecemeal changes at this time was the creation of Haverfordwest as a county borough in its own right, in 1542. In 1543 the second 'Act of Union' was passed, by a parliament which already held Welsh members as a result of 1536. This act was stated in its preamble as intended to establish 'good Rule and Order' in Wales. It confirmed the statutory duty of the Council in the Marches of Wales as the judicial and administrative organisation for Wales and the English border shires of Cheshire (until 1569), Shropshire, Hereford, Worcester and Gloucester (an aspect which these counties would increasingly contest). Working in conjunction with the Council were the Courts of Great Session, operating independently of the royal courts in London. The residual legal functions of Marcher lords were closely defined, restricting their authority to matters below the value of forty shillings (still no mean sum to the average Welsh peasant). The office of Keeper of the Rolls, *Custos Rotulorum*, was instituted, in order to keep a record of justices of the peace, who were not to number more than eight in any Welsh shire. Two new officials were appointed to each shire, escheators, whose function was to maintain the Crown's interest in estates where there was no heir to inherit; and coroners to uphold other legal interests and perquisites of the Crown. In each local area, or hundred, two prominent landholders were to be appointed high constables, 'with special regard to the conservation of the King's Peace'.

THE EFFECT OF THE ACTS OF UNION

The legislation of 1536–43 was wide ranging, and probably sought to be all embracing. Despite the insistence on complete 'Union', it specifically preserved the identity of Wales. This was done principally through the existence of the Council, and the arrangements for provision of justice. Welsh and English now had equal rights, but it was not a matter of adding thirteen counties to the realm of England. The Acts of Union were to control and define the way in which

Wales would be administered for almost three hundred years. A whole range of motives has been imputed to Henry VIII and his government, including a legendary deathbed injunction to his son by Henry VII to 'look after Wales'. The need for internal security undoubtedly played a large part, influenced both by unrest in Ireland and by fear of hostility to Henry's religious policies. But the legislation went well beyond what was needed to provide military security. The desire to reduce the autonomy of the Marcher lordships was also important. For the first time, there was both the royal will to accomplish this, together with the administrative energy and capacity to make it possible.

Perhaps the most vital element in the whole new scheme of things was the attitude of the people who had to make the new system work – the gentry of Wales. Though heavy responsibilities were placed on them, they were now given such opportunities as they had not had since 1282. Many of them had shared the ambitions of William Gruffudd. Now a whole range of public offices, of opportunities for purchase and investment, lay open to them. The dissolution of the monasteries generated a huge new market in land. The *uchelwyr* were not a completely uniform group. They ranged from great landowners, like the Wynns of Caernarfonshire or the Stradlings of Glamorgan, to local chiefs who still maintained an anachronistic rule over a few miles of hill country. These were much less easy to draw into the web of social responsibility. Even in 1555, the 'red brigands' of Mawddwy waylaid and killed Lewis ab Owain, Sheriff of Meirionydd. Bandit gangs were a continuing menace.

Nor could the imposition of English law wipe out the old Welsh social structure, with its basis in the kindred group. Wales remained a land where family feuds were common, usually arising out of disputes over boundaries, rights of way and common grazing. The ownership, and enclosure, of common land was a source of dispute from the later 1400s in such districts as Radnor and Montgomery and western Pembroke, but in many places enclosure was accomplished by tacit agreement of the larger tenants. Although the courts were there, and most disputes were eventually resolved through legal means, there was still an endemic violence which led to brawls and skirmishes when the supporters of rival landowners encountered one another. In 1592, Sir William Maurice, owner of properties in Eifionydd, was taken into custody by his local sheriff for violent crimes. He got his own men to free him, and later on the same day, was said to have sat as a justice of the peace at Caernarfon. He was a deputy vice-admiral for North Wales, with responsibility for security of the coast, and a deputy-lieutenant with powers to raise troops. Even those who lived within the law were competitive and ambitious; if they were not, their fortunes were likely to decline. Many were poor anyway; in sixteenth-century Wales, it was still the case that a long ancestry conferred more status than did wealth.

SOCIETY AND TRADE IN THE SIXTEENTH CENTURY

For all its defects in organisation and execution, the system brought relative peace to the country. The population began to grow again. But what was the general condition of the Welsh in the mid-sixteenth century? The top bracket, the *uchelwyr*, who figure so large as the benefactors of, and operators of, the Union arrangement, were at most 5 per cent of the total population. A rather larger proportion would still have considered themselves among the *bonheddwyr*, free tenants and farmers. Often they would be able to claim relationships with the *uchelwyr*, and their own genealogies could be as long. Arising from the old tribally organised society, based on the land, often inhabiting successive dwellings on the same site, they were deeply rooted in the land and the old culture. They may have amounted to another 20 per cent or so, some of them extending their lands and wealth through marriage and opportunistic purchase; others heading down in the world. New inheritance laws certainly sent many of their younger sons out of Wales as professional men of one sort or another, or as soldiers of fortune.

The towns experienced fluctuating fortunes. Some of the boroughs set up by Marcher lords disappeared, or failed to grow. The same happened with numerous castle-towns, where the location was unhelpful to trade, or too near a stronger centre. Other towns grew substantially. Whatever the reaction of English or Flemish burgesses to the extension of rights to the native Welsh, the effect on the towns themselves was a positive one. But the largest towns were still small by European standards. Only the four chosen as legal centres could offer anything beyond the basics of a market-place and a few taverns. The seaports were small. Cardiff and Carmarthen both had charters as wool staple towns, concentrating the wool trade through their harbours, but maritime trade was dominated by the great English port of Bristol, from which small vessels plied to Welsh ports.

There had been no move to create a Welsh university since the time of Owain Glyndwr. Welsh students went to Oxford or Cambridge, or to a European university; or studied law in London. Wales remained overwhelmingly a rural nation. The urban population in the early sixteenth century was around 25,000, less than 10 per cent of the total. The largest town was probably Carmarthen, with a population in excess of 2,000; Brecon, Haverfordwest and Wrexham had slightly under 2,000; Cardiff, Kidwelly, Swansea, Tenby, Denbigh and Caernarfon had over 1,000; the other seventy-odd towns were smaller. There was no place within the country that could have been called the capital; the administrative centre of Wales was in England, at Ludlow; itself a sort of out-station of the true capital, London, while Chester,

Shrewsbury and Hereford also remained important market centres for Welsh trade.

The majority of the Welsh were landworkers, a peasantry who lived in a state somewhat above serfdom, but in most years not far above subsistence level. Their efforts were concentrated on working in the lands held by the aristocracy and the gentry. In return they were allowed their own plots and enough time to cultivate them. Arable farming and stock-rearing were their main concerns, but the estates and larger farms were labour-intensive in a variety of ways, and work had to be done by everyone from small children to the aged. Geese and ducks had to be watched, hives tended, wood cut, animals slaughtered and butchered, dairy work done, fish traps maintained, domestic repair work carried out, domestic service done. Cloth was woven and made into garments. Military skills remained important, with archery practice demanded from those of age to serve. All estates of any size had an industrial dimension, most often concerned with the fulling of cloth, which had become a mechanised process from as early as the fourteenth century. Much of the cloth industry, in the second part of the sixteenth century, was controlled from Shrewsbury, where the Drapers' Company had a monopoly on Welsh cloth; and a cloth-finishing industry grew up in Oswestry.

Life in Wales in the mid-sixteenth century – a carved scene from the bed of Rhys ap Thomas in St Fagans Castle

In some parts of the country, notably Glamorgan, metal-working was important. The demand for iron was increasing, not only for iron cannon and armour
but for a steadily widening range of tools and implements for agriculture and
industry. Mineral working was still on a modest scale, but the combination of
ore deposits at sites like Llantrisant, with abundant trees for the necessary charcoal, encouraged pockets of industry, and Cardiff added iron plates and bars to
its exports. Guns were also cast there. Coal, which had been dug from outcrops
and small open-cast pits in Flint and Glamorgan from at least the thirteenth
century – there had been something of a hiatus after the Roman era – was seen
as a domestic rather than as an industrial fuel, and was not regarded as a major
asset until later, when unrestricted burning of the tree cover was creating a
shortage of charcoal for ironworking.

This picture of an orderly, busy society, while it expresses the essence of what
was going on, is not complete. At the upper end of society, as we have seen,
there was ample opportunity for acting outside the law, or for hijacking the
process of law for personal gain. At the opposite end of the scale, Wales also
possessed a large under-class, of the dispossessed, the diseased, the despairing,
as well as the blatantly criminal. Failed tenant farmers, men who had got on the
wrong side of the local baron, lepers, half-wits, layabouts, returned mercenaries
who could not settle down – these and their families roamed from town to town
and from parish to parish, dependent on charity and on what they could steal.
Con-men, quack doctors, street entertainers, prostitutes and their pimps generated a 'black economy' at a low but cumulatively significant level of cash. A
statute providing for the punishment of vagabonds was enacted in 1572, but
the Council in 1575 still complained that in the shire of Radnor '... diverse
vagabonds, sturdy beggars and others having no master or entertainment to live
are daily allowed to wander... without apprehension.'

CHAPTER ELEVEN

Cultural and Religious Life in the Sixteenth Century

THE BARDIC TRADITION

Be it known to all persons, both gentry and commonalty, that an Eisteddfod of the Professors of Poetry and Music will be held in the town of Caerws, in the county of Flint, the 2nd day of July, 1523, and the fifteenth year of the reign of Henry the VIIIth, King of England, under the commission of the said king, before Richard ap Howel ap Ivan Vaughan, Esq., by the consent of Sir William Griffith, and Sir Roger Salsbri, and the advice of Griffith ap Ivan ap Llywelyn Vaughan, and the Chair-Bard, Tudor Aled, and several other gentlemen and scholars, for the purpose of instituting order and government among the professors of Poetry and Music, and regulating their art and profession.

This advertisement, quoted by Edward Jones in *An Historical Account of the Welsh Bards*, is of interest in that it shows there was nothing underground or furtive about the maintenance of Welsh vernacular culture. Further *eisteddfodau* under royal patronage would take place, as late as 1597.

If the bards in the preceding centuries had been, in the words of Victor Durkacz, 'the ideologists of medieval Wales, preserving intact a sense of Welsh nationality' (p. 1), the *eisteddfodau* played an essential part in their activities, not merely by providing a platform and a festival in which the old tradition could be celebrated, but by providing 'order and government' among the bards. With no fixed and permanent location, such as might have been provided by the universities mooted by Glyndwr, the examinations, contests and elections of the *eisteddfodau* provided a structure which maintained the dignity and prestige of the bardic profession, as well as the standards of performance. The training of bards was done on a piecemeal and small-scale basis. An established master might take on a handful of pupils; perhaps only a single pupil. Wales does not seem to have possessed the kind of small bardic colleges known in Ireland and the Scottish Highlands, kept by hereditary bardic families like the MacVurichs. But the *eisteddfod* provided the forum through which the young bard could progress, either in poetry or music, until he in turn became one of the leading figures.

During the disturbances of the fourteenth and fifteenth centuries, the tradition of the *eisteddfod* had long periods of abeyance. But the bards flourished in the courts and halls of Welsh leaders. In the cause of Welsh freedom, and to invoke a tradition of heroic independence, many songs written at the time were attributed to the 800-year-old tradition of Taliesin.

By the Tudor era, life in Wales was regulated by its landowners and country squires rather than by princes, chieftains and bishops. Some of these families could still trace, or claim to trace, their descent back to medieval princes; others, like the Salesburys and the Stradlings, were incomers. In the seventeenth and eighteenth centuries, these families would become increasingly anglified in their attitudes and interests. In the sixteenth century, despite the government's pressures towards assimilation, they retained a strong sense of Welshness. The implication of the announcement of the *eisteddfod* of 1523 is that order and government among the bards was lacking, and that the gentlemen and scholars were taking it upon themselves to reinstate it. Some bards, like Lewis Morgannwg, though household bard to Sir Edward Stradling for a

THE 'THREE CLASSES OF BARDS'

According to the Welsh, the metrical bards were divided into three Classes, and the Subjects they treated of were as follows.

The *clerwr*, or Circuit Vocal Songster; to Satirize; to Ridicule, or Taunt; to Mimick, or Take off; to Sue for, or Intreat; to Lampoon; to Reproach.

The *teuluwyr*, Family Songster, or Bard of Domestic Eloquence: to dwell with, and solace, his patron; that is, to divert and enliven the time by mirth and pleasantry. To infuse liberality, to receive guests, and to solicit, in a polite and becoming manner.

Prydydd, a Bardd; or a Poet, and Bard, whose occupation was versifying, etc., to which appertained the following branches: to Teach aright; to Sing aright; and to Judge properly of things. His three excellences were: to Satirize without ribaldry; to Commend a married woman without obscenity; and to Address a Clergyman suitable to his calling.

He was to commend a pleasant disposition of mind; to praise Liberality; and to celebrate the Science of Music, and the Art of Poetry. To delight his hearers; to oppose the bitter invective of the *clerwyr*; and to avoid satirizing any other person. To be obedient, liberal, chaste, and to make himself perfectly beloved.

He was to avoid the seven deadly sins, which are Extortion, Theft, Pride, Fornication, Gluttony, Indolence and Envy; because these things destroy the Genius, Memory, Imagination and Fame of the Bard.

Translated from Dr J. D. Rhys's
Welsh and Latin Grammar, in Edward Jones,
Musical and Poetical Relicks of the Welsh Bards (1808)

time, continued to lead an itinerant life, visiting the homes of gentry through-out the country and composing songs in their praise. Throughout the century it was a necessary part of the style of a Welsh notable to have a resident bard, or to offer generous hospitality to a recognised professor when such a one appeared. In return the bards provided complimentary verses, wrote out genealogies, and copied manuscripts. They were still the recounters of history, albeit usually the fabrications of Geoffrey of Monmouth when it came to earlier times (though in London, Polydore Vergil had already published his refutation of Geoffrey in 1534).

THE NEW ORDER IN LEARNING AND WORSHIP

The development of printing was a blow to the bardic tradition, which had prized its exclusivity. Although books were produced at first only in small quan-tities, they were acquired by the same social class which supported the bards. These upper-class families, their sons educated in Oxford, Cambridge, London and at European universities such as Paris and Bologna, were literate, open to the ideas of the Renaissance, often keen to build up libraries. The idea of read-ing, on one's own, as distinct from listening to a public declamation, began to take hold. The new humanist learning, with its interest in the recently rediscov-ered world of classical poetry, history and philosophy, attracted the scholarly minded in Wales as elsewhere.

With it arose the doctrines of the reformation. The old church order in Wales had perished with scarcely a sigh. The forty-seven religious houses of Wales, in 1535, enjoyed a combined income less than that of some of the individual great abbeys of England – around £3,200. But the church in Wales had always been relatively poor. The diocese of St Davids, though by far the richest in Wales, was less wealthy than any English diocese. The monasteries themselves were under-manned; it was a long time since the wave of enthusiasm that had built the Cistercian houses and filled them with Welsh-speaking monks. Their affairs were already to a great extent controlled by prominent laymen whose roles as semi-official protectors or official commendators enabled them to appropriate much of the abbeys' wealth and place themselves favourably for acquiring the abbey lands and its many subsidiary rights as a property holder when dissolu-tion came in 1536. The last to be dissolved were Neath, Whitland and Strata Florida; one or two which were daughter-houses of English foundations, like Ewenni, lingered on until the mother abbey was suppressed. By 1538 the abbeys, priories and friaries of Wales had ceased to exist.

The abolition of monasticism was accompanied by Henry's establishment of the Church of England with himself as its Supreme Head, and consequent significant changes to the liturgy and forms of worship. Henry's reforms were energetically promoted from 1536 by William Barlow, Bishop of St Davids from 1536 to 1548. The short reign of Edward VI, from 1547 to 1553, saw the imposition of a Protestant reformed religion under Thomas Cranmer, Archbishop of Canterbury. Edward's half-sister Mary, who became queen in 1553, made a determined effort to restore the Roman Catholic religion. In November 1554 the church was restored to its allegiance to the Pope, and in 1555 severe laws against heresy were introduced. During Mary's five-year reign three heretics were burned in Wales; one of them was Robert Ferrar, who had succeeded Barlow as Bishop of St Davids and was executed at Carmarthen in 1555. With the accession of Elizabeth I in 1558, the reforms of Cranmer were reintroduced.

The fluctuations of religious policy between 1534 and 1558 did not provoke any great reaction among the people of Wales. This may reflect a general sense of dissociation from a church whose leaders were almost invariably English appointees whose knowledge of Wales and of Welsh was non-existent. Some bishops were non-resident, like John Salcot of St Asaph, Barlow's contemporary. For the vast majority of the population, their acquaintance with the church was strictly at a parish level. They paid their tithes to the officer of the abbey (or often by this time of the abbey's lay tenant) which controlled the parish church. The incumbent there was as likely as not to be an ill-educated, ill-paid priest who fulfilled the office on behalf of an absentee who might also be the beneficiary of several other livings. Whoever presided at Canterbury, the rite in such places might be unchanged over a lifetime.

However, there was significant change in Edward VI's reign, where an officially inspired iconoclasm encouraged the despoiling of many church interiors, with the breaking of statues, the covering-up of wall-paintings, and the smashing of decorative features. Certain sites which had been venerated by many generations, probably back to pre-Christian times, like St Winifred's Well at Holywell and the shrine of Derfel Gadarn at Llanderfel, were closed down by the reformers, but, in a familiar pattern, official policy and legislation had little effect against deeply entrenched folk belief.

In the course of the sixteenth century, a new emphasis on education arose. Partly driven by humanism and the range of classical learning available, partly driven by the sense that education was needed to support the reform of religion, there was also an official sense that an educated element in society was ever more necessary to maintain an increasingly complex social life. It was also assisted by the relative peacefulness of society and a steady growth in the size and influence of the towns. Before the reformation, the church had been the main source of education, though on a small scale. Grammar schools are known to have existed in such places as Haverfordwest, Wrexham and Montgomery. In the more lordly households, tutoring might be undertaken by a bard. After the dissolution of the monasteries, some towns, such as

St Winifred's Well

ST WINIFRED'S WELL

Water, both still and running, played an important part in Celtic mythology and religion. Lakes, wells and waterways were seen as having their own protective deities, to be worshipped and propitiated. Of the more than two hundred holy wells in Wales, this one is the most celebrated. Its legend is a Christian one, but showing pre-Christian elements. The story is of the holy maiden Winifred, niece of St Beuno (sixth century), whose beauty attracted the Prince Caradog. When she resisted his advances, in rage he cut her head off. For his action he was struck dead, but St Beuno followed Winifred's head, where it had rolled down the hill, retrieved it, re-attached it to her body, and she came back to life. Where the head had come to rest, a spring welled up, with wonderful healing properties. Although Christian pilgrims are only recorded from the twelfth century, there is a strong suggestion of an earlier pagan head cult linked to the tutelary spirit of the spring. Thomas Pennant notes that 'all Infirmities incident to the human body met with relief: the votive Crutches, the Barrows, and other Proofs of Cures to this moment remain as evidences pendent over the Well.' However, writing in the eighteenth century, he also observes that fewer people come these days. The least fortunate pilgrim was Sir George Peckham who came in 1635 and: 'having continued so long mumbling his Pater Nosters and *Sancta Winifreda ora pro me*, that the Cold struck into his Body, and after his coming forth of that Well he never spoke more' – the tale has more than a whiff of anti-Catholic propaganda about it.

Abergavenny, Brecon and Carmarthen, set up schools in the empty monastic buildings. The languages of education were Latin and English. To successive Tudor governments, the schools were an important agency in spreading the use of English through the leading elements of Welsh society. This official policy was supported by a number of wealthy individuals, who set up free schools in different parts of the country. Geoffrey Glynn founded the grammar school at Bangor in 1557. John Beddowes established the one in Presteign in 1565. The grammar schools were still thinly spread. Dr Gabriel Goodman, the Welsh-born Dean of Westminster, who sought to establish a school at Ruthin, referred in his petition to Queen Elizabeth I to the fact that in the six shires of north Wales there was only one free school 'for ye virtuous and godly education of young children whereby they may know their duties to God and your Majesty and thereby be able to serve in God's church and the commonwealth'. (The children, it may be noted, were of the male sex only. Education, outside the richest and most progressive households, was not available for girls.) Such schools as existed, were small-scale institutions, with perhaps a single teacher and an assistant, but they were nuclei of learning and produced a small but important cadre who went on into positions in the church, the law and education. Wealthier families sent their sons to be taught at Shrewsbury and Hereford, and even as far afield as Westminster and Eton. There was still no new move to create a Welsh university, but Jesus College at Oxford, founded in 1571, accommodated many Welsh students. Many endowments were made to support students there, a typical one being that made by one Lewis Owen who founded two scholarships for scholars of Beaumaris School, with preference to 'my own kindred if any be found fit'.

THE LAST DAYS OF THE BARDIC TRADITION

One effect of the new 'new learning' and the various forms it took, was to precipitate the decline of the old Welsh bardic tradition. By the end of the sixteenth century, the bard was an archaic, if not an anachronistic, figure. The upper-class families who had maintained and entertained bards were becoming increasingly English in their way of life. The bardic repertoire had become tired and formalised. The praise poem and the carefully compiled pedigree were also in danger of abuse by poets who, whatever lip service they paid to the concept of gentility by long descent, were willing to invent a lineage for well-off upstarts, some of them not even of Welsh origins. Gruffudd Hiraethog, a bardic leader who flourished between 1520 and the mid-1560s, headed a school of poets who included the last competent bardic genealogists. But one of his pupils, Sion Tudur, a graduate of the 1568 Caerws Eisteddfod, found it necessary to inveigh against such practices:

> ... base-born ploughmen, now, we
> Poets turn into gentry,
> Give pedigrees to blazon
> Jack with praise the same as John.
> Every turncoat filches bits
> From verses of good poets
> To flatter some low fellow,
> This painful bribe paints the crow.
> Plumage from each brilliant bird
> Makes even a crow be-glittered.
> (*An Ode Warning the Poets*)

Though the bardic tradition lingered on into the seventeenth century, a new kind of poetry was gradually appearing in Welsh. Drawing on the work of Dafydd ap Gwilym, and with a more personal and lyrical attitude, it also included religious verse, psalms and carols. The poets, still part of an oral tradition, who composed these works were not bards and did not seek the recognition of bardic status with its degrees and separate departments. The tradition of the *eisteddfod* dwindled away; the last one of the old style was held at Caerws in 1568, though more local ones may have continued in some areas.

SCHOLARS AND GENTLEMEN: WELSH LANGUAGE AND LITERATURE

The bardic tradition had nevertheless performed a very important service in maintaining the prestige of the language during a long period when it was under attack, with many of its official uses being supplanted by English. It was known, and accepted, that Welsh was an ancient language and the vehicle of a great literature as well as of a national tradition. Even though Welsh grammar school boys might receive an imposition if heard to speak Welsh on school premises, the Welsh language was regarded with respect. In this it was very different to Gaelic in Scotland, where there was a profound gulf of ignorance between the speakers of Scots in the south and east, and the Gaelic culture of the Highlands and Islands. Bilingualism was far more common in Wales. It was as a result of this continuing awareness of the qualities of Welsh as a literary language, and as an acknowledgement that most of the population spoke Welsh only, that the first books in Welsh were published. They were the work of humanist intellectuals and designed to spread knowledge. Sir John Price published *Yn y Llyfr Hwn*, an anthology of passages from the scriptures. William Salesbury published *Oll Synnwyr Pen Cymro*, a collection of Welsh proverbs. Salesbury also produced the first Welsh–English dictionary, in 1547, intended to help the Welsh to learn English. An important step was taken when, in 1563, Elizabeth I's parliament authorised the publication of a Prayer Book in Welsh. The previous Prayer Books, of 1549, 1552 and 1559, were all in English. It was accepted that the best way to ensure that the Welsh people embraced the Protestant religion of the Church of England was to expound the creed in their own language. In 1567 the Prayer Book was published, along with a Welsh New Testament, the work of William Salesbury and Richard Davies. In 1588 the complete text of the Bible, translated by William Morgan, was published in Welsh. In the preface to the Welsh Bible of 1588, Salesbury explained the thinking behind it: 'Although it is much to be desired that the inhabitants of the same island should be of the same speech and language, it must equally be borne in mind, that to effect this end, so much time and trouble is required, that to be willing to suffer God's people to perish in the meantime from hunger of His Word, were both barbarous and cruel.' To the exponents of Protestant reform, the Word was fundamental. In all, twenty-three books were published in Welsh between 1531 and 1600, a modest total, but in Gaelic there were none at all. There was no press in Wales, and the printing of Welsh books in London owed much to the presence there of a substantial Welsh community of courtiers, lawyers and merchants who were willing to help underwrite the costs involved.

Several writers of the time showed a scholarly interest in Welsh history and literature. Whilst the majority of the squirearchy were primarily concerned with outdoor pursuits of one sort or another, a few preferred to pursue intellectual and antiquarian interests. Among their number were Robert Vaughan of Hengwrt, who assembled a notable library, David Powel of Rhiwabon, who published a *Historie of Cambria* (1584), Rhys Meurig of Y Cotrel, author of *Morganiae Archaiographia*, and Sir Edward Stradling, who collected many monastic records and manuscripts – all of whom made their own collections available to other scholars. Several of them took up their pens to refute the *Anglica Historia* of the Italian humanist, Polydore Vergil (published in 1534 and 1555), which dismissed the time-honoured fabrications made or passed on by Geoffrey of Monmouth, relating to the roles of such as Brutus and Arthur in the history of Wales. The scholars and copyists of the sixteenth century are responsible for preserving much earlier material that might otherwise have been lost. No doubt much had already been lost before the humanists began their researches. Also of immense value are the commentaries on his own time and circumstances of George Owen of Henllys in Pembrokeshire. Owen was an inveterate researcher and correspondent, whose *Description of Penbrokeshire, Dialogue of the Present Government of Wales, Treatise of Lordships Marchers in Wales*, and *Description of Wales* are invaluable guides to the state of the country and to the activities of the time.

KNAPPAN

. . . [In] these matches the gentlemen would divide the parish hundreds or shires between them, and then would each labour to bring the greatest number, and would therein entreat all his friends and kinsmen in every parish to come and bring his parish wholly with him, by which means great numbers would usually meet, and therefore against these matches there would also resort to the place divers victuallers with meat, drink and wine of all sorts, also merchants, mercers and pedlers would provide stalls and booths . . . after a cry made, both parties draw together into some plain, all first stripped bare, saving a light pair of breeches, bare headed, bare bodies, bare leggs and feet, their clothes being laid together in great heaps under the charge of certain keepers appointed for the purpose, for if he leave but his shirt on his back, in the fury of the game it is most commonly torn to pieces . . . This ball is of some massy wood, as box, yew, crab or holly tree, and should be boiled in tallow for to make it slippery and hard to be holden. This ball is called *Knappan*, and is by one of the companie hurled bolt upright in the air, and at the fall, he that catcheth it hurleth it towards the country he playeth for, for goal or appointed place there is none; neither needeth any, for the play is not given over until the *Knappan* be so far carried that there is no hope to return it back that night . . .

George Owen of Henllys (1552–1613),
The Description of Penbrokeshire

Plas Mawr House, Conwy, built between 1576 and 1585 for the influential Welsh merchant, Robert Wynn

HOUSES AND HALLS

The biggest buildings in Wales, the castles of the thirteenth and fourteenth centuries, built to support colonisation, or to oppose it, were now in most respects redundant. Some, like Dinas Bran, crumbled into ruin. Caernarfon continued as a royal administrative base. All of the Edwardian castles were too big for the requirements of the sixteenth century. Beaumaris, never completed, had five sets of state apartments. Many castles which dated back to Norman times were still inhabited. By this time, however, fortifications and defences were becoming less important to landowning families. Old, cold, uncomfortable castles were adapted or abandoned. From 1536, the residential parts of some abbeys were also taken over. But there was also much new building. The first style of sixteenth century 'big house' was the hall house, still in many respects a primitive building.

Its main feature was a big central hall which occupied the full height of the house and had a central fire whose smoke found its way out without the benefit of a chimney. Originally this single room constituted the entire house, but gradually further rooms were added, and the hall itself became increasingly reduced to a central passage. The supporting framework at each end was a simple cruck, a V-shape of stout, roughly shaped tree trunks. By mid-century, this model was obsolete, and new houses were built with two or more storeys, a staircase, fireplaces and chimney stacks.

By late in the century, the wealthiest landowners were building substantial manor houses with fine brickwork or stonework, glazed windows and considerable ornament (see p. 139). But such houses were always rare in Wales. The income of most landowners did not allow anything like such opulence. A conservative and traditional style of building was common across the country, in which houses would be gradually altered and enlarged from generation to generation. The original core of the old hall was often preserved, subdivided by wooden screens and often with a new upper floor put in. The labouring population continued to live in huts and hovels of the simplest type, often extended into a byre of identical construction.

CHAPTER TWELVE

Elizabethan and Stewart Wales

'THE GREAT DISORDERS IN WALES'

The reign of Elizabeth I was far from being the serene progress through life of a Gloriana, adored and obeyed by her people. Wales was probably among the most peaceful and loyal of her dominions. But Wales did not escape the backwash of troubles and violence caused by loyalties and betrayals at the last Tudor court. In *Wales and the Tudor State*, J. Gwynfor Jones identifies six separate 'factious groups' led by local magnates in different parts of Wales in the years prior to 1588. The Council was hard put to control the personal animosities and political rivalries between these groups. They were not all Welsh squires; some of them were dominant figures in English politics, among them Robert Dudley, Earl of Leicester, a favourite of Queen Elizabeth ever since her accession in 1558. Dudley became by far the most powerful man in north Wales, and an enemy of Sir Richard Bulkeley of Beaumaris, with whom he disputed land tenure in the Snowdon Forest. In Carmarthen, Walter Devereux, a cousin of the queen, soon to regain the family earldom of Essex, allied himself with Sir John Perrott, who was at odds with most of his Pembrokeshire neighbours. Another powerful noble, though one whose sphere of activity was concentrated in Wales, was the Earl of Pembroke, who exercised influence over the gentry of Glamorgan from his base at Raglan. His son, Henry Herbert, also Earl of Pembroke, would follow Sir Henry Sidney as Lord President of the Council in 1586. No aspect of life seemed too small for these notables to control, or attempt to control, to their own advantage. But the rivalries of powerful men were reflected all the way down the scale. One of the informants of Sir Francis Walsingham, Elizabeth's Secretary of State, was Dr David Lewis, who wrote to him in 1576:

> *The great disorders in Wales, especially south Wales, have grown much of late days by retainers of gentlemen whom they must after the manner of the country bear out in all actions be they never so bad ... The authority of the Council there is not regarded as it hath been for neither Sheriff, Justice of the Peace, Mayor, Bailiff or officer of any town corporate, will so carefully apprehend or take any such persons as hath any friend of any account,*

although their faults be never so grievous and apparent, yea though he hath the said Council's letters to that end; but will play bo peep, seest me and seest me not, and this have grown by impunity whereof do proceed all manner of disorders.

The picture painted here seems to show little improvement on that of a century previously. Even allowing for exaggeration, it seems likely that things had deteriorated, owing partly to Sidney's failure to preside regularly over the Council, together with the sense of being above the law that might affect the retainers of such figures as Dudley or Essex.

Under the threat of invasion from Ireland, or in the Armada year of 1588, the discontented and mutually hostile barons nevertheless united in organising the defences of Wales. Wales also continued to supply fighting men. Leicester's ill-fated expedition to the Netherlands of 1585–86 was largely manned by troops summoned or drafted from his large estates in Wales.

The kind of attitudes deplored by Dr David Lewis in 1576 were still reflected in 1601 among the numerous Welshmen who formed part of the retinue of the Earl of Essex. His ill-judged effort to stage a *coup d'état* in London in February 1601 led to his execution and the discrediting of those who had formed his party. In the same year Henry Herbert, Earl of Pembroke and Lord President of the Council of Marches, died. Although the Herberts would remain powerful and influential, the era of domination by great aristocrats was ending. The transition from Tudor to Stewart rule effected on the death of Elizabeth I caused no problems in Wales. The Tudor ancestry of James VI of Scotland was well known in England and Wales long before he made his progress from Edinburgh to London. In Wales, too, the Men of the North, and the old Cumbric-speaking kingdom of Strathclyde, were prominent in people's minds thanks to the work of the sixteenth-century antiquarians. To Welsh members of the House of Commons, like Sir William Maurice, it seemed like a further stage in the process of unifying the British Isles under a dynasty whose ancestry went back into the mists of Cambrian history.

WELSH ASSIMILATION

As represented by the political classes, the *uchelwyr* and the yeomen or tenant-farmers, Wales was royalist and conservative. This almost certainly reflected the views of the great mass of the people. In Scotland, since 1560, religious divisions had opened up sharply between Presbyterian Calvinist reformers and the Episcopalian views of the king. These did not only affect religious belief but engaged the critical issue of whether the church or the secular monarchy was to be supreme. In the Church of England, that issue had been firmly decided by

Henry VIII. In Wales, the existence of the Welsh Bible and Prayer Book helped to consolidate the position of the Anglican church. This was further helped by the policy of Elizabeth's government, of appointing Welshmen to Welsh bishoprics, and Welsh-speaking clergy were to be found in many parish churches. If the Welsh extended no threat to the new king, it was at least partly because he extended no threat to them. Rather, James I was encouraged by what he found, a land at peace under its bishops, lords, judges and squires, in many ways well-integrated with life in England. He was accustomed to regarding the Celtic speech of Scotland and Ireland as both barbaric and subversive, but in Wales, though the native language was spoken by a higher proportion of the population than Gaelic was in Scotland, it appeared to offer no threat to good order. In *A History of Wales, 1485–1660*, Hugh Thomas traces the careers of a number of Welshmen who achieved high office in England during James I's rule, in the church, the royal service and the law (pp. 185 ff.). These successes reveal not only the acceptance of Welshmen at a high level in English society, but the increasing assimilability of the Welsh. By education, family background, and expectation, they were treating Wales and England as a single identity. Inevitably, in this process, despite many examples of local charity, like Goodman's school at Ruthin, they became less distinctively Welsh.

The instrument of control of Wales remained the Council, but in the early seventeenth century the Council was increasingly assailed. It enemies were chiefly in the English border shires, who resented its control. This was by no means because of a Welsh dominance in the Council itself. Though Pembroke, as Lord President, might be seen as more of a Welshman than an Englishman, the Council did not have more than 20 per cent of its members from Wales, and complaints about representation might more readily have come from the Welsh side. The Council was also becoming somewhat unwieldy in its structure. Its function was still to administer on behalf of the Prince of Wales; following the death of Prince Henry in 1612, this was the future Charles I, then aged twelve. Some of its offices were held by absentee courtiers; others had been purchased by officials who expected to make a profit out of their investment and were much more concerned about that than the effectiveness and reputation of the Council. In 1641, during the Long Parliament, the Council was abolished, though it would be revived in 1672.

The end of the Council removed any vestige of an institution which treated Wales as a distinct political entity. There was no national forum. At Westminster, there were twenty-seven Welsh members, voted in by the tiny electorates of shires and boroughs. Although most of them were of broadly similar views, they did not constitute an organised phalanx. They might sit in committee on certain Welsh questions, but these were of strictly local importance, like the Bill of 1597 for bridges over the Usk. In the increasingly strained relations between

143

king and parliament, the majority of Welsh members found themselves increasingly out of sympathy with their English colleagues, though a small strongly Protestant group did align itself with those who opposed royal policy. Charles I's taxes and enforced loans were as unwelcome to the Welsh as to any other group. The successive attempts to raise the Ship Money Tax were progressively less successful, until by 1639, every Welsh shire failed to come up with the required amount. For lengthy periods, of course, Charles was engaged in personal rule and dispensed with a parliament altogether. By no means everyone in Wales welcomed the end of the Council, which had been notably active, if also somewhat corrupt, in its last decade. Now cases which once went to Ludlow would have to go to London, at far greater trouble and expense.

THE CIVIL WAR

In the early years of his reign, Charles I had provoked some opposition among prominent Welshmen, largely through the policies of his favourite, the Duke of Buckingham. John Williams, Archbishop of York, Sir Robert Mansel, Charles's Vice-Admiral, even the Earl of Pembroke (once his keen supporter), were to suffer through their opposition to Buckingham. Buckingham's assassination in 1628 restored better relations between the king and the leaders of Welsh society. For eleven years, from 1629 to 1640, Charles maintained a personal rule, until the 'Bishops' War' with the Calvinist Scots forced him to recall parliament. As relations between king and parliament came to a head, it was clear to both sides that Wales, by and large, was a stronghold of royalism. In a sense, the Civil War was brought into Wales from outside; supporters of the king far outnumbered those of his opponents. Much of this support was latent, or low-key, however. There were committed and active royalists, like the Vaughan family, and Sir John Owen of Clenennau, but many more whose support was passive, and based chiefly on a wish to preserve their now-traditional governance of the Welsh shires. But war was inescapable. As a source of fighting men, as a reservoir of royal support, as a land dominated by substantial castles, and with a strategically important coastline, neither side in this essentially English conflict could ignore the potential of Wales.

The main centres of parliamentary support were in the more English areas, notably Pembrokeshire and the north-east. Apart from their English links, these were also areas where trade and commerce were more firmly established than in the rest of the country, and the interests of merchants were firmly identified with parliament. For the same reason, a number of prominent Glamorgan families supported the parliamentary cause.

When war broke out in the summer of 1642, Charles established bases at Shrewsbury and Chester, and sent his son, the Prince of Wales, to Raglan, seat of the royalist Earl of Worcester, to recruit fighting men. At least half of the royal army at Edgehill, the first, indecisive engagement of the Civil War, was made up of Welshmen, most of them untrained and ill-prepared. Another army was raised in south Wales by the Marquis of Hertford, to be defeated at Tewkesbury, though it went on to capture Hereford. In these early stages of the war, though there was much campaigning on the Welsh border, especially around Bristol and Gloucester, there was no fighting in Wales itself. This changed in the summer of 1643, when a parliamentary force invaded north Wales and captured Hawarden, Mold and Flint before being repulsed by royal troops returning from Ireland. Action also began in Pembrokeshire, where the Pembroke Castle, under Rowland Laugharne, was held for parliament. Under the Earl of Carbery, royalist forces occupied the rest of the county. In the first half of 1644, a parliamentary army under Sir Thomas Myddelton of Chirk and Sir Thomas Mytton took possession of much of the Marches, defeating the royalist forces at Welshpool, Tarvin, Montgomery and Powys Castle. In February of the same year, Laugharne broke out of Pembroke Castle and, aided by the parliamentary fleet's control of the coast, cleared Carbery's men not only out of Pembrokeshire but out of much of the territory to the east, as far as Cardiff, which was captured from the sea. A strong royalist push from the east, under Colonel Gerard, regained most of the lost ground, though Laugharne continued to hold Pembrokeshire.

Pembroke Castle

In the summer of 1645, following his disastrous defeat by Cromwell's 'new model' army at Naseby, Charles retreated to Raglan Castle, his old recruiting ground. This time volunteers were hard to find, and men were pressed into service. Their reluctance resulted in the presentation of a set of grievances to the king, who eventually departed with far fewer men than he had hoped for. Fighting continued in the south-west, where a series of royalist victories by Gerard gave them temporary control of Pembrokeshire again. But the fall of Bristol to parliamentary forces was a fatal blow. Laugharne struck back at Colby Moor, defeating a royal army, and terms of surrender were made with the royalist command in Glamorgan. By autumn 1645, parliament controlled all of the south, except for Monmouth. In February 1646, an attempt at a royalist uprising in Glamorgan, led by Edward Carne, the Sheriff, and supported by Monmouthshire royalists, was suppressed by Laugharne. In August of that year Raglan Castle was captured by a parliamentary force. King Charles had already surrendered himself to the Scottish army in May. The fall of Chester in February 1647 cleared the way for parliament to invade the north. Under Sir Thomas Mytton they fought a methodical campaign which ended with the fall of the last royalist redoubt, Harlech Castle, on 1 March 1647.

Few parts of Wales escaped involvement in the fighting, even if it was involuntary involvement. The aftermath of the Civil War was uncertain and bitter. The king was a prisoner but it was by no means clear that he should not resume

Raglan Castle

his position. There were many dissatisfied people, apart from the defeated royalists. The troopers who had fought for parliament were infuriated by the delays and possible reductions in their payment, and their anger came to a head with the disbandment of the army in February 1648. In Pembroke, John Poyer, governor of the castle, took up their cause, and declared for King Charles. He was joined by two other erstwhile parliamentarians, Rowland Laugharne and Rice Powell, but at the battle of St Fagans, in Mahy, they were heavily defeated by troops of Cromwell's new model army under General Horton. This was the largest battle of the war in Wales, and it was followed by the arrival of Oliver Cromwell in person to ensure the suppression of royalism. On 11 July, he obtained the surrender of Pembroke Castle. In the north, too, a succession of small-scale royalist outbreaks, often prompted by personal factors, such as the Bulkeley family's loss of power in Anglesey, were contained with relative ease.

ADMINISTRATION UNDER THE COMMONWEALTH

The agrarian economy of Wales was not greatly affected by the Civil War. As in the time following the Glyndwr rising, there was a legacy of bitterness in some places between neighbours and even family members who had taken opposing sides. The more prominent royalists faced forfeiture of their estates or heavy fines. But it became increasingly clear that there was going to be no return to the state of things before the war. This was underlined by the execution of King Charles in January 1649. Two Welshmen, John Jones and Thomas Wogan, were among the regicides who signed Charles I's death warrant, but many others who had fought against him, including Sir Thomas Myddelton, were opposed to putting the king on trial. Despite his important contribution to parliamentary victory, Myddelton was 'purged' from parliament in December 1648 and deprived of influence.

Myddelton was one of fifteen Welsh members to be expelled from the 'Barebones Parliament'. For the authorities of the newly established Commonwealth, the administration of Wales, as a predominantly royalist society, and remote from London, was a difficult problem. The basis of their solution was the 'county committee'. The origins of this lay in the early days of the Civil War, in Pembrokeshire, when parliamentary sympathisers had formed a committee to support their own party. In the other shires of Wales, the existence of one or two parliamentarian families helped to make the nucleus of a post-war committee. In addition to these county committees, there were two sequestration committees, one in the north and one in the south, until they were combined in 1650. The purpose of these bodies was to examine and assess the roles played by Charles's sympathisers, and the damages that they should pay. Inevitably the

147

members of the committees profited from their involvement, and there were many accusations of corruption. In such counties as Cardigan, Carmarthen, Brecon and Radnor it was hard to find enough gentry members who had supported parliament, and the committees contained known royalist sympathisers.

THE REFORMED RELIGION

The basic issues of the war between king and parliament in England had been mainly political and economic, and as such had relatively little relevance to the people of Wales. As the war continued, and especially in the years after 1647, the ideological aspects became increasingly apparent. Before 1642, religious life in Wales had been quiescent, with the great majority of the population in membership of the established church, with its Welsh Bible and Prayer Book, and a largely bilingual clergy. Puritan sects had been confined to small and uninfluential groups in towns, mainly in the south-west and north-east. The course of the war brought religious issues out into the open. Charles's employment of Irish Catholic troops had brought fears of a Catholic restoration which alarmed even strong royalists, most of whom had their share of former abbey property to protect. Within the parliamentary armies, there was intense discussion on ideological issues, among many different groups. Official policy of the Commonwealth government was Puritan and anti-Episcopalian, and in 1650 a Committee for the Propagation of the Gospel in Wales was formed. Its aim was to teach doctrines which went far beyond the Welsh Prayer Book in their insistence on the individual's direct relationship with God. The Committee's job was to examine, approve or eject the clergy of Wales. Commissioners decided on what action should be taken. Two hundred and seventy-eight clergy were ejected from their livings between 1650 and 1653, for delinquency, scandal and non-residence, but also in some cases for 'malignancy', the label for actual or supposed Catholic belief. It was often found difficult to find suitable replacements or new appointments, and teams of itinerant preachers, paid for by funds taken from Anglican resources, were recruited to help spread Puritanism throughout Wales. Education also fell within the Committee's remit, and some sixty free schools were founded, mostly in towns which did not have a school. Some of these schools were open to girls as well as to boys, but two-thirds of them had closed by 1660, probably due to the funds being channelled elsewhere by self-interested local committeemen. The national commissioners also had a wider role: a quorum of five could form a committee of indemnity with authority to rule on all kinds of complaints arising in Wales. Its rulings were subject to appeal to a parliamentary committee of indemnity in London.

The Cromwellian government soon began to backtrack on this ambitious

VAVASOR POWELL

The most celebrated of Welsh Puritan travelling preachers in the seventeenth century, Powell (1617–70) was 'converted' as a young man by the ex-Anglican curate Walter Cradock and became a protégé of the Harley family of Brampton Bryan in Herefordshire. He began his travels in Wales around 1639. On the outbreak of the Civil war in 1642 he fled to London, returning to Wales in 1646, where he became an influential member of Colonel Harrison's team of commissioners 'for the Better Propagation of the Gospel'. Powell was a doughty traveller, often travelling a hundred miles in a week across rough country, stopping to preach in each place he came to. His religion was a fiery one; he shared the belief of the 'Fifth Monarchy' men, that the Day of Judgement was close at hand, and he shared the political radicalism of the 'levellers'. He supported Cromwell until the erstwhile Parliamentary leader became Lord Protector, at which point Powell preached and wrote vehement diatribes against him. The title *A Word for God . . . Against Wickedness in High Places* is an indication of Powell's fearlessness. After the royal restoration of 1660, he was to spend most of the rest of his life in jail in London. Released in 1668, he returned to preaching Puritanism, now as a Baptist, and was re-imprisoned until his death.

scheme for propagating reformed religion. Instead of a uniform, sober and law-abiding new sense of devotion and spiritual solidarity, the Puritan movement split into a variety of forms. Some of these were highly subversive of established law and order. Others fostered an extreme religious excitement which drew their adherents away from a sense of daily responsibility and duty. After three years, the act creating the Committee for the Propagation of the Gospel was allowed to lapse.

AN UNPOPULAR GOVERNMENT

The Commonwealth and Cromwell's Protectorship did not win widespread support in Wales. The majority of Welsh had after all, adhered to the losing side in the Civil War and could only look on the new order as the result of defeat. The royalist families who had been fined or sequestrated after the war had had considerable influence, and their decline was shared in by their retainers. There was a constant stream of complaint, sometimes in the form of petitions to the authorities, sometimes as published pamphlets, occasionally as riots and skirmishes, relating to the injustices, maladministration, peculation and incompetence of new officials. Much of this perhaps represented the jealousy of those who had profited from their former positions, but there may also have been expectations of more honest administration, which were not always fulfilled. A prominent case in point was that of Colonel Philip Jones, who had been Governor of Swansea in 1644, and who, as the leading parliamentary official in south Wales, and a member of Cromwell's national Council of State, enriched himself greatly on fines and appropriated church funds. His example was imitated on a lesser scale by others throughout the country. Many of the new officials and justices were Englishmen, often former parliamentary soldiers, and resented by the locals on both counts. Others were seen as 'jumped-up' Welshmen and if anything resented even more. Satirical squibs appeared, mocking the pretensions of those who had been labourers or stone-masons before the fortune of war turned them into leaders of society. The most powerful man in Wales, Major-General James Berry, the military commander, had been a clerk in a Shropshire ironworks before the war. Despite his ability and generally affable attitude towards the Welsh, he headed an unpopular regime. One effect of the changes was to enhance the use of English instead of Welsh. This, if not official policy, was certainly something the Commonwealth did nothing to discourage. Many of its Puritan missionaries were ex-army men who knew no Welsh and preached in English. Although the government came to no fixed view on the form of religion, it was resolute in its wish to stamp out such ancient pleasures as maypole dancing, Robin Hood fairs, and other gatherings which had enlivened country and town life for centuries. Justices of the peace were instructed to use their powers to ban and stamp out such practices. Like all governments with an ideological bent, that of the Commonwealth encouraged spying and delation. With a large standing army to maintain, as well as a network of spies and informants, it was also more efficient in tax collecting than any previous regime in Wales, something which endeared it to nobody.

THE RESTORATION

The restoration of the monarchy in 1660 was warmly welcomed in Wales by everyone except those who might expect to lose some of what they had gained from buying up sequestered estates or misusing church funds. The old county families speedily regained their position, but many of the newcomers also retained theirs. Those who wished to turn the clock back to 1640 found that too many things had happened in the interim for that to be possible. Wales had changed in the course of the Civil War and the Commonwealth, most notably in the growth of Puritan sects. Most of these had a strong democratic tendency, and their leaders were often men of humble background. Part of their preaching was that one man is as good as another, not only in the sight of God, but in secular life. Although their numbers were still very limited, their ideas were well known, and helped in the erosion of the ancient reverence for rank and status which had sustained Welsh society for so long. The more extreme sects, like the Baptists and Quakers, now found themselves liable to prosecution. New acts of parliament sought to enforce the liturgy of the Church of England, and to ensure that all public office-holders were communicants. The four bishops of

Wales were of course reinstated, their sees still part of the province of Canterbury, and in the latter part of the seventeenth century they were, for the most part, Welsh-speaking. Many of the Puritans accommodated themselves within the established church. Others found it impossible to square their independent convictions either with the dogma of the official church or with its structure of bishops and king, or with its interposition of a hierarchy between the individual conscience and the divine. It was hard for Puritan ministers to keep their livings; now it fell to their turn to be examined and often found wanting. More than a hundred and twenty were expelled from their pulpits. The reinforced state orthodoxy also turned on the schoolmasters, and more of them were driven out after the restoration than under the Commonwealth. In these campaigns, the fear of social upheaval, together with a certain revanchism against those who had trumpeted so loudly when Cromwell ruled, perhaps counted for more than the defence of the faith. In that latter respect, the church was compelled to tread a careful middle course. As a result of constant propaganda from the days of Henry VIII on, there was a greater ideological fear of Catholicism than there was of Puritanism.

ATTITUDES TO CATHOLICS AND PURITANS

The number of committed Catholics in Wales in the later part of the sixteenth century was not large, perhaps hardly more than a thousand people. But some of them were important persons, such as the Earl of Worcester. Despite his English title, his seat was at Raglan, and he was a fluent Welsh speaker. For those who could see it, the sympathy at the court in London for Catholicism was clear enough. It was for the benefit of Catholics that the Declaration of Indulgence was made in 1672, though the Puritan sects could not be excluded from its effects. Despite occasional plots both real and imaginary, the Catholics of Wales offered no real threat to established order. This did not protect them in 1678–79, in a time of hysteria occasioned by the 'Popish Plot' of 1678. The Catholic seminary at Cwm was wrecked, and four priests were hanged. The campaign to exclude the openly Catholic Duke of York from succeeding his brother, Charles II, found support even in loyalist Wales, eleven of whose twenty-seven members of parliament voted in 1679 for his exclusion from the throne.

Of the more extreme Puritans, many came from the lower, though not lowest, reaches of society. Their presumption in choosing a personal form of religion affronted the squirearchy quite as much as their opinions. In the mid-1670s their numbers have been variously estimated between 4,000 and 15,000 (out of a total population of around 341,000), but they were far from being a united group. Baptists, Presbyterians and Independents were the main branches, but all had a tendency to separate into schismatic factions. The Quakers especially were treated with as much hostility by fellow-dissenters as they were by the Anglican majority. Many of them, attracted by the prospect of religious freedom, emigrated to the new colonies of North America, especially Pennsylvania. For those dissenters who stayed behind, whatever their disadvantages and sufferings, there was an important positive point. They had exercised independent choice. To that degree, they were more in control of their lives and ultimate destinies than were the free electors of the Welsh parliamentary seats, who voted on instruction. Naturally enough, the majority of them were town or village dwellers, artisans and tradesmen whose skill could guarantee them a livelihood and who were not at the mercy of a master who might not share their views. Whatever their attitude, they were still compelled to pay tithes to the established church, and had to pay their own pastor, if they could, on top of that.

THE 'GLORIOUS REVOLUTION'

Although he bore the title Duke of Monmouth, the connection between Charles II's bastard son and Wales was purely titular. On the death of his father in 1685, he attempted to seize the throne from his uncle, the heir apparent, James II, but the venture failed and Monmouth was duly decapitated in the Tower of London. Wales played no part in his rising and no part in the next political convulsion, the replacement of the Catholic James II by the Protestant William and Mary in the 'Glorious Revolution' of 1688. By this time Wales had seen neither a reigning monarch nor a Prince of Wales on its soil since the days of Henry IV. Perhaps Mary I, when still Princess of Wales with a court at Ludlow, made some visits into her Principality during the 1520s; and Charles II came very close in his escape after the defeat at Worcester in 1644, but loyal, reliable Wales could be taken for granted by a centuries-long succession of kings. The pro-Catholic policies of James II provoked surprisingly little adverse reaction in Wales. In the only election held in his reign, supporters of the 'Court Party' were successful in both north and south Wales. But there was no positive reaction either; the Welsh magnates wished James II well, but above all they wished that he would not rock their comfortable boat too much.

The installation of William and Mary caused something more than a flurry in Wales. The Duke of Beaufort – formerly Marquis and Earl of Worcester – set about raising an army to support James II, and the head of another prominent Catholic family, Thomas Carne of Glamorgan, also came out in public support. But the reaction was brief. James's flight to France brought their efforts to an end, and the support of his sympathisers in Wales did not extend to significant help in his abortive Irish campaign of 1689. Although Wales would remain an area of hope for future Jacobite claimants to the throne, its Jacobitism was largely nominal.

Under William and Mary, the Council in the Marches (revived from 1672) was finally abolished. In politics, the Welsh members associated themselves with English-based factions and saw no reason to form a separate body. In the emerging Whig–Tory scheme of things at Westminster, the majority of them would become Tories, supporting the e stablished church in its most traditional form, and harbouring a strong sympathy with the exiled Stewarts. For most, however, this sympathy expressed a hostility to the 'revolution settlement' and its religious toleration, rather than an active wish to bring in 'the Pretender'.

CHAPTER THIRTEEN

The Era of Improvement

WALES IN THE SEVENTEENTH CENTURY

One hundred and one years elapsed between the 'Glorious Revolution' of Britain and the French Revolution of 1789. Both of these events were significant milestones. The accession of William and Mary, and the manner in which it was accomplished, marked the beginning of the end of royal autocracy. Increasingly, the country would be ruled by an oligarchy of rich landowning families whose expansionist approach at home and abroad would result in the dramatic extension of the British Empire and the steady growth of an industrial economy.

A complex set of changing and developing ideas, at different levels, underpinned the changes that took place during this period. Wales, still lacking a university, with no town to compare with Dublin or Edinburgh in size and national importance, was still a largely rural and agrarian society, whose small towns provided a focus for commercial life on a local basis with markets and fairs. The largest town in 1700 was Wrexham, with about 3,000 people. The capital of Wales continued to be London, and as such it continued to attract many ambitious Welshmen. The nucleus of a Welsh community there, established since Tudor times, made it all the easier for new members to join. From this community emerged such figures as the architect Inigo Jones (1573–1652), one of whose patrons was the Earl of Pembroke, and Edward Lloyd (c.1688–1726) whose city coffee house developed into the dominant shipbroking and marine insurance business. In the course of the eighteenth century, the London Welsh would exert considerable influence on life in Wales, and on the concept of Welshness.

During this period, Wales contributed relatively little to the philosophical 'enlightenment' that arose, partly in reaction to the religious obsessions of the seventeenth century, and partly as a consequence of ideas first mooted at that time. The intellectual excitement generated in England, Scotland and Ireland by such figures as Newton, Berkeley, Locke and Hume, failed to kindle a comparable Welsh mind, though the non-conformist academies followed new ideas keenly. Irish and Anglo-Irish writers like Farquhar, Steele, and, later Sheridan, established great reputations, as did incoming Scots like James Thomson and Tobias Smollett. Wales provided no poet or novelist of note in English. This is in part a tribute to the fact that the vast majority of Welsh people still spoke only Welsh, but it also indicates that ambitious Welshmen did not at that time

---

THE NON-CONFORMIST ACADEMIES

If Wales in the eighteenth century still had no university, it was not without sources of higher education. Non-conformists, debarred from the two English universities, set up their own teaching centres. Ousted ministers often made up the teaching staff in the early days, during the 1660s and 70s. The academies were not large, but the best offered a four-year course and a varied range of subjects, including mathematics and natural sciences as well as Hebrew and divinity. At the Llwyn-llwyd Academy, medicine also was taught. The Academy founded near Bridgend by Samuel Jones, a Fellow of Jesus College, Oxford, became so renowned that it even attracted Anglican students. In the eighteenth century the Academy settled permanently in Carmarthen and, under Thomas Perrot, became famous or infamous for its nourishment of independent religious thought, notably Arminianism, which played down such pillars of Calvinist belief as predestination.

---

see a satisfactory career in assimilating themselves into the intellectual life of the capital. In business and commerce, it was different.

CHANGES IN UPPER-CLASS LIFE

The spirit of life in Wales was driven from two very different and mutually antipathetic directions. The dominant factor in society remained the gentry but there was a change in the composition of this class in the later seventeenth and through the eighteenth centuries, as estates tended to get larger. An important cause of this was the large number of families which failed to provide male heirs, and the resultant marriages of girl heiresses both enlarged the holdings of individual families and brought in more English landowners. Whilst some of these were from the recently rich, the process also brought an influx of the English aristocracy: between 1721 and 1760, Lord Talbot, the Earl of Plymouth and the Earl of Jersey arrived in Glamorgan. As a result, the slow trend towards anglicisation speeded up. By the 1770s, most members of the Welsh upper class would no longer find it necessary to speak Welsh. Even before this, they would take elocution lessons in order to make sure that their English did not let them down. The focal points of their lives were not in Wales, but the annual season at Bath and even in London. In *When Was Wales?* Gwyn A. Williams refers to Welsh heiresses being 'marketed' at Bath; certainly the marriage process was run much more by arrangement than on romantic attachment.

The Welsh seats at Westminster were controlled by fewer than forty dominant families, who negotiated and wrangled among themselves to decide who the representatives would be. Many elections were uncontested. Only a few areas, such as Glamorgan, had relatively large electorates – men who qualified by having an annual income of forty shillings a year, or more, from their land. The lesser gentry, increasingly demarcated from the very rich, still filled the justice of the peace posts, though many hardly participated in the process of justice. With increasing ownership of more than one estate, many landowners were absentees.

The political tradition of Jacobitism lingered until the 1745 Rising. But neither then, nor in the earlier 1715 and 1719 Risings, was there any real Welsh contribution. Only a few Welsh supporters turned up to join Prince Charles Edward Stewart at Manchester. Families such as the Bulkeleys of Anglesey and the Williams Wynns of Denbighshire, the Philippses of Pembrokeshire and the Beauforts in Monmouthshire, though they remained ostensibly Jacobite through several generations, used their Jacobitism more in maintaining mutual bonds and to control local politics than to promote a change of kingship.

By 1720 the already moribund tradition of the bards had ceased. Even the conservative-minded among the aristocrats and squires regarded the notion of the praise-singing bard as something belonging to an earlier era. The last of the genuine old poets was Gryffydd Phylip of Ardudwy who died in 1666. With the end of patronage, poetic production did not stop but became a localised pursuit. With exceptions, the intellectually minded members of the upper class were more attuned to what was going on elsewhere. A rich young man of good family would be expected to make a tour of European centres of culture – Paris, Rome, Florence – with a tutor in attendance, after attending Oxford or Cambridge. Not exposed to Welsh since the time he was wet-nursed, he would regard the Welsh books and manuscripts in his library as curiosities, and it is unlikely he would be able to read them.

Among the clergy there were Welsh writers of note, including Theophilus Evans, author of *Drych y Prif Osoedd*, 'The Mirror of the Early Ages', almost the last work (1716) to treat Geoffrey of Monmouth as a reputable source; and Ellis Wynne, author of the satirical *Gweledigaethau y Bardd Cwsc*, 'The Visions of the Sleeping Bard'. These were exceptional men, and ecclesiastical patrons of traditional Welsh culture like Humphrey Humphreys, Bishop of Bangor between 1689 and 1701, were becoming increasingly rare. Humphreys used the Welsh language in the course of his official duties, and accepted the tributes of bards, but his chief interest was antiquarian and lay in the Welsh past and the ancient achievements of the Welsh language. In this he was a forerunner, but not among bishops, however – after 1720 no Welsh-speaking bishop would preside over a see in Wales for 150 years.

ANTIQUARIANS: THE LONDON WELSH AND OTHERS

Though the leaders of society played very little part, there was an intense spirit of inquiry into Welsh culture and history during most of the eighteenth century. It received much support from the mercantile community of the London Welsh, who, established in the increasingly vast and cosmopolitan capital, were keen to remember their own roots and perhaps to exercise some reverse influence into the old country. Both in the north and the south, researchers delved into the linguistic tradition. In Anglesey, Lewis Morris (Llywelyn Ddu o Fon, 1700–65) uncovered many old manuscripts in country houses, and set up the first printing press in north Wales, in 1735, to make books available in Welsh. These included his own poems. Lewis's appointment as Collector of Customs at Holyhead gave him the income and leisure to pursue his interest. His brother Richard (*c*.1705–79) went to London to work in the Navy Office, and founded the Honourable Society of Cymmrodorion there in 1751. It was not the first London Welsh society – the Ancient Britons had been founded around 1715 – but it was the most distinguished and influential in publishing Welsh-language material. In 1758, Lewis Morris brought the sixth-century text of *Y Gododdin* to public notice, claiming it as a Welsh national epic of equal standing to the *Iliad* and the *Odyssey*. The Morrises – they were first of their family to employ a surname rather than a patronymic – gave support to numerous writers, though their interest was centred in the north. Indeed, they regarded the revivalists of Welsh culture in the south with some doubt, both as 'fanatical' Methodists and as purveyors of what they considered a decadent tradition. Morris referred to the Welsh of south Wales as 'hodge-podge' or 'Hottentotice'.

Hodge-podge's chief purveyor was the Morrises' younger contemporary, Edward Lewis (1747–1826), better known under his pen-name of Iolo Morgannwg. Born at Llancarfan, Glamorgan, the son of a stonemason, he was deeply influenced by his mother, who had links to a gentry family. He worked with the Reverend John Walters, who began publishing a Welsh dictionary in 1770, and in 1773 moved for a time to London and was active in the Gwyneddigion Society, another literary coterie, but one that had a strongly radical political tinge. One of its members, the wealthy furrier, Owen Jones (Owain Myfir), was to remain a patron of Iolo's after he returned to Wales. Iolo studied the poems of Dafydd ap Gwilym and produced a set of 'newly discovered' verses by the fifteenth-century poet. Back in London from 1791, he claimed to have had discussions with the last upholders of an ancient druidic and bardic tradition in the uplands of Glamorgan – of greater lineage and importance than the northern traditions explored by the Morrises and their circle. To supplement his discoveries, he forged numerous documents purporting to set out the bardic tradition. In 1792 he organised a Gorsedd, or bardic gathering, on Primrose Hill in London, the first of many. He published a volume of English verses under his own name, *Poems Lyrical and Pastoral*. Back in Wales, he was given a post by the Board of Agriculture, to inspect farming methods and customs, which enabled him to traverse the country. Iolo published a further collection in Welsh, *The Myvyrian Archaiology*, named in honour of Owain Myfir, between 1801 and 1807. Ostensibly a collection of verses from the sixth to the fourteenth century, many of them were entirely his own work. More of his work was published by his son Taliesin in 1829 as *Secrets of the Bards* (under the impression that they were genuine manuscript copies from the bardic epoch) and the extent of his forgeries was not appreciated until the early twentieth century.

Among the pioneering antiquaries, the greatest was Edward Lhuyd (1660–1709), born in Ceredigion, and educated at Oxford University. In 1690 he became Keeper of the Ashmolean Museum in Oxford. In 1697–1701, he undertook a tour of the Celtic lands, collecting manuscripts and studying the languages and customs. His *Archeologia Britannica* of 1707 was the first to put study of the Celtic languages on a scholarly basis, although those who had subscribed were somewhat dismayed by the implacably comparative-linguistic approach of its first – and only – volume. Lhuyd's work was instrumental in demonstrating the age of the Welsh language and its links with Breton and Cornish. His work on manuscripts was continued by the Morrises.

With the loss of the Stationers' Company monopoly in 1695, it became possible to print and publish books outside of London. Shrewsbury, still a dominant town in the economy of mid-Wales, became a centre for Welsh publishing, and the first Welsh press was established in 1718 in the village of Trefhedyn, near Newcastle Emlyn. Eventually Carmarthen became the main centre of Welsh printing. Between 1710 and 1730, 330 books in Welsh were published, the great majority being devotional writing in prose and verse. The next largest category was the almanac, collections of folk-tales, popular wisdom and proverbs, with a more-or-less moral flavour often dressing up rude and bawdy content. Contemporary literature was rare.

Throughout the century, the awareness of Welsh as an ancient language and the repository of a vivid and exciting history grew steadily. In the latter half of the century, the climate of European thought was not quite ready for such knowledge, but welcomed it warmly. France, which had a Celtic tradition of its own to rediscover, had seen the Abbé Pezron's *L'Antiquité de la Nation et la Langue des Celtes* appear in 1703. Jean-Jacques Rousseau's works, from 1750 onwards, which promoted the concept of the 'noble savage' and the purity of earlier civilisations, struck a responsive chord in England and helped to spark off a new interest in the ancient cultures of Wales and Scotland. The researches of Henry Rowlands, of Anglesey, into the actual traditions of the druids, were important in their own right as well as supplying much useful material for Iolo Morgannwg to adapt. Thoroughly English poets like Thomas Gray were inspired to write verses like *The Triumphs of Owen*:

> Owen's praise demands my song,
> Owen swift, and Owen strong;
> Fairest flower of Roderic's stem,
> Gwyneth's shield, and Britain's gem.

SPREADING THE WORD IN WELSH

This pre-Romantic enthusiasm might not of itself have arrested a decline in the Welsh language; many of those smitten had no actual knowledge of it. It did perform a useful service in exalting the status of what otherwise might have been regarded as a rustic speech for sheep-tenders and rough mountainy folk. (Even so, as Geraint Jenkins notes in *The Foundations of Modern Wales*: 'Many of the gentry and *nouveaux-riches* affected to despise it. "Why should we use or think in such a poor, anonymous tongue?" they declared to Lewis Morris. "English is the language of this kingdom."' [p. 222].) A much more positive force for the preservation of the language was set in motion by Griffith Jones of Llandowror (1683–1761), an Anglican priest of the evangelical wing. Even before Jones, the Reverend Stephen Hughes had established the Welsh Trust, with Thomas Gouge, in 1674. In its seven-year life, the trust financed an 8,000-copy print run of the Bible in Welsh, and supported many schools. Hughes, however, appears to have favoured the established notion of teaching children in English. From 1699, the Society for Promoting Christian Knowledge (SPCK) began to open schools and distribute Welsh Bibles in Wales, and some of its schools, especially in the north, did at least some teaching in Welsh. From 1713, Griffith Jones was a corresponding member of the SPCK. Himself a successful – and to his own church controversial – itinerant preacher, he conceived the notion of 'circulating schools' during the 1730s. He realised that intensive, short-term teaching of literacy in Welsh was the best answer to bringing up a generation of Welsh people in true religion. Saving souls was Jones's business, not preparing pupils for a career; nothing was taught in his schools but the catechism, prayer and reading. And the language was Welsh. Jones published a journal, *Welch Piety*, to propagate his views and help in raising funds for his teachers. Typically they would stay in one place for from six to nine months, then move on. The circulating schools were highly successful within their limited aim. As welcoming of adult as of child pupils, the schools ran evening adult classes which were often better attended than the day classes.

Although Griffith Jones remained an Anglican, he was on excellent terms with the leaders of Welsh Methodism, and many orthodox Anglicans blamed him for seducing people away from the established church. The London-Welsh Anglican vicar John Evans wrote in a hostile pamphlet: 'These south Wales enthusiastick itinerants pretend to be Church of England people, and come to church, but at Nights they creep into such Houses as they are able to work themselves away to, and there delude ignorant men and lead captive silly Women and Children …'

After Griffith Jones's death, his friend and patroness, Mrs Bridget Bevan, of Laugharne, maintained the schools until her own death in 1779. The circulating schools, of which there were around 250 operating up to 1779, are estimated to have taught reading to perhaps 180,000 children and at least 250,000 adults. With a total population of under 600,000, literacy in the national language was at an exceptionally high level in Wales compared to virtually all other European countries.

THE FOUNDATIONS OF DISSENT

There can be little doubt that the circulating schools played an important part in the steady increase of dissenting religion in Wales. In *The People of Wales* (Elwyn Jones and Smith), Philip Jenkins refers to the religious revival as 'perhaps the most important single cultural event in eighteenth-century Wales' (p. 98) and also notes that: 'the areas in which the revivals were burning most brightly by 1740 were exactly those regions of the south where Jones's charity schools were also being founded.' Despite official toleration of religious dissent, those who did not conform were still restricted in many ways. They could not attend an English university (a Scottish one was another matter), nor could they hold political office. But for long, the revivers remained within the Church of England, to the fury of those who saw them as a church within the church. Such is exactly what they were, their organisation set up by Daniel Rowland and Howell Harris through the local *seiat*, or society. The charisma of the preachers and the sense of keen spiritual unity felt by the congregations (the fanatical 'Enthusiasm' so despised by John Evans) helped to attract and hold converts. By 1752, Howell Harris, one of the leaders of Welsh Methodism, had set up his remarkable ideal community at Trefeca in Brecknockshire, a secular monastery where services alternated with farm work, weaving, shoemaking and printing. A third key figure in the movement was William Williams of Pantecelyn, whose magnificent hymns promoted a new wave of religious enthusiasm in the 1760s, following a time when arguments between Rowland and Harris had alienated some of the faithful. The great age of non-conformism in Wales still lay ahead, but the ground was prepared. In addition to the older dissenting tradition of the Baptists and Congregationalists, with their roots in the previous century, there were more than 400 Methodist societies within the established church, numbering something between 7,500 and 10,000 members.

THE DAWN OF INDUSTRIALISATION

If Wales remained a political backwater, some of its landowners showed themselves more modern-minded when it came to the development of industry and the exploitation of the country's natural resources. When silver was discovered on his estate at Gogerddan, Ceredigion, Sir Carbery Pryse fought and won a historic court case in London in 1693 to establish his right, rather than the Crown's, to mine it. Most often, however, they leased these resources to incoming entrepreneurs. The coming dominance of industry in the Welsh economy was far from apparent, though certain localised areas were already industrialised and suffering from the side-effects of uninformed and uncontrolled chemical and combustive action. Pontypool, where water power was used to operate an iron-rolling mill, was also a centre of tinplate production. Until the late eighteenth century, most ironworks remained relatively small-scale. The Welsh ironmasters were slow to turn to the use of coal, despite the successful experiments made at Coalbrookdale on the English Severn. But, driven by the reduction of the once-extensive forests, and by new processes, the iron-making industry presently settled itself on or close to the coalfields. Deposits of iron ore stretched along the heads of the valleys of Glamorgan and Monmouthshire, and ironworks were set up at sites such as Hirwaun, Dowlais, Merthyr, Sirhowy, Beaufort, Ebbw Vale and Blaenavon. Names like Beaufort and Plymouth indicate the involvement of aristocratic landowners. Landowners with coal reserves underground found themselves sitting on diamond mines – but the diamonds were black and produced by the ton rather than the ounce.

The existence of coal deposits had been known for centuries, and it had been extracted in easier places since Roman times. Until the late seventeenth century, its use was very largely as a domestic fuel, and a modest export trade had been established from ports along the south and north coasts. Difficulties of land transport meant that mines tended to be close to the sea. But by the later seventeenth century, inland pits were being dug in Glamorgan and Monmouthshire. Steam power, then very new, was chiefly used for pumping engines which helped keep water out of the increasingly deep pits. A new drive came into the industry with Sir Humphrey Mackworth, who married into the Evans landowning family of the Gnoll. An apostle of mechanisation, he installed pumps and wooden tramways. Coal was run straight from his pitheads to the quays of Neath from the late 1680s. Around Neath and Swansea the houses of the colliers formed drab little industrial communities, an indicator of things to come.

Mining was a physically exhausting task. Hewers dug out the seams with picks, working by candlelight, hoping not to encounter pockets of explosive firedamp. Women and children dragged out the coal in baskets and sleds, and bore it in creels up the rickety ladders lining the shafts. More advanced pits had windlasses or gins worked by horses or donkeys. Coal was normally moved on the surface by packhorse. Even though the very low wages paid held down costs, it was a slow and labour-intensive business to bring every ton of coal to the surface.

Mackworth was also involved in other forms of mining. In 1693 he bought the Pryse family's rights to mine copper, lead and silver at Gogerddan in Ceredigion. Lead was mined also in Pembroke, Flintshire and Caernarfonshire. Lead mines were often sunk in remote mountain sites where deposits were tenuous or of poor quality, and opened and closed again sometimes with great rapidity. In Flint especially, lead-smelting became a significant industry, with coal used to heat the reverbatory furnaces. The necessary capital was raised not in Wales but by the London Lead Company. The discovery of substantial copper reserves at Parys Mountain on Anglesey enabled the Mona Mine Company to dictate prices and supply for almost three decades from 1760. Copper smelting was carried out largely in the south, first at Neath, which in the early 1700s was the most industrialised place in the country, and later around Swansea. A smelter opened at Llangyfelach in 1717, and by the end of the century, the lower Tawe Valley had a succession of them. The investment was largely made from outside Wales.

Bristol and Liverpool were growing very rich on the proceeds of colonial trade generally and the slave trade in particular. Profits from this were ploughed into

Parys Mountain, Anglesey, as it looks today

new industrial ventures which were expected to pay back handsomely. In most cases they did, helped by the wars of the eighteenth century. Shipbuilding became important in the sheltered reaches of Milford Haven, and a royal dockyard was established at Pembroke. In 1746, Lord Mansel sold 90,850 cubic feet of timber, chiefly oak and elm, from Margam forest to the Admiralty for shipbuilding.

In the early years of the eighteenth century, the slate industry began in small pockets in the Nantlle Valley of Caernarfonshire. Thatching with reeds or straw was the normal way of roofing a house, and the market for slate was not a large one. But an export trade with Ireland began, taking about half the production, and boosting the fortunes of the port of Caernarfon. The growth of the industry was gradual but by mid-century quarrying had spread to Llanberis and other locations in Snowdonia.

ROADS FOR THE MODERN AGE

The landscape of Wales had more than once shown in previous centuries that it was inimical to those who wished to cross it. English armies had been turned back, to the relief of Welsh commanders. But it was equally unfriendly to the Welsh themselves. No roads had been constructed in Wales between Roman times and the eighteenth century, other than purely local ones. Overland transport of goods was mainly by packhorse, or by horse and sled. The vital export of cattle into England did not follow the packhorse tracks but was conducted over long-established drove routes through the hills and valleys, converging on the border market centres of Wrexham, Shrewsbury, Hereford and Monmouth. The key strategic routes remained as they had always been, that along the north coast from Chester to Holyhead and the sea-link to Ireland, and its parallel in the south from Monmouth past Cardiff and Carmarthen to Pembroke and the anchorage of Milford Haven. Throughout the country, muddy, stony, ill-made tracks linked one community to the next. Whenever possible, journeys were made by sea. It was always easier to travel from the north or south into England than it was to journey cross-country from Cardiff to Aberystwyth or from Swansea to Machynlleth. Roads that were no more than ill-maintained tracks hampered the movement of heavy items like slate, but also of everything else.

Little change in an essentially medieval network came until the turnpike trusts began to be set up, from 1750 onwards. The new toll roads, reaching in from Chester and Shrewsbury, and linking towns in mid and south Wales, made transport easier. Wheeled vehicles, previously rare, appeared in increasing numbers, both for goods and passengers. Stage coaches began to ply, more (and wealthier) travellers prompted improvements in the often dismal and vermin-ridden inns and hostelries and new inns were established.

AN EIGHTEENTH-CENTURY 'CHARACTER'

Marged uch Ifan was a well-known figure in north Wales for most of the eighteenth century. Born in 1696, she is first heard of as keeping the Telyrnian Tavern in the Nantlle valley in Caernarfonshire. Able to make fiddles and harps, she could also play these instruments, and often provided music for her clients to dance to. The copper mines of Drws-y-Coed were busy at that time and she had no lack of customers. Later she moved to Penllyn, at the end of Llyn Padarn, where she ferried copper ore down the lake for onward transport to the coast. According to the traveller Thomas Pennant (though she was not at home when he called) she kept her own pack of foxhounds, had a great repertoire of old musical airs, could build a boat, and shoe a horse. Even at the age of seventy she could throw any man in a wrestling match. According to some authorities, Marged died in 1788, aged 92, but an early nineteenth-century *Cambrian Traveller's Guide* says that she died in 1801, at the age of 105.

Cultivated people's perception of landscape changed radically during the century, to the benefit of Wales. Mountain scenery, earlier regarded as gloomy and desolate, was viewed with new, romantic eyes, as picturesque, grand and thrilling. Relative ease of access had something to do with this, as well as a new appreciation of wild nature. Coming to Wales was still something of an adventure for the English traveller, but the Welsh tourist industry had its modest beginnings at this time.

THE CHANGING FACE OF FARMING

Traditional agriculture-based industries also flourished in the eighteenth century, notably cloth and wool, both dependent on the sheep stock. By the seventeenth century, its main centres of production had moved from around Carmarthen to Meirionydd, Montgomery, and Denbigh. The cloth and wool industries were cottage-based industries, both for weaving and for knitting. The income they generated was low, and the quality of Welsh wool and cloth products was rugged rather than suitable for high fashion. The main markets were the growing population, slave and free, of the American colonies, together with Ireland, another area of population growth.

Agriculture itself, still the chief activity of the people, followed a roller-coaster path through the eighteenth century. Though the underlying trend was towards greater productivity and a wider range of crops, this was often reversed for years at a time by prolonged winters, excessively wet autumns, and other climatic difficulties. Food shortages happened at intervals through the eighteenth century, the worst periods being 1739–41, 1751–53 and 1766–67, when serious and successive harvest failures led to a shortage of flour and an inflation in the price of bread. Such famine periods often coincided with epidemics of disease, when smallpox and typhus struck down many people already weakened by lack of nourishment. Tenant farmers found life a struggle, made worse by landlords' demands for higher rent – rents went steadily upwards after 1750, at a rate faster than the tenants' income, until by 1790 they had doubled. Leases were granted for shorter periods and on stricter terms. The landlord's steward or agent became an ever-more oppressive and hated figure, even when he was honest. Another group which found life hard was that of the small-scale squires. Many of them forsook their aspirations to gentility, as the gap between them and the very rich widened, and became working farmers, the mansion demoted to a farmhouse. Many others had to sell up. But thrift, perseverance, and application of new techniques helped farmers to survive. Scientific crop rotation, fertilisation with lime and manure, and new crops, all helped. The use of turnips as winter fodder (once their novelty had worn off and they were no longer eaten as dessert!) helped maintain cattle in better condition through the winter. Farmers got together to discuss and compare progress; the Breconshire Agricultural Society, founded in 1755, was the first of many such groups. With an expanding population and better communications, the basic conditions for agriculture were good, so long as the farmer was not squeezed too hard financially by rent or debt.

A VIEW OF WALES IN THE EIGHTEENTH CENTURY

In the eighteenth century, to a large degree, north and south were separate entities: densely populated groups of communities separated by mountains which were threaded only by the often-impassable tracks. North met south in Shrewsbury, Hereford or even London, rather than anywhere in Wales itself. Their trading links ran east–west into England and over to Ireland – and south to Bristol for the southern shires. Denbigh, Caernarfon, Brecon and Carmarthen remained the law centres, with the Great Sessions still taking place. The four bishoprics, each answering separately to Lambeth Palace, perpetuated the divide. There were no political institutions to unite the Welsh. The factors promoting a sense of wider unity were unofficial ones. First was the possession of a national language. Although spoken somewhat differently in north and south, it was mutually intelligible. And two hundred years of grammarians, translators, writers and teachers had established a written Welsh common to all. Second was the network of shared thought and experience present among the dissenting and Methodist societies. Neither flood nor landslide, nor any vagaries of weather, long deterred the wandering preachers and teachers from reaching places that had not yet been given their own form of revelation. Inevitably they brought news and stories with them, accounts of great things done in other communities, of sacrifices and victories in the cause, all helping to create a sense of mutual effort and involvement.

In the course of the century, the science of political economy was developed, and in *The Wealth of Nations* Adam Smith sought to explore the reasons for the apparently ever-expanding wealth of Great Britain. But successive governments, though confident in waging war, found it less easy to maintain an economic equilibrium. Harvests were still subject to the weather and crop disease. There were times when food supplies ran dangerously short, or the price of grain and flour soared to unacceptable heights. In the 1790s, food riots were commonplace events among the urban population of Swansea and Merthyr.

CHAPTER FOURTEEN

Industrial Wales. The First Phase: Primitive Industrialism

A SCENE SET FOR INDUSTRIAL DEVELOPMENT

In 1780, despite the smoke rising from places like Neath, Wrexham and Merthyr, the country was set out in a human pattern that had been very much the same since Tudor times. Most towns had grown, but the largest, Wrexham and Merthyr, still had fewer than 10,000 people; and their growth was being accelerated by a demand for industrial workers. The old country towns, with their trading roots in agriculture and rural industry, were still of very modest size, Swansea and Carmarthen the largest with around 4,000 people; most others had fewer than 2,000 inhabitants, with many under 500. The countryside was still firmly under the control and management of landowning families, some of them old-established like the Wynns of Wynnstay and the Pryses of Gogerddan; others were new, the product of heiress-marriages or straight land-purchase. Notable among these were the Cawdors of Colden Grove and the Butes of Cardiff, in both cases members of large Scottish landed families, Campbell and Stewart respectively. As before, their control of local appointments and local events was absolute, and they continued to dominate the election of Wales's twenty-seven members of parliament.

In 1780 the population, estimated at 580,000, was more or less evenly divided between north and south, largely spread along the fertile coastal plains and valleys. Rural areas were well-populated. Though agricultural techniques had improved dramatically throughout the century, farming was still unmechanised and required large teams of men and horses. More labour was required for the extraction of timber from the hillsides and peat, then still a common source of fuel, from the uplands. There was a range of rural skills in virtually every parish: blacksmith, farrier, joiner, drystone dyker, shoemaker, tailor, tinsmith. Lack of communications compelled communities to be self-sufficient. Where there was a concentration of 'big houses', notably in Flint, Monmouthshire and Glamorgan, there would be more skilled workers available: carriage-builders or repairers, cabinet-makers, dressmakers. The wealthy also imported a great deal. They bought their clothes and quality furniture in

England, and brought in specialist builders and decorators to enlarge and embellish their houses.

Events and developments outside Wales were to condition what would happen within the country. The notion of an 'industrial revolution' has been largely discarded by historians, as research has shown how industrial techniques and production developed steadily from the mid-seventeenth century onwards. Many factors played a part. The establishment of transatlantic colonies, with the consequent expansion of trade, was important. The growth of the Empire encouraged greater imperialism. It was in order to feed the slave population of Jamaica cheaply that HMS *Bounty* was sent to the South Pacific to collect breadfruit plants. The rivalry between Britain and France that lasted throughout the eighteenth century and into the nineteenth fuelled an arms race that required an ever more efficient and versatile metals and chemicals industry. The development and improvement of new tools in science and industry demanded greater production of copper, brass, iron and tinplate. Improvements in medical science cut the infant mortality rate and ensured that people lived longer. Except among the poorest, people's expectations from life rose, and standards of living improved. Houses were enlarged and better furnished. The 'Welsh dresser' was installed in many farmhouses, and required good plates for show. Windows were glazed. Bedrooms and beds replaced the box-beds set into the wall of the single kitchen-cum-living room. The tenant farmer might still drink home-made ale in the morning, but by the mid-eighteenth century, his wife was more likely to drink tea. Coffee and chocolate remained luxury drinks, but tea increasingly became a staple drink, which people saved

---

PONTYPOOL IN 1801

Pont y Pool is a large straggling place, containing 250 houses and 1,500 souls. Several neat habitations, and numerous shops, present an appearance of thriving prosperity, notwithstanding the dusky aspect of the town, occasioned by the adjacent forges. The inhabitants derive great support from the ironworks and collieries, and have been recently benefited by the trade of the canal. The place is the principal mart for the natives of the mountainous district, and the weekly market is not the least considerable, and the cheapest in Monmouthshire. It was a pleasing amusement to mix in these crowded meetings, to observe the frank and simple manners of the hardy mountaineers, and endeavour, in asking the price of their provisions, to extract a *Saxon* word from this *British* progeny. The women were mostly wrapped in long cloth cloaks of a dark blue or brown colour; all of them wore mob caps neatly plaited over the forehead and ears, and tied above the chin; several had also round felt hats like those worn by the men, or large chip hats covered with black silk, and fastened under the chin. This head-dress gives an arch and lively air to the younger part of the sex, and is not unbecoming.

William Cox, *An Historical Tour in Monmouthshire* (1801)

---

up for and used sparingly. Its 'cheering' capacity, combined with its associations with feminine sociability, made it a suspect drink to many old-fashioned males.

In the late eighteenth and early nineteenth centuries, the rate of population growth accelerated dramatically throughout Europe. It was not necessarily related to industrial development: growth in non-industrial Ireland was as notable as that in England, Flanders – or Wales. Except in some of the soon-to-emerge urban slum districts, more newborn babies survived, and they themselves had a longer expectancy of life. Inevitably the birth rate went up.

Whilst many of the factors promoting industrial development were to operate in Wales, very few originated there. In the metallurgical industries, the entrepreneurs and craftsmen tended to be incomers. Wales was a small country and a small market. Set between the burgeoning commercial ports of Bristol and Liverpool, Welsh harbours had remained small and local, with minimal participation in the lucrative Atlantic trade that flourished until the hiatus caused by the American Declaration of Independence in 1776. Wales was to be a key area in the rapid expansion of industrial growth that happened between 1780 and 1840. It has been variously described as a crucible and a cradle of the new industrial world. But if it was a cradle, then the baby was a foundling, put in from outside. Large-scale industry was thrust on Wales.

THE ERA OF THE INDUSTRIALISTS

The impact was greatest on the south. The necessary conditions were present. Ironstone contained workable ore at the northern rim of the coalfield. The coal itself, mixed with wide beds of shale, dipped deep under the ridged plateau but the coal measures were often near the surface in the valleys, and again close to Swansea. There was still extensive tree cover and water power. Natural energy was available in large quantities. The will and economic resources to take advantage of this came from outside. A new generation of names came to dominate large areas of Welsh life – this time of industrial developers: Guest, Crawshay, Bacon, Bailey, Wilkinson, Homfray and others. Their wealth was often generated from colonial estates in the Americas and India, and their techniques of large-scale management of workforces owed much to the same experience. The slave-operated plantation was a vertically integrated enterprise in which the owners provided everything and dictated the terms on which it worked. Feeding, housing and clothing hundreds of workers was part of the business, to be managed along with production, harvesting, processing and transport. The lessons of this were not lost on the entrepreneurs in their home-based activities. There was one important difference – Britain was a 'land of the free'; only recently a patriotic imperialist Scot had written *Rule Britannia*, with its chorus: 'Britons never, never, never shall be slaves'. In Britain, workers had to be paid.

In fact, to lure potential employees to the new communities at the heads of the valleys, in high and unpopulated country, it was necessary to pay wages well in excess of what they would have received in any other form of labouring. News of this encouraged others to come in search of work. For their money, they put in ten or twelve hours a day, six days a week, of physically hard and often dangerous work. The ironmasters built houses to rent out to the workers – quite substantial houses at first, on the farmhouse model, though they soon became heavily overcrowded, with tenants compelled to sublet – and set up shops to sell them food, clothes and other basic necessities. This was the notorious truck system: the shops supplied on credit, and the debt was removed from the pay-packet before it was handed over. Skilled workers were made to sign legally enforceable contracts to ensure that they could not take their knowledge elsewhere for more cash.

The growth of the iron industry created further jobs. The packhorse was an obsolete form of transport, and the roads, despite improvement, were not suitable for bulk haulage. From 1790, following pioneering work in England, canal construction got under way, with the Glamorganshire Canal obtaining its Act in that year (it opened between Cardiff and Merthyr Tydfil in 1794). The Neath and Monmouthshire Canals were authorised in 1791 and 1792, the Brecknock and Abergavenny in 1793. Canal building offered many jobs, taught new skills, and many Welshmen became professional 'navigators' who followed the contractors and engineers from project to project, in England and abroad. The

Pontcysyllte Aqueduct , near Llangollen, in Victorian times

greatest engineering feat in Wales since the construction of the castles gradually rose above the Dee Valley near Llangollen, as the Pontcysyllte Aqueduct, built between 1795 and 1805, took the Ellesmere Canal on what still seems a waterway through the air. It also pioneered the use of iron to form the trough that held the water. The Glamorganshire Canal needed many locks to hoist barges from sea level to the 500-foot contour at Penydarren, near Merthyr, but it and the other canals had a dramatically lowering effect on the cost of haulage, and on the time taken. The canals also opened up the coalfield, though at first most of its production still went to the ironworks.

POLITICAL REVOLUTIONS AND THE WAR WITH FRANCE

'Politics in Wales begin with the American Revolution', wrote Gwyn A. Williams in his stimulating history *When was Wales?* (p. 167), unperturbed by the fact that he had already been describing Welsh political life in some detail prior to the crucial date of 1776. But in at least one important respect he was right. To the Welsh, the American Declaration of Independence, with five signatories of Welsh origin, was a reminder, if one were necessary, that for a hundred years, their countrymen had been emigrating to the New World in large numbers, and that many districts in the United States were almost wholly Welsh in population. Especially among Dissenters, there was considerable sympathy for the American cause. Political tracts arguing the case for and against American independence were published in Welsh and English. Dr Richard Price (1723–91), a London Welsh Unitarian minister, wrote *Observations on Civil Liberty* (1776) arguing for the sovereignty of the people. Not everyone approved. The war and its resulting economic blockade cut off trade, except for the lesser trade with Canada, and lost an important market to the woollen and cloth industries. Within a few years, a headier political brew was being stirred. Its origins were in France. Price's response to the French Revolution, the sermon, *On the Love of Our Country*, in 1789, directly prompted Edmund Burke to reply with his *Reflections on the Revolution in France*. Another notable radical was David Williams, friend and correspondent of Benjamin Franklin, whose ideas anticipated much of the Chartists' agenda. Like most British supporters of the Revolution, Williams turned against it, but not until he had been to see for himself how the surge of idealism and democracy was crusting into oppression and tyranny. Men such as these took the Welsh dissenting tradition up out of the parish level and indeed out of Wales altogether, into an international community of radical thought. Inside Wales their influence was great. A growth in the network of Freemasons' lodges helped to spread this influence. Price was elected Grand Master of the

Bridgend Lodge in 1777. Such semi-secret societies, with their rituals and devices for recognition, were a phenomenon across Europe at the time, spanning the political spectrum. In Wales, their predecessors had been the ultra-Tory Jacobite societies, where glum squires drank to the king-over-the-water and did little or nothing to ensure his return. At the other end of the political spectrum, in the same way, the Freemasons and other societies prompted intense discussion but little action. But the topics of discussion, and the excitement they provoked, were a novelty in themselves. 'Liberty, Equality, Fraternity' was a heady slogan, heralding a future that seemed entirely possible.

When Britain and revolutionary France went to war in 1793, however, the government took action, or rather intensified a campaign which had been under way since 1791. Known radicals and Jacobins were subject to official harassment and arrest under often vague charges. Patriotic mobs were whipped up to terrify their families, disrupt their meetings, and wreck their houses. Civil rights were put into suspense. Once again there was a watch on the coast. Deputy lieutenants assumed purposeful expressions and drilled the scarlet-coated Volunteers. In the seaports, the press gangs were on the hunt for able-bodied men. Landlords found a new market in flesh, with government bounties payable to them for each youth or man delivered up to serve with the colours. Such a blend of political repression and patriotic fervour added its strains and stresses to a confused period in which industrialisation was being accomplished at an ever-increasing pace. Every event had a political slant imputed to it. If the workers of the vast village – for it was in no sense a town – of Merthyr rioted against food prices, there must be enemy agents or sympathisers at the bottom of it. In places like this, the county magistrates were out of their depth. No such community had ever existed before in Wales. Nowhere had been big enough to have a mob. Their fear made their sentences harsher, with troops standing by to back them up. Faced with war, and with the collapse of the great French experiment, where Terror was giving way to dictatorship, many who had celebrated the revolution now protested their patriotism. Despite the hazards of crossing the Atlantic, many other religious and political radicals left for North America, leaving Wales, and Europe for that matter, to sort itself out as best it might.

The war with France produced an exciting episode centred on Fishguard, where, in February 1797, a small French invasion force, commanded by an Irish–American, was landed. It had no obvious purpose, except perhaps to create a diversion from more serious French operations in Ireland. If local support had been anticipated, none was forthcoming. The militia were sent for, and in an almost bloodless confrontation, the French surrendered. Rumours and reports exaggerated the affair, which caused more alarm in other places than it did in Fishguard, but the very fact of enemy troops landing on a British shore helped to raise patriotic fervour and further discredit political radicalism, firmly identified with French revolutionary sentiments.

IRON, COAL AND THE CHANGING LANDSCAPE

By this time, the first, or primitive, phase of industrialisation was well advanced. No one quite knew what was going on, or where it would lead. Each man knew his part of it, whether it was leasing his ground for iron mining, or investing his capital in the new technology, or fitting in as a foreman, artisan or labourer to the complex structure of employment within the ironworks, where a 'gentleman puddler' with a gang of his own might act as one of a whole range of subcontractors to the owners of the works. But the whole picture was still obscure, characterised by the unplanned, unimaginative spread of factory villages in the valleys.

Just as in politics, there was excitement and novelty, and sometimes the grand gesture. Until recently, the non-conformist, Puritan tradition has somewhat obscured the fact that historically, the Welsh have always been keen on gambling. In February, 1804, the owner of Penydarren Ironworks made a hefty bet with a local rival. He wagered the sum of 500 guineas that a steam-powered 'travelling engine' set up on his mining tramroad by the Cornish engineer Richard Trevithick, would pull a load of ten tons from Penydarren to Abercynon, a distance of just under 10 miles. The bet was taken. The locomotive, first in the world to run on rails, made the journey in four hours and five minutes, with seventy men clinging on to the wagons, as well as ten tons of pig-iron. The flanged track was broken and cracked by the wheels, and Penydarren went back to pony-hauling for thirty years. But that day, on this bleak plateau, the steam railway was born. In a few decades, south Wales would have one of the densest and busiest railway systems in the world.

While the shape of things to come was briefly made apparent in Glamorgan, rural industry was also changing fast. War and empire together created a strong demand for cloth and wool, and these industries flourished. Increasingly they moved from rural cottage bases to more concentrated centres of production in towns like Dolgellau, Newtown and Llanidloes. Although much of the finished product went out through Liverpool, the port of Barmouth also benefited. Further north, in the slate mountains, organisation of the industry into large quarries had begun at Penrhyn under Richard Pennant in 1780. The farming landscape was changing in appearance. Enclosure of common land by land-lords and tenants became more and more frequent, and field boundaries were pushed further up the hills. Drystone walls or thick hedges surrounded larger fields. At Traeth Mawr, in the angle of the Llyn peninsula, even the coast was

Restored cottages at Rhyd-y-Car, Cardiff, typical of cottages in the factory villages of the nineteenth century

made to change shape, when the salt marshes were drained by William Maddocks, and new settlements made at Tremadog and Porthmadog.

Throughout the country, there was industrial activity. Yet Wales was still a land of farms and farmers, with large patches of forest. But the forest cover was diminishing rapidly in some places. Thomas Mansel Talbot planted over a million trees at Margam between 1780 and 1813, and Iolo Morgannwg, on one of his national tours, reported that at Carreg y Gwalch, in the Forest of Snowdon, there was 'a very fine grove of many thousands of beech planted within the memory of living'. But in Brecknock, the great forest established in Norman times by Bernard of Neufmarché was completely wiped out by 1815. In Anglesey, while the great copper vein at Parys Mountain remained unexhausted Amlwch was an industrial centre comparable with Neath, but as workable reserves ran out, the industry declined, and by 1844 the copper industry of Anglesey was no more. Swansea and Neath however continued as a major centre of copper smelting, though raw ore was now imported from abroad. Nine-tenths of the British output of refined copper came from south Wales during the nineteenth century. Other metals were also produced in the Swansea area, chiefly zinc and nickel. The district around Landore and Llansamlet became a region of smoke by day and flame by night. Rivers turned black and the atmosphere was a cocktail of poisonous fumes on – fortunately rare – windless days. In the first two decades of the nineteenth century, the coal industry was seen chiefly as the supplier of fuel to the furnaces of other industries, especially the ever-growing iron industry. But in the 1830s, coal began to establish a dominance that it would retain for nearly a century.

This dominance was closely linked to the development of the steam engine. By 1829, Trevithick's lumbering machine had been developed into George Stephenson's 'Rocket', with flanged wheels running on bullhead track. The locomotive had come of age. In 1819, the first steam-assisted passage of the Atlantic had been made by the US ship *Savannah*. In 1822 the first iron steamship was launched, drawing on Wales's two major new industries. Stationary and mobile, on land and sea, the steam engine was at the basis of all industry and transport. And it needed coal. The eastern coalfields of south Wales produced good-quality steam coal, eminently suitable for the purpose. In the early 1830s an enterprising woman landowner, Lucy Thomas, had established a coalmine on her land near Merthyr and was sending coal down on the canal to Cardiff, for export. Her pit at Abercanaid was one of the first to be sunk for uses other than that of the ironworks. The example was soon followed. In 1840 more than a million tons of coal were being shipped from Cardiff, mostly on the short routes to Bristol and Plymouth. At first the export of coal in British ships was hampered by government duty, but with the lifting of this in 1842, trade began to increase. As the Royal Navy increasingly began to use steam power, coaling stations were set up in remote places like Aden, and vast stocks were shipped out there. In 1836 the Taff Vale Railway was incorporated, its main line running from Cardiff Docks to Merthyr, with a short branch up the Rhondda Valley, and opened to business in April 1841. In 1844 the first Welsh trunk route, the Chester and Holyhead, was incorporated, in the expectation of making a good income out of carrying the Irish mail. The Taff Vale's prime concern was with moving coal. From 1845 the 'railway mania' began, pushing up the demand for iron rails, iron tubes, all manner of iron and other metal products, and of course for steam coal.

THE HUMAN FACE OF INDUSTRIALISATION

In the new centres of industry, new social skills had to be found, or learned by the community. In the early phase of industrialisation, the majority of Welsh workers were labourers. The small element of skilled operatives were brought in from the English midlands, or the Forest of Dean, or the now-declining Sussex iron industry. The even smaller element of managers were also incomers. Merthyr, the early model, was new, raw and remote, a group of villages whose only reason for existence was the ironworks. Here an urban army of several thousand men, women and children lived, their existences focused on the works that provided their livelihood. Their language was Welsh (90 per cent of the population of Merthyr spoke Welsh in the 1840s), their religion was based on the chapel. The Church of England, comfortable in its long-established parochial structure, was very slow to adapt to the fact that new communities were springing up in areas far from a parish church, where before only shepherds and foresters had wandered. Unitarians, Baptists and Congregationalists were far quicker to respond. Work was welcome, the pay, especially at the start, was good; the houses, in the beginning, were often superior to what their occupants had grown up in. Enthusiasm for the social benefits of industry, and interest generated by the continuing stream of mechanical inventions and improvements, encouraged many people to improve their own skills, at evening classes often sponsored by the chapel or even by the management of the works. But it was apparent from the beginning that the works had not been constructed for the benefit of the workers. Like the coal, the ironstone, the limestone, to the proprietors the workers were a resource; like the minerals, there was an apparently inexhaustible supply of them. But they were people – they could protest. Through such a close-packed community, rumours, ideas and urgings could sweep at high speed.

The food riots in Merthyr, in 1800, had an economic basis. But the authorities found it easy to suspect, identify and magnify a political agenda. Anonymous leaflets had been passed around whose authors wanted nothing less than a nationwide rebellion and the overthrow of king and government, a rerun of 1789 in Paris. Official alarm led to the hanging of two rioters. By 1811 a new barracks was being constructed at Brecon to ensure that permanent military support for civil law and order was close by. The policy of authority was clear, and developed naturally enough from the attitudes long held by the squires who still controlled local government, and which were readily absorbed by the incoming ironmasters, with substantial interests to protect. But whilst the countryside dwellers, conditioned by generations of acceptance and deference, rarely challenged the power of the squirearchy, a different social climate was being created in Merthyr. Over these years, a sense of community among the workers was developing, in different ways. Where there was money, businesses arose to recirculate it. Pubs and beer shops were established, and the range of retail outlets soon went beyond the company store. Moneylenders appeared on the scene. A vibrant popular culture arose, with a strong musical element, rich in ballads both topical and romantic. Although some of the proprietors might retain a squire-ish paternalism in their attitude to the workers, the attitude and discipline of the factory floor was very different to life on the land. There was a daily urgency and compulsion. And each day's task was essentially the same as that of the day before. For a people familiar with the proverb also known in other Celtic languages, 'It's a whole day's work, getting started', this constant repetitiveness took more getting used to than the noise, the fumes, the blasts of heat and the danger of splashing from molten metal. Pride in the job came, even pride in the primitive and dangerous conditions in which the job was required

---

WORKING IN PARYS MOUNTAIN, ANGLESEY

To my grandmother fell the task of tending the two cows, two pigs and three dozen chickens on the homestead, while her husband was employed in the Parys Mountain Copper Mines, where he had started work at the age of eight for a wage of fourpence for a twelve-hour day. He was only twelve when he went 'down below' to mine copper, and there he toiled like a galley slave for the rest of his life. On many a 'settling-up Saturday' he used to return home withpout a halfpenny to bless himself with, after a whole month of accursedly hard toil, for the owners followed a system of 'stoppages' against the cost of candles, powder, sharpening augers and hoisting the ore from the mine. There were times, indeed, when my grandfather returned home, at the month's end, actually in debt to his owners, since this shameful levy totalled more than the wage he had earned in a month of sweated, sweltering labour underground. My grandmother tried to induce him to give up the work, but they could not make a living out of the homestead with its three small, mean fields, and food had to be provided for themselves and their two children . . . And every morning at six, in the Prayer Meeting that was held in the smithy on the surface, he gave thanks to God that he was able to keep his children from starvation.

T. Rowland Hughes (1903–49),
From Hand to Hand, translated by Richard C. Ruck

to be done. Compared, say, to serving on a warship, it was far safer and vastly better paid, and women were employed as well as men. Compared to life on the land, it was even better paid. Gwyn A. Williams provides a reminder that while one man might be a skilled operative working at the forefront of the technology of the time, speaking a 'world language' and learning to cope with a new kind of society: '… a brother or sister would be tramping after sheep in some barren and cloud-capped valley and trying to live according to the rules of a people's law, graced with the name of Hywel Dda, in a people's now essentially oral language' (p. 182). (There were times also when the valley was fertile, sunny and green.) Stresses and strains between industrial and rural areas worked their way increasingly deeply into society. However strong the job market in new industry, it could not take in everyone. Nor did everyone go looking, though very many did.

THE RISE OF RADICALISM

The kind of theoretical debates stimulated by the American and French revolutions took on a more practical tone in the industrial communities. At first, the way in which work was organised, the voluntary arrival of the workers, the owners' control of housing, and the truck system all combined to prevent unified action except in the most obvious cases, like the price of a loaf or the non-availability of flour. The earliest protests were against profiteering shopkeepers rather than the masters of industry. The social and political predicament of the workers was most clearly seen by the Unitarians, whose pared-down view of religion seemed to expand their political horizon. They upheld a stoutly radical tradition. Among their leaders was Zephaniah Williams, not an ironworker but a pub owner and mineral agent, one of those who might have been typified as an exploiter: no one's role could be taken for granted. Although strikes had occurred since 1800, the moment of discovery for most of the workers came with the end of the Napoleonic Wars in 1815. The massive slump in demand which followed was a frightful shock to the confidence of everybody. The owners responded by cutting wages by as much as 40 per cent. It was a stunning realisation for the workforce: their labour too was a commodity, whose supply could be controlled. Demonstrations, marches, meetings took place, but the message was clear. Following the disastrous years of 1816–17, which affected every other industry in the country, not least the cloth industry which had been sustained by military demand for so long, a greater degree of organisation and politicisation began to emerge. One aspect of this, stemming from the Jacobin-Unitarian tradition, developed into the Chartist movement. Chartism was a political movement with its roots in working communities in England, Scotland and Wales. Through the 1820s

---

ZEPHANIAH WILLIAMS

A native of Argoed, Bedwellty, born in 1795, he became a master-collier at Blaina. He kept the Royal Oak Pub there (it was usual to pay workers in a public house). Despite his position as an employer, he was a radical in politics and a freethinker in religion. Gwyn A. Williams records that he kept a picture of Christ, with the inscription: 'This is the man who stole the ass'. He allowed his house to be used as a meeting place for the Working Men's Association and participated fully in the aims of the Chartists. Following the ill-fated Newport March of 1840, he fled, but was arrested on a ship at Cardiff. On trial, he was sentenced to death, but the sentence was commuted to transportation to the Antipodes. In Tasmania, he used his old skills to prospect for coal, found large deposits, and made a fortune. In 1854 his wife and daughter went out to join him. He died in 1874.

---

and 1830s its message was still being worked out. But although it was 1838 before the 'People's Charter' was published, the Chartists were active long before that, advocating a range of reforms from universal suffrage to outright republicanism.

In the 1820s the graphs of production and wages ran like magnified saw-teeth in reaction to rises and falls in demand for iron, and therefore coal, and all the services which had sprung up to sustain the new industries. (The economy of adjoining rural areas had been wrenched into support of industry. The increase in demand for ponies and horses is one example.) Perhaps the most volatile area at this time was the Monmouthshire coalfield. This had developed as a system of independent collieries and colliery groups, fiercely competitive, dedicated to minimising their costs and making the most of their often marginal profits. Safety, at a discount everywhere, partly through ignorance and largely through indifference, was even more neglected here, and no formal welfare system existed to care for those who were injured, or the dependants of those who were killed. In specific response to conditions in Wales, two distinctively Welsh protest movements arose.

DIRECT ACTION: 'SCOTCH CATTLE'

The first one was the 'Scotch Cattle' movement, with its roots set in the Monmouthshire mining communities, though it spread westwards into Glamorgan. Organised into lodges, secret, anonymous, the Scotch Cattle picked targets both among the mine and factory owners, and among those in their own community who tried to avoid the sacrifice or exposure created by local strikes, boycotts (a name not yet in use but a well-known process), and pressure-groups. Although the basis came from the Freemasons' lodges and political debating societies, they were dedicated to direct action. Anonymous letters and threats were followed by threatening visits made under cover of darkness. The visitors had blackened faces and some wore animal hides; their first calls were restricted to gunshots, loud mooing noises, and clashing metal, but if the display got no result, then violence to property and persons would follow. Blacklegs and informers were especially detested and often had to flee the area. The Scotch Cattle maintained operations through the 1920s and 30s. While a range of motivations can be detected, including hooliganism and perhaps a Luddite element too (although the destruction of machinery was more likely to be as valuable property than as a supplanter of manual workers), they show the first instance in Wales of people taking affairs into their own hands, not to over-throw society but to apply a corrective to injustice at a local level. The effect of the Scotch Cattle was sporadic and localised. It was mainly focused on indus-trial disputes, although blatant offenders against accepted standards of moral behaviour might also be visited. The movement certainly did not provide an alternative law-and-order system. The conventional courts continued to oper-ate, though the oath of secrecy usually stood up against the hectoring of magis-trates and counsel. One Edward Morgan was hanged at Monmouth in 1834, as a result of Scotch Cattle activities, but such a judicial victim was exceptional. The degree to which the Scotch Cattle were actively supported by their commu-nities is difficult to assess. The numbers of activists has been put as high as 9,000 in their own propaganda, suggesting that the real total may have been considerably less. Nevertheless the movement survived through some twenty years.

WORKERS REVOLT

The 1830s were to see another secret society rise, but before that happened, the cross-currents of unchannelled discontent and futile protest came to a devastating climax in the heartland of the new industrialism, at Merthyr Tydfil. A curious combination of alliances brought this about. At Westminster, after thirty years of Tory rule, the battle for the first, modest, steps in electoral reform was joined, between those who saw ruin for Britain if it succeeded, and those who equally clearly saw ruin for Britain if it failed. The House of Commons passed it; the House of Lords rejected it. Everywhere the local significance of the proposed redrawing of constituencies was worked out with care, but in few places more carefully than Merthyr, which despite being the largest centre of population in Wales, had no representative in parliament. The industrial bosses and commercial interests of Merthyr wanted an MP, who would, of course, be selected and elected on their terms. The iron industry was in one of its periodic recessions, debt was at a high level among the 9,000-plus workers, and a sense of crisis was in the air. An ambiguous role

180

was played by one of the ironmasters, William Crawshay, more radically minded than his peers, who had made encouraging noises about trade unions. The spark was provided by bailiffs who, on behalf of the Court of Requests – the debtors' court founded in 1809 – began to claim property owned by debtors. One of these was Lewis Lewis, a radical known as Lewsyn yr Heliwr, 'the huntsman', who mobilised a crowd on 31 May 1831 to restrain the bailiffs.

By the next day, the situation had become revolutionary. The town was firmly in the control of the workers, who began the restoration of goods already distrained by the court. The magistrates sent to Brecon for troops, and a detachment of Highlanders was faced by the mob. Under attack, the troops opened fire. Twenty-six people died. Sixteen soldiers were injured. But the soldiers withdrew. When the hastily mustered Swansea Yeomanry appeared, they were driven away. Supporters began to approach Merthyr from Monmouthshire, to find that the town was being ringed by the military. For four days, the workers held the town. There were reports from England of other revolts, in Bristol, Nottingham, Derby. But the nation did not rise. Isolated, hungry and disconsolate, the people of Merthyr abandoned their stand. As a thousand armed soldiers manned the streets, the forces of law and order came back. After the trials which followed, Lewis Lewis was transported to Australia. Another man, Richard Lewis, known as Dic Penderyn, was hanged at Cardiff.

The battle fought in Merthyr had a deep impact. It taught the new Welsh industrial community its strength and its weakness. Its strength was solidarity and unity. Its weakness was complete powerlessness in the face of employers, magistrates, government – the whole Establishment of the United Kingdom. This was rubbed in by the defeat of a bitter coal strike organised by the newly formed National Association for the Protection of Labour. Meanwhile in 1832 the Reform Act was finally passed, and Merthyr duly gained its new MP, in the person of J.J. Guest, proprietor of the Dowlais Ironworks, who represented the Liberal interest, as the old Whig party was now known.

DIRECT ACTION: CHILDREN OF REBECCA

Anonymous, secretly organised protest and direct action continued. A new movement, this time to the west of the industrial districts, arose. The core of its membership was among small farmers. For them the final straw was the erection of toll-gates, beginning in 1839, and intended to finance the construction of new roads. But the contracts for the road-building, and the control of the funds, were all with the same little group of landowners. Other discontents had been around for longer: farm prices had soared and plummeted, while rents had mostly just gone up. A new Poor Law, in 1834, required the setting-up of workhouses in each district, or union of districts, to hold the able-bodied poor. Resentment was aroused not merely because of the cost of the workhouse system, but because, in country areas, charity, if sparse, had been traditional and voluntary. The movement was known as the Children (or Daughters) of Rebecca, a name variously said to come from the lady who had lent her dress to its first known leader, Tom Rees; or from the Book of Genesis: 'And they blessed Rebecca and said unto her, let thy seed possess the gates of them that hate thee …'

Posses of Rebeccas, dressed in women's clothes, with blackened faces, turned up on horseback at newly erected toll-gates and tore them down. Although they often appeared in daylight, their movements, like those of the Scotch Cattle, were unpredictable, and their local intelligence network was highly effective. Their activities spread rapidly west across Carmarthenshire into Pembrokeshire. An attempt was made to burn down the new workhouse at Narberth in 1839 and the Carmarthen one was attacked in 1843. The campaigners also targeted high-rent landlords, merchants who pursued their debts too vigorously, and, of course, those who were believed to be informers and stooges of the magistracy. They, too, to a greater degree than the Scotch Cattle, began to operate as arbiters of popular morals. The Rebeccas were not 'new people', they were the traditional backbone of rural society (some of them might have been members of that Swansea Yeomanry which was outfaced by the people of Merthyr) and undoubtedly had substantial support. In June 1843 they staged a public parade through Carmarthen before the attack on the workhouse. Especially in Carmarthen, a town with a strong radical tradition, the Rebecca's Children movement was taken up by people with a different agenda to that of the farmers. Efforts were made to broaden the scope of Rebecca's large family:

> Oh yes, they are all my children. When I meet the lime-men on the road covered with sweat and dust, I know they are Rebecca-ites. When I see the coalmen coming to town clothed in rags, hard-worked and hard-fed, I know they are mine … If I turn into a farmer's house and see them eating barley bread and drinking whey, surely, say I, these are members of my family, these are the oppressed sons and daughters of Rebecca.

Such writings as this, from a proclamation in a radical newspaper, *The Welshman*, of September 1843, made some of the early Rebecca-ites feel anxious. The lime-men and other members of the agricultural labouring class had grievances which could only be satisfied at the expense of the farmers. Already the Rebecca-ites had attracted favourable attention from an early crusading journalist,

Thomas Foster of the London *Times*: their grievances were laid out on the breakfast tables of the governing class in a manner very different to that of the ironworkers, or, for that matter, the cloth-workers of Llanidloes, who had erupted in a Merthyr-style rising in 1839, which was put down by the army after a week of heady freedom. Indications of positive government action to come, plus fear of the climate of revolt spreading to the labourers, brought the Rebecca episode to an end by 1844.

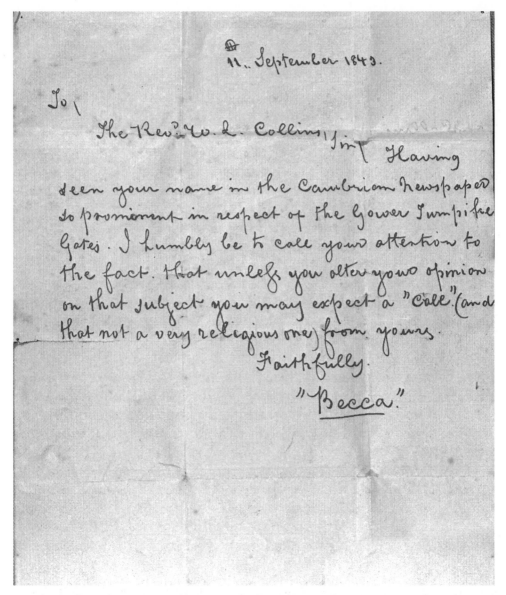

A threatening letter sent to the Rev. W. L. Collins of Oxwich from the Rebecca movement

OLD TRADITIONS AND NEW MOVEMENTS

Historians have noted how much such popular movements as the Scotch Cattle and the Children of Rebecca owe to a strong and old-established tradition of social control from within the community. Social sins and shortcomings – excessive drunkenness, scolding women, the irresponsible fathering of illegitimate children, petty theft – might be punished by a gathering of neighbours who made a public example of the culprit by mounting him or her on the *ceffyl pren*, a roughly shaped wooden horse, and parading them down the street. Other folk traditions made their contribution. The women's dresses and horsehair wigs of the Rebeccas, though partly disguise, were prompted by the Hallowe'en tradition of youths masquerading as women in order to play tricks. Old forms of behaviour were drawn on in order to fashion new forms of protest.

By 1844, too, Chartism had reached a peak and fallen back. In the course of 1838, the movement had at last been able to concentrate its agenda into five points: universal manhood suffrage, voting by secret ballot, the abolition of property qualifications for prospective MPs, equal-sized constituencies, and annually elected parliaments. All but the last of these are now unquestioned elements of the democratic system, but in 1838 they were a threat to the established and undemocratic order. A Chartist demonstration in Newtown in 1838 drew substantial crowds, and the movement was supported throughout the country. In Merthyr especially, Chartism was seen as the answer to the workers' predicament. If the five points were granted, then people, not property, would be in control. One of the leading English Chartists, Henry Vincent, was jailed in Monmouth in May 1839, provoking large protest demonstrations. In that year, a Chartist Petition was presented to parliament, and rejected. In November, a further demonstration was planned to take place in Newport.

By this time, south Wales was seen by the authorities as the most turbulent part of Great Britain. It was seriously proposed to put the entire region under martial law, and a large military presence was maintained there. The whole area was also planted with police and informers (the presence of three London policemen had helped inflame the situation at Llanidloes). The Newport demonstration was awaited by a tense detachment of troops. Rumours, information and disinformation all played a part in events. There was a division of intention among the leaders of the three groups converging on the town. John Frost, an advocate of Chartism's 'moral authority', led those from Blackwood, Zephaniah Williams led those from Ebbw Vale, and William Jones, once an actor, was to lead those from Pontypool, but this contingent failed to join the others. Frost was no revolutionary; Williams may have had other ideas, but it is most likely that the march was always meant to be a peaceful one: 'moral authority' meant a great deal to most leading Chartists. The marchers arrived in Newport in pouring rain, to be fired on by waiting troops. Around twenty people were killed, and the marchers dispersed in panic. Their leaders were arrested, tried and transported to Australia, though supporters of the *status quo* would have very much preferred to see them hanged.

CHAPTER FIFTEEN

Industrial Wales. The Second Phase: 1840s to 1880s

THE WELSH PEOPLE IN THE MID-NINETEENTH CENTURY

As a domestic market, for domestic products like food and cloth, Wales in the late 1840s was in real terms much bigger than it had been two generations before. But a comparable rate of increase was also under way in the very much more populous England, and in Ireland as well. That of Ireland was to endure a shattering blow in the potato famines of 1848 and following years. Wales, with its mixed farming pattern of sheep, cattle and cereal crops, had never come anywhere near the utter dependency of the Irish country people on the potato crop. And the population of England kept on rising. Welsh farmers enjoyed the presence of an ever-growing market on their doorstep for meat and dairy products, at the same time as railway lines, gradually pushed through the interior from Chester, Shrewsbury, Craven Arms and Hereford, made it easier to deliver their produce to the rapidly growing conurbations in the English west midlands and even to London. There were fluctuations in the story of relative prosperity, linked to phases of recession in the wider economy, and to changes in the international pattern of production and distribution (the rise of the Australian wool trade and the invention of the refrigerator ship would not be good news for the Welsh sheep farmer). In the early 1840s, and again in the 1880s, farmers had a lean time of it. But even in the worst years of depressed prices and low demand, a farm would provide subsistence for a family, so long as the landlord remained reasonable in his demands. Most of the small farmers in Wales were tenants. Few owned their land, though their families might have worked it for many generations. In many valleys they formed a cohesive social group, combining to cope with the principal tasks of the agricultural year, especially the harvest. Their chief problem was lack of capital and land. Improvement-minded squires might nag them to improve their stock or try new crops, but they resisted both through ingrained conservatism and lack of capital. Sporting squires insisted on strict observation of the Game Laws, which until 1880 refused tenants the right to pursue game on their land; game was reserved for the landlord, who had open access. Those cottagers who did own their land tended to have tiny properties, only a fraction of an acre, and would have relied on weaving, road-mending, or some other additional source of income to survive. They were particularly vulnerable to local squires' attempts to enclose common land, often finding it hard to prove their title, and suffering eviction as a result. The old social-agricultural pattern, established before recorded history, of transhumance, of the annual movement between valley and *hafod*, fell into disuse, and the summer hill dwellings and shelters gradually crumbled into ruin. There was also a stratum of 'yeoman farmers', whose holdings might be anything from 50 to 500 acres, and who provided much of the county electorates before the Reform Act of 1832. They were severely reduced in number in the collapse of trade and prices that accompanied the end of the Napoleonic Wars. Many had to sell out to a neighbouring landowner, and moved to an industrial town, or emigrated.

By 1841 the population had well passed the million mark and was still soaring upwards. In 1851 it was 1,153,000, double what it had been only fifty years before. No longer was there an even balance between north and south. Glamorgan and Monmouthshire grew in population at a rate vastly exceeding that of any other county, though Denbighshire and Flintshire also outpaced the rest. Glamorgan in 1851 had a population in excess of 210,000. Much of this additional population was the result of immigration from other parts of Wales, from England, and from Ireland. Up to 1841, population growth took place in all the Welsh counties, though at varying rates. Whilst the overall national rate of increase went on, after 1841 there were a number of counties which showed a steady loss of population: Anglesey, Pembrokeshire, Cardiganshire, Radnorshire, Montgomeryshire. The areas bypassed by industry, or where industry had already declined, were becoming apparent. Their fall in population was compounded by the fact that jobs were available elsewhere. People were becoming more mobile, and the process in which Wales was transformed from a nation of countryfolk to one of town-dwellers was well under way.

Despite official terrorism in 1839 and the early 1840s, support for the Chartists remained strong in the years after Newport. The principles of Chartism continued to imbue radical political thinking even when the movement itself had largely died out. The first steps towards parliamentary reform had been modest; with the increase in population, the proportion of those entitled to vote actually fell slightly between 1832 and 1852. The gap between actuality and aspiration remained enormous, and intense thought went into how it might be bridged – or how it might be perpetuated. These were the years in which Karl Marx and the young Friedrich Engels published *The Communist Manifesto* (1848) and expected the British people to produce the revolution which never happened. By 1850, the first generation to experience industry on a large scale had died out. Their grandchildren were now entering employment in a world whose features had become familiar, and in which change was normal and expected. Even though many were still streaming in from the rural areas, and from outside Wales, they mostly had a clear idea of what they were doing, and why. The scale of industry had continued to grow. The rise of an industry-based economy, and especially the spread of railways and the switch from wood to iron in shipbuilding, had meant boom conditions for the iron works in the 1840s. Through the 1850s and 60s, the economy continued to expand. As more and more people joined the ranks of industrial workers, there came about, if not a tacit acceptance of the scheme of things, an awareness that change was not going to happen suddenly. The political agenda became less immediate. This did not mean greater deference among the workers. Confrontation in labour disputes remained sharp and fierce, often violent, but concern focused on workers' organisation in order to achieve work-related aims: resisting cuts in pay, seeking better conditions of employment, demanding pay rises to match a rising cost of living and rising standards of home life.

A LAND SHAPED BY COAL AND STEEL

The pattern of industry changed. Increased demand and improved mining techniques enabled deeper seams to be opened in the coalfields. From the later 1830s on, exploitation of the coal went on at an ever-increasing rate. The Glamorgan valleys began to fill with terraced streets of colliers' houses, while the wider parts of the valley floors were packed with hurriedly built sheds, engine-houses and warehouses, threaded by railway tracks, with smokestacks and pithead winding towers rising above. In the early 1850s, the first pits were sunk in the Rhondda Valley. The iron towns were joined by coal towns, like Aberdare, Abertillery, Treherbert, Tonypandy. To the stranger, one community merged seamlessly into the next. To the local, each had its own identity. In the course of little more than ten years, Welsh coal became a world commodity. Its reputation as the world's best steam-raising coal was sealed by British Admiralty tests. Demand rocketed. The port of Cardiff became one of the busiest harbours in the world, and the town itself grew enormously. From less than 4,000 people in 1821, it had reached 60,000 by 1868. The Bute West Dock opened in 1839 and was soon inadequate to deal with the volume of shipping and the amount of coal coming down. New docks were built in Newport in 1842, and Cardiff's Bute East Dock followed in 1859.

Steel is iron hardened by the presence of a small proportion of carbon. Although it had been known since ancient times, its manufacture had always been in very small amounts. This changed in 1856 with the invention of the Bessemer process, which enabled steel to be produced in industrial quantities.

Bessemer's interest was principally in gun barrels, but steel plate and steel rails were soon in great demand. Further improvements and inventions followed. The new Siemens steel plant at Landore (1868), set up by three German immigrant brothers, using an early form of the open-hearth furnace, was another major step forward; the Siemens process was to be used all over the world by 1900. Although initially ironmasters sought to convert or extend existing works to produce steel, the age and location of the plants usually made this uneconomic. The Penydarren ironworks closed down in the 1870s, as the focus of steelmaking transferred to the coastal strip. With high-grade imported ores, and a manufacturing process that led the world, the steel industry was poised to undergo massive expansion. A substantial part of the demand for steel would be in the form of thinly rolled sheet for tinplate. Tinplate works were mostly located in the Swansea–Llanelli area; unlike the steelworks, these were individually on a modest scale and their numbers became considerable later in the century. The swathe of country to east and west of Swansea was dotted with industrial sites, often quite small, each with its furnace, chimney, spoil heaps, ore dumps, and tramroads, while the rivers and streams bore away chemical residues. This was the heart of the specialist smelting area, where the chief metals produced were copper, zinc and nickel. The bulk of British production of these metals was concentrated around Swansea; especially in the case of copper.

INDUSTRIALISATION: THE HUMAN COST AND THE GLITTERING PRIZES

The infrastructure to support ever-growing production – railways, docks, steelworks, new pits – developed at a much faster rate than that which supported the people. The new deep mines encountered problems of flooding and methane gas – the dreaded firedamp – and there was a succession of accidents. Sir Humphry Davy's safety lamp had been invented in 1816, but safety was given little more than rudimentary consideration in mine development. Miners, who were often organised as sub-contractors with their own gang of loaders, were expected to look out for themselves. Acts to promote safety in mines were passed in the 1840s, 1855 and 1860, but inspection was frequently cursory and it was often difficult to prove negligence on the part of managers. In town building, few lessons had been learned from the iron towns. The vast majority of new houses were built by works proprietors or ground landlords, as an investment, for rental to the workers. Hygiene was ignored. The close-packed new streets, built to inferior standards, rapidly became squalid. There were no sewers, and water was drawn from wells which became polluted and spread cholera in a series of epidemics beginning in 1831. Smallpox, typhoid fever, and tuberculosis also raged through the towns. Doctors were few and largely confined their services to those who could pay. The greatest time of danger in life was early infancy; though this was true at all levels of Victorian society, it was most apparent in working communities, where almost half of all deaths were of children aged under five. Members of the urban labouring class who survived childhood might expect to live until their mid-thirties; hardly more than half the life span of those who led a less strenuous life. It was only in 1872 that it was made illegal for women and children to be employed in 'metalliferous mines'. Health care was always dragging behind the rate of progress in England; this would be a source of contention right up to the introduction of the National Health Service by the Welshman, Aneurin Bevan, in 1948. A hundred years before that, the Public Health Act of 1848 was passed, to promote the formation of local boards of health. As these were financed by a local rate paid by property owners, their implementation was stoutly resisted, notably by the Marquess of Bute's agent in Cardiff, at a time when Bute was the richest man in Wales and one of the richest in the world, and getting steadily richer on coal royalties, harbour dues, and house rents.

In the same league as Bute were other families which had grown rich on the combination of landowning, mineral extraction, and ironworking. A new generation of stately homes arose, like the Crawshay castle at Cyfarthfa. The second Lord Bute, like a Norman baron in the centre of his domains, occupied the greatly modernised Cardiff Castle. His son moved out to lead a fantasy life in the hills at Castell Coch. The Guests of Dowlais and Vivians of Swansea, whose fortunes were based on iron and copper respectively, were among others who built castles and took on the roles of landed gentry. The real plutocracy was very

---

CASTELL COCH

The original Castell Coch was a small triangular castle built in the thirteenth century by the Norman de Clare family, controlling the point where Taff Vale debouches into the coastal plain. By the nineteenth century it was a picturesquely sited ruin, and as such it caught the eye of the Third Marquess of Bute and his architect, William Burges. Bute and Burges shared a fascination with the 'Gothic' Middle Ages. In 1871, the Marquess decided to restore the castle. Burges made the plans, and in 1875 work commenced. The architect died in 1881, ten years before the castle was finished, but work went on according to his drawings. Although it sits on the old foundations, there are few of the original elements in Castell Coch; it is essentially the product of two intense imaginations set not only on reproducing the authentic architecture of the thirteenth century, but also on creating a spiritual atmosphere, both ascetic and emblematic, which really only existed in their minds. Vast amounts of money were spent to achieve Burges's exacting requirements, but Bute was immensely rich from coal royalties, dock fees, and rents. Travellers who seek out its pointed towers from the M4 can still cross the drawbridge and savour the somehow rather dull mysticism of the Marquess. He rarely visited the completed castle.

Castell Coch

small in numbers. In a paternalist way, and very much on their own terms, they were often philanthropic. Amenities at workplaces, like canteens or pithead baths, were non-existent. But they set up or subscribed to schools, very much with a commercial ethos. Increasing numbers of clerks, accountants, solicitors, letter-writers were necessary as businesses became more complex and more involved in a worldwide export trade. Libraries were more suspect; they could be the seeding ground for political agitators.

INDUSTRIAL DEVELOPMENT IN THE NORTH: SLATE

Whilst the south had the greatest concentration of industry, the greatest growth of population, and the greatest wealth, there was parallel development on a smaller scale in the north-east. The Flint-Denbigh coalfield was smaller than the south Wales one and did not provide coal of such good quality. Also it was nearer the English midland coal deposits. Its trade tended to be mostly with Ireland and internal. It had its own iron industry, and towns such as Wrexham, Hawarden and Mold developed in the same way as the industrial towns of the south, though on a smaller scale and with a greater proportion of English immigrants. The north never developed a port, however; the Dee estuary was heavily silted, and Liverpool too near. Further west, in Caernarfon and Meironydd, another mineral deposit enabled Wales to take up a monopoly supply position even more dominant than that of coal. This was the slate industry, which had been in existence on a relatively small scale since the early eighteenth century. The difficulty of access to the slate quarries had always been a problem. The limitations of transport raised the price and increased the amount of breakage. Two things now transformed the industry. One was the vast increase in the number of houses being built to accommodate the ever-growing population of Britain and Europe. Thatched roofs were obsolete; slate roofs were laid faster, lasted longer, and were at that time cheaper than tiles. The other factor was the narrow-gauge railway. The Ffestiniog Railway was opened in 1836. At first a horse-and-gravity powered tramway, it introduced steam traction in 1863, which vastly increased its carrying capacity. In 1865 came the Tal-y-llyn Railway, and numerous other lines followed, all intended as mineral carriers, though some also introduced passenger services on the lower sections. New harbours were built at the seaward end of the tracks at places like Towyn and Porthmadog, and the export trade flourished.

Slate never came near employing the numbers that coal did, but around 1880 – one of its peaks – the industry employed some 14,000 quarrymen, which means that it sustained a population of around 45,000 people in a region which otherwise could have accommodated only a small fraction of that number. They were almost all employed by two families, the Pennants of Penrhyn and the Assheton-Smiths of Llanberis, owners of the world's two biggest slate quarries, at Penrhyn and Dinorwic.

Like most other sites of industry, the slate quarries were highly unhealthy places. The owners at Dinorwic could find doctors who proclaimed that the ever-present dust was positively beneficial to the lungs, even as workers died from lung disease in numbers out of all proportion to the size of the communities in which they lived. They were a highly skilled, tightknit group, most of them speaking only Welsh, owning their houses (but not the land they were built on), in villages such as Blaenau Ffestiniog, Llanberis, or the biblically named Carmel and Caesarea, reflecting the religious dominancy of the nonconformist chapels. At the industry's peak, however, many workers were also housed in bothies or barracks close to the quarries.

WILD WALES

In the course of 1854, the post-Romantic English traveller George Borrow made a lengthy walking tour of Wales with his wife and daughter. The result, published as *Wild Wales* in 1862, serves to show how unindustrial the country could appear to those who wanted to see it that way. Borrow liked the rustic, the traditional, the quaint or curious, and did not care at all for the modern. He found much to engross him. In the countryside, he noted the preservation of a rural costume among women, 'blue tunics and sharp crowned hats'. He went to the trouble of learning some Welsh, to protect himself from '*Dim Saesneg*' – the not always believable 'No English' response of the countryfolk. In some places, he could not escape the contemporary scene. Here he describes a prospect of Neath Abbey:

> *I had surmounted a hill and had nearly descended that side of it which looked towards the east, having on my left, that is to the north, a wooded height, when an extraordinary scene presented itself to my eyes. Somewhat to the south rose immense stacks of chimneys surrounded by grimy diabolical-looking buildings, in the neighbourhood of which were huge heaps of cinders and black rubbish. From the chimneys, notwithstanding that it was Sunday, smoke was proceeding in volumes, choking the atmosphere all around. From this pandemonium at the distance of about a quarter of a mile to the southwest, upon a green meadow, stood, looking darkly grey, a ruin of vast size with window holes, towers, spires and arches. Between it and the accursed pandemonium lay a horrid filthy place, part of which was swamp and part pool: the pool black as soot and the swamp of a disgusting leaden colour. Across this piece of filth stretched a tramway leading seemingly from the*

193

abominable mansions to the ruins. Had it been on canvas, with the addition of a number of diabolical figures, it might have stood for Sabbath in Hell …

(p. 671)

In visiting a number of other places Borrow comments on the sudden contrast between natural beauty and the works of man; many of the latter, like the works he found at Ysbyty Ystwyth, hardly visible nowadays. His observations underline the divisions between town and country, but what they chiefly do is to confirm the dominance of the Welsh language. Without his learned Welsh, or an interpreter, Borrow would have found his tour impossible. The revival of popular culture, expressed in local *eisteddfodau*, in street ballads and vernacular verse, had been going on strongly ever since Iolo Morgannwg's first show on Primrose Hill, London. It is striking, however, that much of the political debate was carried on in Welsh. English-language radical papers and magazines existed, but so did Welsh ones. In the 1790s, Morgan John Rhees had published a radical journal, *Y Cylchgrawn Cyn-mraeg*, suppressed by

---

TWO ANGLO-WELSH LADIES

Lady Charlotte Bertie, daughter of the Earl of Lindsey, came to Wales in 1833, aged twenty-one, as the second wife of Sir John Guest, proprietor of Dowlais Ironworks. Highly intelligent, and intrigued by her new surroundings, she learned Welsh and, in between giving birth to ten children, steeped herself in Welsh history and culture. The Guests were founder-members of the Society of Welsh Scholars, of Abergavenny. Charlotte obtained access to the *Red Book of Hergest*, kept at Jesus College, Oxford, and began to translate its contents into English. The result was *The Mabinogion*, published in seven parts between 1837 and 1845, with great success. It stimulated a great increase of interest in the ancient past of Wales and played its part in the formation of the nineteenth-century conception of Welshness. In 1852 Sir John died and for a time his widow took over the direction of the Dowlais works. Later she married her sons' tutor and forsook Welsh antiquarianism for the study of ceramics and Spanish fans, in which she became an expert. She died in 1884.

Her friend Augusta Hall, Lady Llanover (1802–96), heiress of the Llanover estate in the Usk valley, shared the same interests. She was the moving spirit of a series of *eisteddfodau* at Abergavenny, which played an important part in converting these events from a sort of tavern-based folk-festival into a more self-conscious and sober literary and musical event. Her essay of 1834, *On the Advantages Resulting from the Preservation of the Welsh Language and the National Costume of Wales*, won an *eisteddfod* prize and was influential in wealthier circles. Taking and adapting costume elements from different parts of the country, she virtually invented the 'traditional' Welsh woman's dress with its tall black beaver hat, mob cap, bedgown (*betgwn*), petticoat, apron and shawl; she had her portrait painted wearing it and encouraged her friends to wear it on suitable occasions, and to make their female tenants wear it all the time. Though she spoke little Welsh, she ran her household on what she regarded as traditional Welsh lines. A militant Protestant and temperance crusader, Lady Llanover remained a devotee of Welsh culture to her death in 1896.

government action in 1793. One of the earliest newspapers (1834) was the bi-lingual *Y Gweithywr/The Worker*, published by one of several early trade union initiatives, the Grand Consolidated National Trades Union started by Robert Owen. Owen himself, who was born in Newtown and returned there to die (1771–1858) was more influential outside his native Wales as a practical industrial reformer, especially at New Lanark in Scotland, than he was at home. To some extent, perhaps, Welsh served as a useful cloak for discussing ideas inimical to the anglophone bosses of mines and factories, but it was clearly a medium for creative thought in the political and labour spheres as well as in traditional culture.

Welsh national costume in Victorian times

SUNDAY SCHOOLS AND NATIONAL SCHOOLS

Quite apart from the calculated benevolence of industrialists, Welsh education, or the lack of it, was engaging the attention of some strategic thinkers during this second phase of the country's industrial growth. In the period from 1800 to 1840, education had not been at the forefront of concern. In both the old Wales of rural industry and the new Wales of urban industry, children were expected to start earning their keep well before their ages reached double figures. Children of five and six operated primitive ventilation gates and flaps in mines. By eleven, if fit enough, they would be hauling coal to the base of the pit-shaft. Most of the old grammar schools continued to operate, but despite the free status of some, they were effectively reserved for the children of the better-off: shopkeepers, and the small but growing class of professionals, such as doctors, lawyers, ministers, engineers and administrators. As before, they gave an education exclusively in English. Most children were getting no schooling at all. Now the non-conformist Sunday School movement attempted to remedy this, largely by following the same plan as Griffith Jones in the circulating school of the previous century. The main difference was that although these schools were open only for a short time on Sunday, they were intended to be permanent, unlike the circulating schools. They shared the aim of teaching reading and the catechism – in the Welsh language. A London-based Sunday School Union provided free copies of the New Testament in Welsh. With games, hymns and occasional outings, the Sunday school provided a focus for many children's lives outside the regime of work. They also played a part in recruiting several generations for non-conformism.

An important initiative, the first for a long time, was taken by the church in Wales in 1811 when the National Society for Promoting the Education of the Poor in the Principles of the Established Church was set up, to cover both England and Wales. The church already maintained, in varying states of liveliness and efficiency, around a thousand schools. Behind the venture was the Society for the Propagation of Religious Knowledge, which had done little in Wales since the early eighteenth century. It was based on the concept of the single teacher plus monitors, or teacher-pupils. Each diocese established a committee, funds were actively sought, and provided. The curriculum went somewhat beyond the Sunday Schools, and an assiduous pupil could emerge both literate and numerate, and well-instructed in those principles of the established church most appropriate to the poor. Another Anglican initiative was the setting up of St David's College at Lampeter, the first institution of higher education in Wales (1820). Even if its main function was to provide clergy for the church, these would be Welsh clergy, Welsh-speaking. The National Schools movement was a great success in Wales, and the Society set up training centres

---

CHURCH AND CHAPEL

'That's the difference between "church" and "chapel",' said Will. 'You church people think yourselves good when you are bad, and the chapel people think themselves bad when they are good.'

Daniel Owen (1836–95), *Rhys Lewis*, translated by D. M. Lloyd

---

for its teachers at Carmarthen and Caernarfon. By 1850, 375 National Schools had been established, with pupil numbers approaching 50,000. Led by a Quaker, Joseph Lancaster, the non-conformists set up a rival British and Foreign School Society, but its effects, in Wales at least, were much less evident. In the second quarter of the century, even if most children still escaped education, it could truly be said that the church was doing much more for education than was the chapel.

NEW DEVELOPMENTS IN EDUCATION

The church in Wales maintained its efforts in education, but after a slow and ragged start, the non-conformists also mounted a sustained and ultimately successful campaign to turn the Welsh into an educated nation. Its leader was Hugh Owen (in due course to be Sir Hugh), originally from Anglesey, yet another successful London-based Welshman doing good to his countrymen from afar. Unlike some fellow non-conformists, Owen had no objections to using government money when it was available, and was adept in tracking it down. His *Letter to the Welsh* of 1843 was intended to be a manifesto and a call to action. It was received by a non-conformist community already profoundly concerned by the extent of Anglican control of education. For most children the choice was a church school or no school. A further blow was struck in 1847, when a government commission, composed of three Englishmen of wholly Anglican sympathies, submitted a damning report on the state of education in Wales. Their report was known as 'The Blue Books' because of the blue binding, but to the non-conformist Welsh it was *Brad y Llyfrau Gleision*, 'the treachery of the Blue Books'. Rage and offence at the report, which seemed to regard Wales as a remote and backward colonial territory, was shared by Anglicans as well as non-conformists. The National Schools were condemned for teaching by rote rather than fostering understanding: 'On asking a class, "When can a man be said to be perfect and right?" reported R.R.W. Lingen, one of the commissioners, 'forty children chorused, "And there were born unto him seven sons and seven daughters."' Teaching techniques were to improve, but, despite the hostile reaction, what stuck from the Blue Books was their patronising view of the Welsh language, which was seen not as a unique possession but as a simple hindrance to self-improvement on an individual and national basis. Even as they sought to raise the level of education, the leaders of Welsh opinion accepted the verdict on their language. In the British and Foreign School Society Report of 1848, one official stated: 'So long as Wales is subject to the laws of England, the importance of establishing English schools in Wales can scarcely be overrated.'

Between 1848 and 1870 the British Society opened more than 200 schools, with new colleges for teachers at Bangor (the famous 'Normal College') for men, and Swansea for women, both established in 1858. Prior to that, teachers in British schools had to get their qualifications in London. To cap the school structure, a long-held dream was realised with the foundation of the University College of Wales at Aberystwyth in 1867. Its first building was a disused hotel on the seafront. With no government funding, it relied on donations and subscriptions, and these came in huge numbers. The amounts were mostly very small, but the venture was secured by wealthy non-conformist entrepreneurs like the industrialist David Davies. Kenneth Morgan calls the college 'the creation of the chapels', but Gwyn A. Williams points out that the largest single group of subscribers were from the Welsh church. Although it was an all-Welsh institution, when it opened its doors in 1872 there was no instruction in or on Welsh.

In 1870, the Elementary Education Act required the setting up of school boards throughout the country. The arguments among non-conformist groups in Wales that had gone on for decades, about whether church schools should accept state funds, and about whether anything other than voluntary education was acceptable, were stopped, only to reopen on another front – whose form of Christianity should be taught in a publicly funded school? Surely the major-ity's? And everyone knew who was in the majority – or did they? In 1851, non-conformist places of worship totalled 2,769, compared with 1,180 for Anglicans. Non-conformists undoubtedly outnumbered those who attended the established church. But the largest single cohesive religious group was the Church of Wales. For a time, the issue did not arouse controversy, as the new scheme of things continued to fund both the National and British schools. Local school boards were established in areas which had no schools. Under heavy pressure from both sides, many of the new boards opted for a 'secular' policy in religion, in which either no religious instruction was given, or nothing more than Bible readings.

A great deal of this school development would have come about anyway. In its needs no less than its aspirations, the more mobile, commercially and industri-ally based society of the railway age could not function without a solid cadre of educated people. Whereas before, education was only required by those at the

Old College Building, Aberystwyth University

THE WELSH MORMONS

In the mid-nineteenth century, missionaries from the Church of Jesus Christ of Latter-Day Saints, established in the United States in 1830, were so successful in Wales as to cause concern to the traditional religious groups. Their efforts were mostly in the mining districts of the south, but even country villages, like St Brides Major in south Glamorgan, were visited and many of the population emigrated to join the Mormons in the USA, in the anticipation of an imminent Day of Judgement. The old fervour of Vavasor Powell and the Fifth Monarchy men had clearly not entirely gone away. Events like the Crimean War and the appearance of Donati's Comet after it were blamed for increasing people's susceptibility to new cults. But the sense of apocalypse being at hand was always one of the strands in Welsh non-conformity.

---

top of the pyramid, the new circumstances demanded a far greater number of people with a basic education. For the reactionary-minded in high places, the problem was that once people had learned to read and write, they could read and write anything, not just invoices and commercial correspondence. As a leisure pursuit, this could mean the novels of Charles Dickens or Thackeray, or the less memorable works of romantic novels and 'penny dreadfuls'. It also meant reading newspapers, magazines and journals of all kinds. The population was becoming better informed. In 1855 the tax on newspapers was abolished, and the duty on paper prices was also lifted in 1861 following the establishment of free trade by the Liberal government under Gladstone. Many new papers were founded in Welsh and in English, usually stirringly named, like *Y Gwladgarwr*, 'The Patriot'.

THE LIBERATION SOCIETY AND LIBERAL VICTORIES

One aim of Chartism had been achieved in 1858, with the abolition of a property qualification for MPs: the others, unforgotten, were incorporated into the aims of new bodies like the Liberation Society. This had existed from 1840, but it rose to national prominence in the 1850s and 60s. It was concerned not with self-government but with the extension of civic rights to non-conformists, the disestablishment of the Church of England in Wales, and the self-expression of a growing middle class through the vote. Branches were set up throughout the country. The Society was well run at a tactical level and each modest step towards electoral reform, like the Act of 1867 which extended suffrage to artisans in towns, was seized on locally, ensuring that eligible names were actually added to the electoral rolls.

This began to make a difference in elections. In that of June 1859, which brought an overall Liberal victory and the promise of further reforms to come, the Tory candidates put up by the landowners found themselves facing opposition. Seats like Meirionydd, where the Watkin-Williams-Wynne family candidates had been unchallenged for more than a century, came within a few votes of being won by an upstart Liberal. The infuriated landowners evicted some tenants who had dared to oppose their will, and raised the rents of others. These revanchist actions brought a storm of protest focused on the little town of Bala. Coercion continued in the elections of 1865. But by the 1868 general election, with an enlarged voter's roll bringing artisan householders into the electorate, the Tory candidate for Meirionydd withdrew from the contest rather than face an inevitable defeat. Elsewhere the landed interest fought harder to hold on to the parliamentary influence it had controlled for so long, and there were instances of pre-election pressure and intimidation, followed by post-election eviction or victimisation, throughout rural Wales. The Ballot Act of 1872, providing for a secret ballot rather than the old public vote, put a stop to much, if not all, of this kind of thing.

The general election of 1868 has been seen as a watershed in Welsh political history, the moment at which the popular vote became more important than the influence of landowners or factory owners. It was dramatised at Merthyr, a two-member constituency since 1867, with the largest electorate in Britain, where the poll was topped by Henry Richard, from Tregaron, a leading member of the Liberation Society and an uncompromising upholder of Chartist values. The former MP, Henry Bruce, a prominent Liberal and industrialist in the J.J. Guest mould, lost his seat. All told, the Liberals had twenty-one Welsh seats, the Tories twelve. But the change ran deeper. Among these new MPs were Liberals of a new kind. They had emerged through the hard work of the Liberation Society and bitter confrontations not only with landlords great and small, but also with the masters of industry who had for fifty years upheld their own kind of paternalist, Whiggish Liberal tradition in borough seats, especially in the south. With Henry Richard, they could reasonably describe themselves as representing the 'working man'. One of the reasons for Bruce's defeat was the issue of mine safety, on which the coalowners were all too clearly unwilling to take real action.

WORKERS: PROTEST AND REFORMS

The industrial workers of Wales, many of them still women and children rather than men, were fighting their own battles in the workplace. Their labour remained a commodity, to be reduced when demand or prices fell, to be rewarded only when boom conditions created a shortage of jobs. The concept of 'industrial relations' scarcely existed. Even the benevolent capitalist, on the Robert Owen model, set out to give the workers what he thought they should get, on the basis that this would make the business prosper. The general atti-tude of management was that the workers should accept their lot, and the majority of workers did just that. Most industrial units were relatively small, employing a hundred or so people. Those who stood up to represent the inter-ests of their fellow workers were considered troublemakers and liable to be reported to the police, or dismissed. In the face of this, it is not surprising that periodic outbreaks of Scotch Cattle activity continued well into the 1850s.

In parliament, the political battle to legitimise trade unions waxed and waned through the 1860s. In 1859, peaceful picketing during a strike was made legal. In 1867 trade unions were declared illegal. In 1871 they were finally given legal recognition. It was around this time that the coal industry, still bedevilled by frequent accidents and disasters, began to consolidate both in terms of manage-ment and in terms of unionism. The Powell–Duffryn amalgamation of 1864 created a major employer. The Amalgamated Association of Miners, from an English base, won many Welsh recruits from 1871. By 1875 it had vanished, the victim of a recession in demand with the resultant inevitable pay cuts for the workforce. In its place there rose a multiplicity of local unions, which might have been subjected to a divide-and-rule policy by the coalowners, but for the emergence of the celebrated 'Mabon': William Abraham, a negotiator and crowd-handler of genius, who represented the union side in negotiations with the newly formed Coalowners' Association in 1875. These broke new ground in their establishing of a wage agreement that would be standard – in its imple-mentation if not in its rates – across the south Wales coalfield. It introduced the 'sliding scale' of payment, which linked the colliers' pay to the price obtained by the owners. Its effect was to enable the workforce to share in success as well as in recession.

By 1880, a sense of structure was appearing in Welsh society quite different to that of forty years before. It was based around certain 'pillars' or established facts: heavy industry in the form of mining and metal production; a system of elementary education for virtually all children; the general acceptance of what might be termed 'non-conformist values', though many of them were equally Anglican values; and a new style and content to politics that, though still infused with a somewhat paternalistic liberalism, increasingly identified with the interest of the working class. They added up to a mix that was peculiarly Welsh and which created a distinct sense of community and culture, which was underpinned by the uniquely Welsh foundation of language and culture. Noth-ing in all this structure was permanent. Each aspect was in a continuous state of development, and so therefore was the whole. In 1880, Wales was on the move, and most of its people would have felt that the movement was in the direction of progress and improvement.

CHAPTER SIXTEEN

Industrial Wales. The Third Phase: Maturity, 1880 to 1920

THE GREAT AGE OF HEAVY INDUSTRY

In 1880, a man or woman of sixty could look back to a time before Queen Victoria's day, when the steam train was virtually unknown in Wales, when Cardiff was a village, and across the land the squire's word was law. Their ten-year-old grandchild, with a life expectancy of another fifty-eight years, if a boy, or sixty-two, if a girl, would live into the era of the aeroplane, the radio, electric power and nuclear fission. The years 1830 and 1930 could touch hands: a reminder of the brevity of human history, packed with events as it might be. David Lloyd George, born (in Manchester) in 1863 and at this time a brilliant and argumentative solicitor's clerk of seventeen, would live until 1945. In 1881 the population of Wales was 1,577,000 people. More than half a million of them lived in the county of Glamorgan. Cardiff had 106,641 inhabitants, Swansea was close behind with 93,001. Despite the absolute increase of more than 150,000 since the census ten years previously, there were areas of decline. In the counties of Pembroke, Cardigan, Montgomery and Radnor the population continued to fall, and Brecon joined the list. Anglesey's fall ceased, but the population did not rise. These were all predominantly agricultural counties. More surprisingly, perhaps, the population of Merthyr Tydfil and Aberdare went down. This fall represented the migration of industry and industrial workers away from the 'cradle' of the iron industry. The ironstone deposits along the northern rim of the coalfield had long since been worked out, and to bring imported ore up to the heads of the valleys seemed a pointless expense when there were greenfield sites for new works close to the docks. The technology of ironmaking had also moved on. Ironworks were getting bigger. There was a steady increase in the demand for steel and tinplate, and the metals industries clustered along the coast.

The 1880s and 90s were not decades of universal economic good fortune. In the middle of the former decade the general recession was severe enough to bring out a royal commission, which noted in 1886 that the Welsh iron and steel industry was feeling the effects of international competition from new plants in the Ruhr and in Pennsylvania. The steel industry fought back; others found recovery more difficult. The decline of rural communities was hastened by a slump in farm prices during the 1880s. The already depleted cloth and woollen industry of Montgomery and Meirionydd was being wiped out by factory-produced competition from Lancashire and Yorkshire. The Welsh producers could not compete on price or quality, and went under, adding to the numbers trekking north or south – or east into England – to where industry seemed unshakeably set on expansion. In the Teifi Valley, by contrast, a modernised flannel industry survived and prospered, using power looms and distributing the finished cloth via the railway network. In the north-west, the slate industry had somewhat over-expanded in the 1870s and its production was cut back until around 1895. Some of its uses were in decline, with earthenware replacing it in public urinals, and exercise books taking over in schools (in some places, though, the schoolroom slate would survive World War II). But the area was still the world's chief source of roofing slate, and provided over 90 per cent of all British slate.

The general picture was one of expansion and success. Historians have referred to this period in triumphal terms: 'In the years from 1880 to 1914 it was amongst the most buoyant growth centres in the world for industrial expansion, and for manufacturing and commerce,' writes K.O. Morgan (p. 59), adding that only the Ruhr in Germany and the industrial sectors of the eastern United States rivalled south Wales as a centre of heavy industry. Describing south Wales as 'an Imperial Democracy', Gwyn A. Williams calls it one British region where 'growth was still breakneck and full of promise' (p. 222). Coal was of course the foundation on which expansion rested, with the rapid growth in the use of electricity and piped gas providing it with two large extra markets. The iron ore was used up, the copper, silver and lead deposits were exhausted or, with minor exceptions, not able to be extracted on an economic scale. But coal extraction went up and up and up. In the early 1870s, it was estimated at around 16 million tons a year. By 1891 that had almost doubled, to 30 million tons. By 1913 it reached a total, never to be surpassed, of 56 million tons. It was the most productive and successful coalfield in Great Britain, and more than half of its output went for export, thereby creating a hugely expanded railway and dockyard industry. At first the export trade was centred on Cardiff and Newport.

With the development of the western anthracite coalfield, Swansea too became an important coal port. In 1898, in the teeth of the Bute interests of Cardiff, and after complicated legal processes and parliamentary machinations, the coal magnates David Davies and John Cory obtained an act of parliament to build extended docks at Barry, tapping the Rhondda coal pits by means of a rail link. Barry became a town almost overnight. In 1913 it overtook Cardiff to be

Coal being loaded at Cardiff Docks

the busiest coal-exporting port in the world. Between 1880 and 1920, some-thing very close to a thousand million tons of coal were hacked out of the strata underlying south Wales. The destiny of all this vast quantity was to be burned, to be transformed into heat and energy, and to make its own substantial contri-bution to the artificial cocktail of gas and dust injected by human enterprise into the earth's atmosphere. Such considerations simply did not arise at this time. Spoil, slack and stone accounted for further millions of tons, in their case heaped up in steep mountains on already steep valley sides above the colliery towns and villages, as short a distance as possible from the pit.

Equally successful were the metal industries. In the north, new steelworks were built: at Brymbo in 1885 and Shotton in 1896. In 1891, the old ironworks at Dowlais were largely replaced by a large new steelworks at East Moors in Cardiff, close to the docks. As in the coal industry, amalgamations and takeovers were leading to bigger companies, capable of larger investment and able to seek markets throughout the world. The same trend was happening in the non-ferrous metals industry round Swansea, where the largest nickel producing plant in the world was opened at Clydach in 1902 by Sir Alfred Mond, son of another immigrant from Germany.

INDUSTRIAL CONFLICTS: AN UNEQUAL WAR

In their mountain enclave, the slate magnates and their army of quarrymen found their market again beginning to expand in the later 1890s. In 1896 the quarrymen formed a union, as they were legally entitled to do. Lord Penrhyn, as the head of the Pennant family had now become, refused to recognise it or to negotiate with it in any way, as he was also legally entitled to do. There was a year-long lockout, ending in a return to work, with Penrhyn still refusing to budge. In 1898 they had a boom year. The Pennants made profits of £133,000. Equivalent to many millions in present-day currency, such a level of income, plus a peerage, might turn many people's heads. Lord Penrhyn did not remain unaffected. The union had not gone away, and now he refused to allow it to collect members' dues on his property. The resulting protests and disturbances provoked a three-year lockout at the world's greatest slate quarry. Lord Penrhyn had plenty of money in the bank; the quarrymen did not. Furthermore, Lord Penrhyn could hire blackleg labour to maintain some kind of output, with police brought in from as far away as Liverpool and Birkenhead and militia standing by to ensure that the slate was moved. There was intense bitterness and much hardship. Virtually all of Wales was on the side of the quarrymen. But law and order were on the side of the baron. At the end, a reduced and dispirited workforce returned, without obtaining any concession whatever. The Penrhyn lockout had a dire effect on the industry, already experiencing competition from US producers. In fourteen years, World War I would all but see it killed off, but the events of 1900–03 prematurely weakened it. The political impact of the Penrhyn lockout was also profound.

The miners of south Wales were a force ten times that of the quarrymen in number. The basically co-operative tactics of Mabon, as leader of a collection of separate but homogeneous local unions, which had established the sliding scale of payment in 1875, were maintained through the 1880s and into the 1890s. In 1888 the employers granted one Monday a month off to the miners, duly named 'Mabon's Day', when special 'MD' trains would take spring and summer excursions to the coast. Though Mabon's hold on the miners' side was firm, it was a personal dominance. Only three of the eight unions were independent; the others were essentially company unions, with limited independence and no funds of their own. The majority of colliery workers were not enrolled in unions at all. During this period the employers' side continued to combine into larger groups and companies. Powell Duffryn were joined by Ocean Coal, the mining empire of David Davies, the benefactor of Aberystwyth's college, by the Cambrian Combine run by D.A. Thomas, and by the Lewis Merthyr group of Sir William Lewis, as the major employers. Lewis became the leader of the Coalowners' Association, and, though less medieval in his attitudes than Lord Penrhyn, he had a clear idea of who were the 'masters' and who were the 'men'. Despite increasing dissatisfaction with the ways in which the sliding scale was implemented, the steady growth of the coal industry helped to keep industrial relations quiescent until late in 1897. The miners gave notice of their intention to end the sliding scale agreement, and proposing its replacement by a 10 per cent pay increase and a fixed minimum wage. In February 1898 negotiations failed, and the coalowners imposed a lockout which lasted for six months. The employers' victory was as complete as that of Penrhyn in 1897. The sliding scale was retained, and 'Mabon's Day' was abolished.

CHEAP LABOUR, HUGE PROFITS

Thus ended the always somewhat uneasy cohabitation between miners and coalowners. To the miners, it revealed the essential facts that in confrontation they had no power, and that their interests would never be taken seriously by the employers' side unless they had such power. To the historian, there is another level of explanation also. The astonishing expansion of the south Wales coal industry between 1880 and 1910 had something miraculous about it. The coal, though of excellent quality, was often deeply buried, in undulating and fractured seams, sometimes thick like the famous 'four foot' of the Rhondda, sometimes thin and narrow. Methane gas and underground floods were constant hazards. It was a labour-intensive industry. The wage bill amounted to almost 70 per cent of the operating costs of a colliery. For those who ran the industry, to hold that wage bill down was a first law. A second law was to keep all other operating costs as low as possible. Cheap labour made the Welsh coal boom possible; once this pattern had begun, it remained in place. Despite the often atrocious working conditions, despite frequent appalling accidents, there was no shortage of recruits to the industry. Apart from the influx from depressed rural communities in Wales, people came from Ireland, England, Spain and Italy. In all cases, the wages of a colliery worker were much larger, and more reliable in their payment, than their previous earnings.

In Wales, particularly south Wales, the gap between rich and poor was wider than in industrial England. It was an area of massive industrial growth, where huge profits were made. What happened to the capital gains? The castles and stately homes of the coal and steel magnates were plain to see, if only through the screening trees of their landscaped parks. A proportion of the profits was reinvested in new plant and new pits. Undoubtedly, vast sums passed out of Wales altogether, into the banking system and evolving money markets of London. There was also large outward investment of Welsh capital, by Welsh entrepreneurs, in coal and steel-related industry elsewhere. Welsh money and

Welsh expertise promoted the growth of Bilbao as an industrial centre in the Basque country of Spain, and helped to develop the network of railways in Argentina, among many other overseas developments. Public-spirited philanthropy within Wales supported causes like the college at Aberystwyth, and other good works, from public parks (Cathays Park was given to Cardiff by Lord Bute) to horse-troughs at street corners. But, on the whole, provision for public welfare was slow in coming, meanly funded, and far behind what was happening in England. K.O. Morgan spells it out in *Rebirth of a Nation*: 'Long before 1914, south Wales lagged behind most parts of Britain in terms of sub-standard working-class housing, in urban overcrowding, in its health and hospital services, in the indices of industrial disease among workers, poverty and ill-health among the old, malnutrition and disease among children' (p. 71). In 1911, in the five largest boroughs of Wales, the death rate among children ran at 380 in 1,000. Once upon a time, Wales could have honestly pled poverty. If, in the first decade of the twentieth century, the picture was as bleak as this, it showed either something rotten in the state, or an alarming imaginative gap in the minds of the people who controlled the Welsh municipalities and country districts.

It is tempting, and not necessarily wrong, to see at least some of the causes stretching back into history. It may exceed any historical licence to look back as far as the medieval period of castle and hut, when the hut-dwellers lived at the orders of the castle-dweller, and also looked up to him as a chief and leader. But the attitudes of Welsh landowners in the nineteenth century show clearly that they continued to expect not only deference and respect, but obedience, from their tenants. In Ireland and in Scotland, apathy among the working people has been partly ascribed to emigration, and the consequent absence of the people of greatest energy and initiative. But emigration from Wales was very much less than from Ireland or Scotland, and the southern industrial area was a zone of immigration. There is ample evidence of people with both energy and initiative, but it was rarely deployed in the sphere of urban improvement. An acceptance-culture among the people clearly played its part. The chief culprits, however, were those individuals and companies paying rates to the local authorities and so providing the income which nourished civic life. Except in small colonies, for example in Swansea satellite towns, such as Gorseinon, and even parts of the Rhondda towns, owner-occupiers were few, and the great bulk of the housing stock was rented, often by coal and steel companies. These, as the prime source of a town's income from rates, kept a steely clamp on development. Managers and agents fought to keep rates at the lowest levels, and protested vehemently at every increase or new development which would not be self-financing. They also campaigned successfully to prevent councils from building houses for workers.

TRADE UNIONS, TRADES COUNCILS AND THE LABOUR PARTY

The reaction of the miners to their defeat in 1898 was different to that of the quarrymen. However passive they were about the amenities of their towns, there was no sense of acceptance of the coalowners' victory. They understood that the economic importance of their industry gave them clout, if only they could deliver its impact. In October 1898 the South Wales Miners' Federation was founded. Though Mabon was made president, his personal authority was greatly reduced. His style of negotiation and collaborative approach to the owners were discredited. In a year the Federation gained over 100,000 members, and these were men who wanted to see results. With tactics including twenty-four-hour strikes, and a far tougher negotiating stance, it forced the abolition of the sliding scale in 1902. From 1899 on, the atmosphere in the coalfield was one of hostile confrontation. Aware of the fact that every improvement would have to be fought for, the Federation's attitude to the Coalowners' Association was militant and suspicious. Within the unions, too, there was a new sense of involvement from individual members. Paternalism had been strong in their leadership, just as it had been among such liberal-minded company bosses as D.A. Thomas (the future Lord Rhondda) of the Cambrian Combine; but now the wisdom of the old guard was under question.

Leaders like Mabon identified thoroughly with the social pillars. A prominent

---

D.A. THOMAS (LORD RHONDDA)

His grandfather migrated to Merthyr Tydfil in 1790 and became a haulage contractor to Crawshay's Ironworks. His father was a shopkeeper who turned coal prospector and opened pits in the Rhondda. Thomas, born in 1856, went to Cambridge University, and on his return to Wales, went to Clydach Vale to learn about mining. He helped build up the family mining business, whilst also taking a strong interest in Liberal politics. He was elected four times at the top of the poll for Merthyr's two MPs. In 1894, the collapse of the Cymru Fydd movement alienated Thomas from Lloyd George. Failing to get a ministerial post in Campbell-Bannerman's Liberal government of 1906, he turned his full attention to developing the huge Cambrian Combine, and became one of the leading coalowners of south Wales, at a time when industrial relations in the coalfield were at their most acrimonious and the Labour-Liberal alliance was breaking up. In 1915 he was brought back into government, entrusted with a vital arms-buying mission to the USA. He returned on the *Lusitania*, surviving (with his daughter) its torpedoing. He was made a peer as Lord Rhondda. Joining the wartime Ministry of Supply, he became Food Controller in 1917, ensuring an efficient distribution of food throughout Britain. He died in office in 1918. His daughter, made Viscountess Rhondda by special dispensation, inherited his toughness and panache, having gone to jail in the 1900s for her part in the women's suffrage movement; and later founding the once-influential weekly journal *Time and Tide*.

D.A. Thomas

non-conformist, active in Liberal politics, fluent in Welsh and a fine orator and singer, his instincts were for consensus. Employers like D.A. Thomas, another leading Liberal, whose 1897 proposal for a voluntary and managed system of controlling coal output and prices was rejected by Sir William Lewis, shared many of the same ideas. There is a faint glimmer of a distinctive Welsh approach to industrial management, rooted in a sense of community values and community responsibilities, though it was never erected into a philosophy. And in Wales as elsewhere, the mutual intransigence of capital and labour, pronounced inevitable by Marx as early as 1848, began to dominate industrial relations.

Though south Wales, from the 1890s on, proved to be highly receptive and responsive to the new drive both to establish trade unions and to provide the workers' movement with its own political wing, most of its ideas were imported from outside. Most unions were linked to unions already established in England. Their number grew rapidly. More than twenty unions were represented on the Cardiff Trades Council in 1902. The trades councils were of great importance in the larger centres, in presenting a united face of trade unionism to the local authorities and gradually ensuring the election or appointment of working people to the committees and sub-committees that ran municipal affairs. Some of these were very new, like the Cardiff Corporation Tramways, founded in 1901 to take over from two horse-drawn tram companies; soon local transport was far more widely available. The most celebrated action by a trades council was that of Merthyr and Aberdare in 1900, inviting the Scottish Labour pioneer, Keir Hardie, to stand as Independent Labour candidate for Merthyr Boroughs, and thus providing Wales's first Labour MP (Hardie's Christian pacifism and teetotal beliefs would have done him no harm among the non-conformists). The transfer of political loyalty from the Liberal Party to the new, inexperienced Labour Party was a gradual and uneven one, not fully accomplished until the 1920s. Well before that, the trade unions were firmly established.

Among the most dynamic trade unionists were the railway workers, in particular those in the short but intensely busy and profitable industrial lines linking the coalfields to the docks and steelworks. (The Taff Vale, with 384 miles of track, ran 2,809,868 train miles in 1909.) The Amalgamated Society of Locomotive Engineers and Firemen, the footplate-men's union, had three of its first six branches in south Wales, and a railwayman from Merthyr, Richard Bell, became general secretary of the Amalgamated Society of Railway Servants, later to become the National Union of Railwaymen. In 1900, a strike on the Taff Vale line led to a historic court case, ultimately decided by the House of Lords, in which the company claimed, and was awarded, damages for loss of income as a result of the strike. The decision rocked the labour movement and speeded up the formation that year of the Labour Party.

LIBERAL PARTY DOMINANCE

Political awareness and debate were encouraged by further enlargements in the electorate. The year 1884 was important in this respect, with the third Reform Act, followed by a new redrawing of constituency boundaries in the following year. Male householders were now enfranchised, giving the vote to thousands of industrial and agricultural workers. Glamorgan now had five MPs. Five small borough seats disappeared, as the realities of political life caught up with Haverfordwest, Beaumaris, Radnor, Cardigan and Brecon. But Cardiff still only had a single member. Most of the Welsh constituencies were by now impregnable strongholds of the Liberal Party. In the general election of November 1885, they won thirty out of thirty-four seats, the others falling to the Tories. When elected county councils were introduced in 1889 (a further blow to the powers of the landowners), the Liberals were the majority party in every one except Brecknockshire. In 1904 Brecknock too went into the Liberal fold. The reasons for this Liberal dominance were many, including a still-vivid recall of the period in which Tory landowners were able to dictate the result in advance. The party leader, William Ewart Gladstone, was a popular and admired figure in Wales, where his brand of idealism was perhaps received with more sympathy than in England. His association with Hawarden, his wife's family home, also gave him an honorary Welsh dimension. A Liberal government in 1881 had brought to the statute book an act framed specially for Wales – the Sunday Closing Act of 1881 which kept all pubs in Wales shut on Sundays: the first piece of legislation since 1542 to treat Wales as a separate entity from England, and a noisy triumph for the non-conformist-temperance alliance. It was only a few years before Oscar Wilde would say 'Work is the curse of the drinking classes.' The reaction of the substantial elements in the population who went neither to church nor chapel, some of whom also enjoyed gambling and already illegal sports like cock-fighting, was more muted, in public at least. Another Liberal measure on behalf of Wales was the Welsh Intermediate Education Act of 1889, which owed a lot to Henry Bruce, summarily dismissed as a Merthyr MP in 1867, but resurrected as Lord Aberdare. He chaired a committee which made a wide-ranging and influential report on Welsh education in 1881. The Intermediate Education Act broke new ground by providing government money for the establishment of secondary schools in Wales (elsewhere, only elementary education was subsidised by the state). This gratified the Welsh concern with education. The Liberal Party was the defender of free trade, on which coal and metal exports were dependent, and it was associated in the minds of the Welsh people with progress and reform.

The Liberal MPs covered a range of views and characters, still including one or two of the old-style captain-of-industry Whigs, such as Sir Hussey Vivian of Swansea. More typical were men like Bryn Roberts, a barrister by profession and a devout Methodist, who defeated Lord Penrhyn's candidate in the Eifion constituency of north Caernarfonshire. He got the quarrymen's vote, but he was not a working man. Equally typical might have seemed David Lloyd George, now a newly qualified solicitor who scraped in as Liberal member for Caernarfon Boroughs in 1890, and would hold the seat for fifty years. But Lloyd George was to reveal himself as a politician of genius who, without severing his links to Wales, established himself as a statesman of Great Britain and the British Empire, to the occasionally baffled but always sincere admiration of (most of) his fellow-countrymen. Despite slight fluctuations, the Liberal hold on Wales seemed as inevitable as the annual increased output of the coal mines. If Wales had had a parliament of its own, there would have been a permanent Liberal administration from 1868 to 1925. As things were, the Welsh Liberal MPs, rarely fewer than thirty in number, formed a solid core of the Westminster parliamentary party. Among them were formidable figures, not only Lloyd George but also Thomas Ellis, the Chief Whip and a dedicated Welsh nationalist. Even in times of travail and division within the party, the Liberal vote in Wales remained essentially dependable. A few seats might be lost, large majorities might drop, but things always came together again. If the support of the electors was steady, so was the cohesion of the members. They did fall out with one another, but the splits did not last.

DIVISIONS IN THE LIBERAL PARTY

They split in 1886 over the Irish Home Rule Bill, when Liberals and Liberal Unionists opposed each other. Seven Welsh MPs voted against Irish Home Rule and helped to bring their government down. But unionism was not a visceral belief to the Welsh Liberals as it was to the Tories. In the 1892 general election, no Liberal Unionist candidate won a seat in Wales. They split again between 1894 and 1896 in a purely Welsh dispute, sparked off by the Cymru Fydd, or 'Young Wales', movement. Established in the 1880s, it succeeded in bringing, after a very long lapse of years, the issue of Welsh nationalism back into the political arena. Cymru Fydd was based on the fact that 'cultural nationalism' in Wales was strong and vibrant – evidence was universal in the form of Welsh speech, the relatively recent but hugely successful choral singing tradition, and the system of local *eisteddfodau* leading to the grand annual National Eisteddfod, held from 1881 in a different Welsh town each year (even unto Birkenhead) – and its supporters felt it was only natural that such national feeling should be linked to some form of self-government. With its beginnings in north Wales, the movement quickly found the support of the Liberal Party there, and the concept of a Welsh Liberal Party independent of the English one found favour. But the reaction of the South Wales Liberal Foundation was entirely different. Here, where the forges of the empire clanged day and night, where the coal that fuelled the mighty Royal Navy was hewn, the concept of a Welsh government was reviled, despite the dominance the heavily populated south would have been able to exercise in it. Although it had been supported by Ellis, Lloyd George and, for a time, D.A. Thomas, Cymru Fydd was abandoned, and with it the prospect of Welsh devolution. The party drew together again, but had been forcibly reminded of the fact that the ancient north–south divide was as strong as ever. They disagreed again in 1899 over the Boer War. At the time, the anti-war faction had the worst of it, but later Lloyd George, an opponent of the war, was to benefit from the unpopular stance he took then. Wars, of course, were always good business for coal and steel producers, but the flood of Imperial enthusiasm, in Wales as elsewhere in Britain, ran far ahead of economic self-interest.

As organised labour grew stronger, it seemed possible that the Liberal Party, always one containing a wide range of sympathies, might provide its political wing. In 1906, six 'Lib-Lab' members, coalminers with impeccable working-class credentials, were elected in south Wales. But that doughty Liberal capitalist, D.A. Thomas, was also returned at the top of the poll in Merthyr. The Liberal Party, though now rooted far more in the middle ranks, of lawyers, shopkeepers and doctors, than among the capitalist magnates, was slow and reluctant to adopt working-class candidates, despite most full-time workers' possession of the vote since 1884. For the emerging generation of trade union and Labour activists, the Liberal Party's long identification with the leaders of industry and commerce marked it, and with policies which backed the interests of big business, stamped it as the enemy almost as much as the Conservative Party. They saw absorption into it as a threat, likely to stifle their own aspirations, and preferred to stick with the long haul, through union meetings, town hall committees, street corner speeches and local elections, of getting their own men into power.

TOWARDS A WELSH IDENTITY

By the turn of the nineteenth century, when Britain was fighting the last of the small, far-off and questionable imperialist wars that characterised the second half of the nineteenth century, against the would-be independent Boers in South Africa, Wales was in political and economic terms an adjunct of the vastly enlarged economy and polity of England. As a major source of primary industrial product – coal, iron, steel, non-ferrous metals and slate – it was an important contributor to the wider economy of the British Empire, not least in its shipping lines. Welsh tramp steamers took coal to anywhere in the world, picked up return cargoes to other ports, and eventually returned to a Welsh home port to load up with coal again. In industrial terms, it was as mature as any other industrial zone. Politically it was growing up fast. Socially, it was more backward than it should have been, especially in matters of health and welfare. The values of 1880 still held up; the pillars of society and community remained the same.

It was those values, and the social culture that produced them, which determined the 'Welshness' of Wales at a time when, after the short career of Cymru Fydd, there was no political Welsh identity and no movement to promote one. Through the nineteenth century, the concept of a 'Celtic' identity, uniting the people of Wales, Ireland, Scotland and Brittany, had arisen. Pan-Celtic congresses were held, though their domination by antiquarians and aristocrats tended to mean that they discussed matters like a suitable national dress for the Irish rather than a practical agenda. Wales, whose aristocracy was very small in numbers and largely absentee, played little part in these games. Far more important within the country was the popularisation of the Welsh past and the new organisation of the *eisteddfod* system. Every community in the country could rise to the challenge of the Eisteddfod, in poetry, prose and song. The ritual of these events, however much it owed to Iolo Morgannwg's imaginative interpretation, provided a social cohesion and a national forum. This was Wales, and it happened nowhere else, except among Welsh communities overseas. At one time, earlier in the century, the *eisteddfodau* had been rather beery events, centred on pubs and with something of a carnival atmosphere. By the end of the century, they had been greatly formalised. Clergymen, both nonconformist and Anglican, had played a major part in refining the procedures and the programme, and saw no problem in robing themselves as 'druids' to run the shows. In addition, the Welsh language in Wales was in a far stronger position than the marginalised Gaelic of Ireland and Scotland. Here, however, the auspices did not look so good. The census of 1891 recorded 54.4 per cent of the adult population as Welsh-speaking; by 1901, it was down to below 50 per cent.

CHURCH, CHAPEL AND
THE SECULAR MAJORITY

Although it remained the largest single denomination (it had 193,000 communicants in 1906), and despite its participation in cultural affairs, and the appointment of Welsh-speaking bishops, the Anglican church occupied an anomalous position in Welsh life. It was still strongly identified with the squirearchy, and the landowners at this time still exercised great local influence. It was still the established church and as such exercised various rights which the much larger non-conformist population, emancipated in other ways, found increasingly intolerable. Chief among these was its right to collect tithes even from those who did not subscribe to its creed. Another grievance was that only Anglicans were allowed burial in parish churchyards. This cause brought the young Lloyd George to national prominence in Wales. The church still controlled many schools, usually the only school in the town or village. Lloyd George, again, though of a Baptist family, attended a church school as a boy in Llanystumdwy. He, and probably most others in a similar situation, found it easy to absorb the secular education without the religious doctrine (Sunday School would provide a hefty weekly antidote), but nevertheless, in the last years of the nineteenth century, the demand for disestablishment of the church in Wales grew steadily more vociferous.

Non-conformism remained the religion of the majority, with its major sects of Baptists, Methodists and Congregationalists all remaining strong. Their need to provide separate meeting places for their adherents, plus the existence of numerous smaller sects, explains the large number of chapels – most now abandoned or in use for other purposes – in every town and village. The influence of religion extended far into daily life. By no means all non-conformists were teetotal, but the temperance movement was closely linked to the chapels. Chapel influence pervaded traditional culture. Not least, in Wales the non-conformists were the Liberal Party at prayer. The link was expressed by Henry Richard as early as 1868; his self-description was as 'a Welshman, and advanced Liberal and a Non-conformist'. Twenty years later, W.E. Gladstone could declare (to a suitable audience): 'The Nonconformists of Wales are the people of Wales.'

The non-conformist-Liberal alliance drew the majority of its activists from a relatively narrow section of society. Nowadays perhaps the majority of Welsh people would describe themselves as 'middle class'. A hundred years ago, this would have been far from the case. The middle class at that time was composed of professionals such as lawyers, doctors and of course clergymen; of shop-keepers; of small-scale entrepreneurs largely in businesses serving heavy industry; of senior managers, clerks and accountants; of the better-off farmers. Their influence was out of all proportion to their numbers. That influence has cast a long shadow over a much larger section of the community, the working class of Wales.

Even in 1851, a census had shown that just over half the population, 51 per cent, did not attend any place of worship on a Sunday. Many of these might have been nominally members of church or chapel, but the majority simply led lives in which religion did not play an integral part. Mostly urban and working class, they maintained a different set of values. Their culture was built around the pub, the boxing ring, and outdoor sports and pastimes. Many of these were either outright gambling games, like pitch-and-toss, or had a strong gambling element, like cockfighting or dog-racing. They would take to rugby and soccer with enthusiasm, both as players and as spectators. Such people did not produce newspapers or journals and their existence is documented more by statistics and by the disapproval of the *bien-pensant* element than by their own evidence. Their language was Welsh, though they were mostly bilingual and had a taste for the new mass-circulation English newspapers like the *News of the World*, whose spicy news items and features were not available in any Welsh-published journal in either language. They worked hard and they played hard, and showed solidarity in industrial disputes. Perhaps in times like the religious revival of 1904–06, inspired by the charismatic preacher Evan Roberts, when chapel membership reached 549,000, some of them were drawn into the world of non-conformist religion, but they mostly dropped out again. The existence of this silent secular majority is perhaps too easily forgotten or underrated. They undoubtedly provided the Liberal Party with electoral fodder, even if they were not activists. But for those who wanted to take a more active role in trade unionism or in politics, the Liberal Party was not welcoming. Its leading figures tried to foster the notion of a 'respectable' working class – chapel-going, domestically minded, socially responsible and of course, Liberal, but in practice working men found it difficult to be accepted by the villa-dwelling merchants and professional men who ran each local branch of the party. The Labour movement, though far from godless – Christian socialism was an important element – was much less concerned with religious belief as part of political life. Atheist and agnostic could make common cause with ardent Methodist or Baptist – or Catholic – in a strictly political context. As the Labour Party increasingly distanced itself from the Liberals, accusations of atheism and rootless internationalism would be thrown at it from the bunkers of community values and Welsh-style Christianity. But with Labour there was no suggestion of siding with the employers and their acolytes, as there was with the Liberals. As a result, the secular majority would eventually shift its political allegiance to the party of the workers, in which it could identify its own people as striving for its own welfare.

It was a male-dominated section of society, probably even more so than the Liberal-non-conformist section. The women of Wales, who shared the toil in the formative years of industry, had been gradually shut out from employment, partly by reformist legislation, partly by a change in social customs, enabled by rises in pay and living standards, which fostered a kind of domestic purdah. However powerful she might be within the family, the wife and mother played very little part in public life. The first Welsh branch of the women's suffrage movement did not appear until 1907, at Llandudno, significantly a town with a substantial English proportion in its population. Health and education were the only professions which actively sought women entrants, although the positions on offer were almost exclusively those of elementary schoolteacher and nurse, with little prospect of promotion in professional structures which were as male-dominated in the upper levels as any other. At the bottom end of the social scale, well past the lowest respectability barrier, prostitution flourished in the ocean seaports. The brothels, drug dens and dubious clubs of Bute Town and Tiger Bay were known to seamen worldwide. Pockets existed in other towns, notably in Merthyr's rackety old central district of 'China'. But this too was a male-run industry which exploited women and girls as victims.

CONTROVERSIES IN EDUCATION

The old anti-church antipathy of the non-conformists became a heated issue in the later 1880s as a result of farmers' sometimes violent opposition to paying tithes to the church in Wales. Their resentment was made greater by the collapse in farm prices at that time. In 1891, a Tory government transferred responsibility for payment of tithes from tenant to landlord, but the movement for disestablishment remained vocal. In 1895, a bill to bring it about was in the committee stage when the Liberal government fell and was replaced by the Tories. Their historical links with the church, together with their Unionist beliefs, put the Tories in total opposition to disestablishment. Another critical period came in 1902 and the years that followed. The Conservative-Unionist government's Education Act of 1902 provided for church schools to be supported from the rates. Fierce parliamentary opposition was led by Lloyd George. When the Education Act became law, most of the Welsh county councils failed to implement it. Pleadings and threats from the Board of Education were ignored, or met with delaying tactics. The councils were determined not to subsidise the church schools without having a say in how they were run – not something the Education Act had allowed for. Several councils were facing a legal challenge from the Board when the general election of 1906 restored a Liberal government in a landslide majority, and the crisis was brought to an end. The Act was not repealed – opposition by the House of Lords made that impossible – but the issue died away. In the previous year the Tory government had sanctioned the establishment of a Welsh National Library in Aberystwyth, and a National Museum in Cardiff, demonstrating that they too were aware of the fact that a Welsh nation could be said to exist. It did them little good: they failed to win a single Welsh seat in 1906.

Under prompting from Lloyd George, who from 1906 to 1916 acted as a sort of unappointed 'Minister for Wales' whatever his other functions, a Welsh Department was set up within the Board of Education in 1907, under its own secretary and with an eminent Welsh educationist and writer, Owen M. Edwards, as its first chief inspector. Although its powers were limited, the Welsh Education Department was another official acceptance of a 'nation' whose requirements could not simply be dovetailed to those of England. Its attitude to the Welsh language was a positive though not evangelical one; it encouraged its use in schools and worked to incorporate the teaching of Welsh and Welsh literature in secondary schools and colleges, though it did not go so far as to promote the teaching of other subjects in Welsh. Edwards himself made a massive individual contribution to the sustaining of Welsh, most notably perhaps through his founding of the first Welsh magazine for children, *Cymru'r Plant*, which survived until 1927. As Chief Inspector, he was frequently at odds with the Central Welsh Board, which had been set up in 1896 to manage the new secondary schools, and with the education committees of county councils. Edwards, fired by a scholarly interest in Welsh culture, found these bodies narrow-minded and unimaginative, over-concerned with the most mundane aspects of the curriculum and in seeing good examination results maintained.

LLOYD GEORGE IN GOVERNMENT: WELSH MEASURES

Already in 1906, David Lloyd George, as President of the Board of Trade, was fighting battles on other fronts than Welsh ones. From 1908 he was Chancellor of the Exchequer, introducing measures, such as the old age pension, national insurance and income tax, which affected all of Great Britain, and led towards the constitutional crisis of 1910–11 which confirmed the supremacy of the House of Commons. In 1911 he found time to mastermind the investiture of Edward, Prince of Wales, at Caernarfon, at which, in K.O. Morgan's words, 'new heights of bathos were scaled' (p. 122).

In 1912 the Welsh Council of Agriculture was set up, in response to many

David Lloyd George

appeals, articles and memoranda stressing the ongoing plight of the Welsh farmers; and in the same year a Welsh commission was established in order to implement the new National Insurance Act in Wales. These again were devolutionary in intention and effect; although of limited impact, they took for granted a separate Welshness in areas far removed from language and traditional culture.

The cap was set on these developments by the success of the long-running campaign to secure the disestablishment of the church. Lloyd George's political skills were fully drawn on here, though the atmosphere of 1912–14 was very different to the rancorous and unpleasant mood of the 1880s and 90s. The view of the church itself had changed. With a huge Liberal majority in parliament, and with disestablishment in the party's manifesto for twenty years, action was bound to come. A certain fatalism prevailed on both sides. The Liberal government took its time, delaying action with a royal commission into the state of all the Welsh churches, in 1907. Among the bishops and their clergy were also some who felt that to give their Welsh church its independence would be a positive move. The passage of the Parliament Act, removing the Lords' veto, took away the last defence of those who wanted to maintain the church as it was. The Act was passed in 1912, and in 1914 the inevitable opposition of the House of Lords could not stop it. On the night it became law, Welsh MPs sang *Hen Wlad Fy Nhadau* in the lobby of the House of Commons. In the event, the outbreak of war delayed the final implementation of the Welsh church's freedom until 1920.

In the shadow of other events of that year, in the end it seemed a small enough victory, achieved very late in the day. But there had been a succession of small victories, each of them serving to reinforce the concept of Welshness, the sense of a Welsh nation. Since the demise of Cymru Fydd there had been no overt Nationalist movement. The victories had occurred on a piecemeal basis, each with its own origin. Certainly no serious Nationalist agenda would have counted any of them as truly important; but there was no such agenda. Among the Liberals, the concept of devolution had been wrecked on the intransigence of the mercantile-industrial community of the south. Among the socialists, communists and syndicalists who formed the political arm of trade unionism, self-government was a distraction and a snare. Their impetus was class-based and internationalist.

THE LABOUR MOVEMENT SHOWS ITS TEETH

A powerful boost was given to the Labour movement in 1908, when the Miners' Federation of Great Britain, with the enthusiastic support of Welsh miners, voted to affiliate itself to the Labour Party. The big battalions were on the move. At this time the total number of miners was around 200,000. The electoral pacts and truces between Liberals and Labour, common in the first elections of the century, gave way to sharp rivalry as it became clear that the Labour activists were not content to take a share of the seats; they wanted them all. In Merthyr, where a Lib-Lab agreement allocated one of the borough's two seats to each party, the Liberals chose a candidate in 1913 to stand against Keir Hardie (who died in 1915 before an election took place). The trade union and Labour movement won scars and battle honours in Wales; but as with all fresh ideological causes, even the defeats and setbacks were turned into martyrdoms and new examples of the awfulness of the enemy.

Inevitably, given its scale and the manner of its running, it was in the coal industry that the greatest confrontations happened. Even reformist legislation like the Coal Mines Regulation Act of 1908, specifying an eight-hour day underground as the maximum, caused furious argument between unions and managements as to what constituted an eight-hour day. Unresolved disputes and temporary settlements over pay rates created growing tensions, and led to the eruption of late autumn 1910, when the miners at the Naval Colliery, Penygraig, refused the price offered for working the difficult Upper Five Foot Seam. A lockout by the owners followed. The owners were the Cambrian Combine, the mining empire of D.A. Thomas MP. Negotiations failed and the dispute escalated until by the end of October all the mines of the Rhondda and Aberdare were at a standstill. Serious violence began at Tonypandy on 7 November, in battles between miners, non-union workers, and the police; one miner died of a fractured skull and many others were injured. Shop windows were smashed and some shops were looted. On 8 November, the Home Secretary, Winston Churchill (at that time a Liberal), authorised troops to be moved into the area. Infantry detachments were moved into the Rhondda, and the Eighteenth Hussars were stabled at Pontypridd. Disturbances went on during November, with angry crowds stoning the police. Churchill spoke in the House of Commons of a 'savage war' being waged in the Rhondda. Soldiers with fixed bayonets patrolled the streets and stood guard on colliery property. It was not the first time a south Wales area had known military occupation, but the episode entered into the folk memory of the Labour movement. In January the troops were withdrawn, but the Cambrian strike went on until August 1911. Riots broke out in Ebbw Vale and Tredegar, their targets mainly Jewish shopkeepers and property owners. Although this is not an episode of the struggle that the Welsh are happy to recall, its motivation seems to have been economic rather than racial. In a tightknit, hard-pressed community the spectacle of 'incomers' requiring their rents or calling in their loans is always likely to cause resentment. The mining valleys were not the only scenes of violence. That same summer, troops sent into Llanelli during a rail strike shot dead two railway workers.

Following the ugly events of 1911, a national coal strike was called by the Miners' Federation of Great Britain in the spring of 1912, in order to procure a minimum wage. On this occasion the Liberal government reacted differently, and the strike was settled on the basis of promised legislation, which took the form of the Coal Miners (Minimum Wages) Act. In 1913 the appalling disaster at Senghennydd Colliery, in which 493 miners were killed, reminded the nation of the true price of coal.

THE REVOLUTIONARY SOCIALISTS

In the intensive researches of historians into the industrial and labour history of south Wales, there has been a strong focus on those individuals and groups within the mining communities whose agitation and leadership helped to bring the miners to a point as near to the revolutionary class war prophesied by Marx as any part of Great Britain ever came. They were certainly influential. Perhaps the most so was Noah Ablett, one of the founders of the ironically named Plebs' League. He was one of a small number of miners who had gone to Ruskin College, a further-education institute for working men set up in Oxford. Dissatisfied with the theoretical and passive approach of Ruskin, he returned to the Rhondda with a sense of commitment to direct action and the overthrow of the capitalist system. Through speeches, pamphlets, and news-sheets like *The Rhondda Socialist*, later to be *The South Wales Worker*, Ablett and his colleagues – Will Mainwaring, Frank Hodges and A.J. Cook among them – kept up a constant pressure. They had learned the power of organisation and education, and their efforts to teach revolutionary socialism to the mining proletariat were systematic and serious. They supported the founding in late 1909 of the Central Labour College in Oxford (it later moved to London), which became an incubator for young left-wing activists, and soon was sending emissaries back to south Wales and other industrial regions.

They had something of an evangelistic fervour, which perhaps struck a stronger chord in Wales than in England (it may be noted that the other area which, in 1919, seemed also for a moment to be on the brink of revolution was Glasgow, in old Strathclyde). There were other fiery leaders not involved with the intellectually based but deadly serious Plebs, men like Charles Stanton, the leader of the Aberdare miners. But their numbers were very small compared with the army of 30,000 and more who went on strike for eight grim and bitter months in 1910–11. They were not leaders but agitators, and their efforts were resisted by the more traditionalist leadership of the Miners' Federation almost as much as by the employers. The colliery workers and their families had a deep sense of grievance, of long exploitation, of neglect of safety – with a new terrible disaster always likely to happen – and this was the most important factor. The fieriest orators and the most skilled agitprop techniques would not mobilise entire communities unless those communities were already seething with half-suppressed anger. And, since it takes two sides to make a war, on the other side of the battle line, the Welsh coalfield possessed the most intransigent employers and managers in Britain. Even General Macready, commander of the troops in the Rhondda, was impressed by the obduracy of such coalowners as Leonard Llywelyn.

By 1913 the impetus of the Plebs' League and of militant socialism had ebbed. The attempt to revolutionise the miners had failed, and such millenarian documents as *The Miners' Next Step*, published in 1912, with its call for a workers' commonwealth of true democracy, already had an air of unreality.

THE FIRST WORLD WAR

In August 1914, the international solidarity of the working classes proved to have the strength of tissue paper in the face of the steely claims of national interest and national duty in Britain, France, Germany and Austro-Hungary. The few voices opposing the war as a purely capitalist crisis were drowned by the tom-toms of militarism and often rabid imperialism. Lloyd George was typical in his initial hesitancy being swiftly replaced by a driving enthusiasm for the war. By November 1914 a new Welsh Division was formed in the army and recruitment was rapid. Proportionally, more Welsh men and boys were to serve in the armed forces between 1914 and 1918 than either English or Scots.

The exercising of total war took a grip on Wales as on every other part of the United Kingdom (with the exception of Ireland). In the course of 1915 and 1916 government control extended itself into areas of life where it would have been unthinkable only a few years before, and, as more than one historian has noted, gave the British executive a degree of economic and social management that Lenin would have envied. The war economy, with its demand for coal, iron,

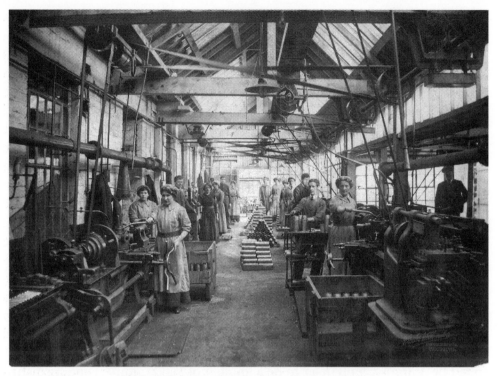

Women munitions workers during the First World War

steel, metals of all kinds, pushed Welsh industry into full production. Mines and railways, agriculture and engineering, all were placed under state control. Once again, women were recruited into industry, to take the places of men or to form the basic workforce in new factories producing munitions.

Support for the war, in Wales, was massive and coherent right to the end. Undoubtedly this owed much to Lloyd George, who, from the post of Minister of Munitions, finally replaced Asquith as prime minister of the Liberal-Tory coalition government in December 1916. With a Welsh prime minister, who also brought numerous Welsh associates into powerful positions, Welsh people could feel a close involvement with the war effort. A long feud with D.A. Thomas ended with Lloyd George's appointment of him first to negotiate with the Americans over arms supplies, then, as Lord Rhondda, to be the Minister of Food, up to his death in 1918. Another vital figure was Thomas Jones, deputy-secretary of the War Cabinet.

Compared to this formidable mobilisation of Welsh energy, courage and talent, the few voices raised against the war were crying into the wind, though they gained volume as time went on and public reaction to the mass slaughter of trench warfare brought about a more sober mood, and an increasing readiness to criticise the way in which the war was being run. Welsh Liberalism had

Men of the 6th Battalion of the Welsh Regiment, 1914

had a pacifist strain at least since the time of Henry Richard, and this often went hand-in-hand with Nationalist sentiment. At Aberystwyth, the journal *Y Wawr*, edited by Ambrose Bebb (later to be a founder of Plaid Cymru) contained articles and poems expressing doubts or opposition to the war, until the college authorities closed it down in 1918. Dr Thomas Rees proclaimed Christian pacifism in the journal *Y Deyrnas*, founded in October 1916. The imprisonment of conscientious objectors and the abrogation of civil liberties in the interest of the war effort caused great unease to some Welsh Liberals and Labour supporters, and this was intensified by the government's introduction of conscription in January 1916. The No Conscription Fellowship found adherents in Wales, one of whom, Morgan Jones, was jailed for publishing anti-war propaganda.

The acquiescence of the great majority of Welsh workers in the war was shown in Merthyr in 1915, when the death of Keir Hardie (a pacifist to the end) resulted in a by-election which was comfortably won by C.B. Stanton. Once the revolutionary leader of the Aberdare miners, he was standing as pro-war Labour candidate with Liberal and Conservative support. He beat the Independent Labour Party candidate, James Winstone, by a wide margin. Winstone was not a pacifist, but his party was identified with such prominent pacifists as Ramsay Macdonald, who had come to Merthyr to speak on his behalf. The bellicosity of the miners did not blind them to the fact that the coal industry was making large profits out of wartime demand. To the vituperation of London newspapers, they successfully went on strike for higher pay in July 1915. In general, the war brought higher pay and greater prosperity to Wales, ending a period that had lasted since around 1900, when living costs had generally risen faster than wages. This new prosperity embraced farmers and landworkers as well as industrial workers. Lord Rhondda's highly efficient methods ensured a steady market and good prices for Welsh milk, beef and cereal crops. Farm labourers benefited from legislation stipulating a minimum wage and an eight-hour working day.

Whatever individuals' attitude to the war had been, the armistice in November 1918 was greeted with huge relief. The war had come home to Wales as to all of Great Britain, in the form of many thousands of deaths, mostly of young men. A generation had been decimated. One small section of society which was perhaps most affected was that of the squires. Their sons, naturally members of the officer class, enlisted in large numbers. But at times in 1916 and 1917, the average life expectancy for an infantry subaltern, from his arrival at the front, was about seven days. The loss of so many had a massive impact on society, not least in the upper social bracket. But it was undeniable that, for the survivors, Wales had done well out of the war.

CHAPTER SEVENTEEN

A New Idea of Wales: 1918 to 1939

THE LABOUR ASCENDANCY

With shrewd political instinct, Lloyd George called a general election in December 1918, before the war machine had rattled to a halt. The overwhelming victory of his 'coupon' candidates – those who had Lloyd George's letter of approval, be they Liberal, Unionist-Conservative or even Patriotic Labour – did not prevent the coalition from falling apart after a Conservative revolt in 1922. After the collapse of Lloyd George's attempt to run the peace on a consensus basis, he had the unusual experience, for the first time since 1906, of sitting on the opposition front bench. Party warfare resumed; in the case of the Liberal Party it was also civil war between the factions led by Lloyd George and H.H. Asquith, whom he had ousted as prime minister. Most Welsh Liberals rallied to Lloyd George – Asquith's remark, that he would rather go to Hell than Wales, did not endear him to the Welsh – but the Liberals were damaged by division and by the post-war failure to provide a 'land fit for heroes', an oratorical flourish of Lloyd George's that was to be quoted against him on countless occasions. Lloyd George was also blamed for the government's failure to implement the majority report of the 1919 Sankey Committee on Coalmining, which had recommended that the mines be taken into public ownership. The Labour movement, on the other hand, had gained in resources, numbers and confidence in the course of the war. It was still very much entrenched in the coalfields and with little strength in other areas, but then Glamorgan and Monmouthshire held over 60 per cent of the total population. In 1923, Labour gained over half the votes in the mining counties of the south. In 1924, briefly, there was a Labour-led coalition government at Westminster. By the election of 1929, Labour had twenty-five of the Welsh seats, the Liberals were reduced to ten, and the Conservatives had one. The pattern of Welsh politics in the rest of the twentieth century was now defined.

TROUBLE FOR WELSH INDUSTRY

The advances and retreats, the unspontaneous and barren couplings, the subsequent recriminations, of political parties during the 1920s and 30s were expressive of the fact that none had the ability effectively to control the economy of Great Britain, far less contribute towards a stabilisation of the wider world economic system. Welsh industry, so vibrant and prosperous right up to 1919, was suddenly revealed in a precarious situation. The overwhelming dominance of coal in the economy now showed as a terrible weakness. By the end of 1919 demand was dropping fast. After 1920, the Welsh coal market declined steadily, year by year. Only the western sector, producing high-grade anthracite, retained any sort of buoyancy, but the great majority of the colliery workers, who in 1920 reached an all-time maximum number of 271,516, were employed to the east of that, in the steam coal and bituminous coal mines. In 1921, the miners of Great Britain went on strike, but with results very different to 1915. April 15 of that year was labelled 'Black Friday' as a result of the miners' own leader, the Welshman Frank Hodges, suggesting a temporary solution that broke the 'triple alliance' of railway and dock workers with the miners. Nothing came of it except pay cuts and job losses. In 1923, Wales still managed to export 35 million tons: rather more than in 1913, but that was a last rally. Now, in an international market of cut-throat competitiveness, the problems of Welsh coal, which had always been there, swelled to giant proportions. It was expensive to extract, the industry inefficient in its use of machines, and extravagant in its use of (albeit cheap) labour. American coal, machine-cut in modern pits, could undercut it in price. So could German and Polish coal. It was a bitter fruit of victory for the Welsh coal industry to see its Italian market taken away by the supply of German coal, as part of Germany's war reparations negotiated by the allies in the Versailles Treaty that had formally ended the war. The same pattern emerged in the steel industry, further reducing the home demand for coal. Another consequence of the war had been a dramatic improvement in the efficiency and use of the petrol engine. New ships were being built with oil-fired furnaces or marine diesel drive instead of coal-fired boilers. Improved road vehicles began to eat into the railways' domination of land transport, and peripheral lines began to close down. A severe blow from outside came when Baldwin's Conservative government returned Britain to the 'gold standard' in 1925. The resultant over-valuation of sterling made exporting even more difficult.

South Wales had grown populous and prosperous on coal, iron and steel. Apart from the non-ferrous metal plants, virtually every other industry existed to serve these giants. When the giants caught a cold, these feeder industries suffered severely. Now that the giants were in serious recession, the repercussions in other industry and business were often fatal.

It became starkly apparent that the failure to achieve industrial diversity in south Wales was a grave disadvantage to the region's economic life. The industrial magnates had seen themselves exclusively as coalowners, or steel-works owners, suppliers of the primary materials of modern industry. Other coalfields had developed manufacturing industries. The Tyne and the Clyde built ships and locomotives; Lancashire and the Black Country had a varied industrial base. South Wales had very little of any of this. They may have congratulated themselves on the fact that there would always be demand for the basic materials, as indeed was the case. The problem was that customers could now buy in a world market, its communications aided by wireless and the electric telegraph. The danger facing the Welsh industries was that demand might fall below a point where it was economic for them to maintain their works.

North Wales fared better in some ways. Its coal industry had always been much smaller, and its steel works were more up to date than those in the south. Even in 1923, new collieries were being sunk in the Wrexham area. Importantly, there was more diverse industry. In 1917 a big factory was established at Flint for making artificial fibres. As the cloth industry in the countryside crashed, the market for rayon grew. Whether driven by Welsh or English initiative, the north moved easily into an era of modern light industry, in a way which the south found hard to emulate. Easy road access into England helped considerably. The door-to-door flexibility of road transport was part of the 'modern' environment in which such industry thrived. West of the industrial area, the coastal resort towns from Prestatyn to Llandudno were sustained by middle-class holiday-makers and the immigration of affluent pensioners.

In the mountains of the north-west, however, the picture was bleaker. The slate industry, weakened ever since the Penrhyn lockout, employed less than half its peak numbers by 1918, 6,600 men. Its export trade had been hit first by import tariffs in its biggest markets, Germany and France; then stopped completely by the war. In 1918, slate export amounted to no more than 1,592 tons, though there was some recovery after the war. For several years after the war, domestic demand went up, and total output rose from 164,000 tons in 1919 to 231,000 tons in 1922. The numbers employed reached 9,500 in 1922, but wages fell. Increases in the use of tiles, corrugated iron, and asphalt roofing, even the import of cheaper slate from Portugal and other countries, also contributed to a continuing fall in demand for Welsh slate.

Drastic change and the uncertainty that goes with it were not restricted to industry. Land-ownership underwent a convulsion in the years after the war. Even before World War I, there had been a trend for landowners to sell off parts of their estates to tenants. Between 1918 and 1922, it is estimated that almost a quarter of Welsh land changed ownership, resulting in a vastly greater number of owner-occupier farmers. The farmers had accumulated some capital during the war, when farm incomes had gone up, but rents had fallen. To landowning interests, land did not seem a worthwhile investment any longer, though few proprietors sold off their entire estates. They preferred to turn land into capital, to reinvest elsewhere. If the farmers had hoped for a continuance of their war-time prosperity, they were disappointed. As the slump of the 1920s continued, prices fell. Many who had borrowed in order to acquire their land were obliged to sell up.

In May 1926, the first and only General Strike in British industrial history took place. It lasted nine days. But it was founded on a miners' dispute that was to continue for six months before the strikers finally gave in and went back to work, again on the owners' terms. Another round of pay cuts, job losses, and victimisation of activists began. The number of trade union members fell dramatically. Almost half the Miners' Federation membership left it between 1926 and 1930 – some 70,000 men. Unemployment rose sharply, year by year. Then, in 1929, prices collapsed on the New York Stock Exchange, and did not recover. The years of the Depression had begun.

LIFE AND LEISURE IN THE TWENTIES

This is the period which is also recalled as the 'Roaring Twenties', and there is no reason to doubt that they roared as loud in Wales as in any comparable region. Fashion was reaching further down the income scale, with the opening of multiple store branches in the bigger towns. Although the wartime jobs for women reverted to men, and tens of thousands of women found themselves relegated to domestic chores, the war had emancipated them in various ways. Women over thirty had the vote from 1918. Women rode bicycles, smoked in public, cut their hair short. Skirts for the first time rose above the knees. Skating rinks were already popular places. Now cinemas and dance halls also competed for the spare cash of a younger generation that wanted to enjoy itself. Buses linked villages to towns and made it easier to get out in the evening. Converted army trucks hauled side-shows and even small circuses from place to place on an annual circuit. At home, recorded music could be played on the gramo-phone. From 1923, those who possessed or had access to a wireless set could listen to the BBC, broadcasting from Cardiff, though the programmes were mostly relayed from London. One effect of the war had been to give greater earning power to the young, and for young workers living at home with their parents, as most of them did, this meant disposable income even after their contribution to the domestic budget.

For the unemployed and the long-term sick, life was grim. Mining families suffered grinding hardship during the long strikes of 1921 and 1926. But despite the pay-cuts, for most of the time, most wage-earners were in work. And there was a steadily increasing number of salaried professionals to administer and maintain an increasingly complex social infrastructure. The numbers of teachers, civil servants, medical staff, engineers, shop managers and other

'middle-class' workers grew steadily. Although very often 'chapel' in their attitudes to certain leisure activities, these were people who could afford to acquire
radios, pianos and gramophones. Leisure pursuits established for two generations or more, like rugby and football, remained universally popular with the
male sex of all classes, chiefly as spectator sports, and new grounds were built,
with very basic grandstands of corrugated iron, for village and district clubs.
Other old-time pursuits like cockfights and dogfights largely died away. Boxing
remained a popular sport, though increasingly organised in gyms and clubs,
rather than in bare-knuckle bouts behind a shed. The rise of league football,
and the widespread use of the telephone, created new opportunities for the old
national pastime of betting. Off-course betting on horse-races was illegal, but
furtive characters on street corners waited to take bets and find out on the
'blower' what the result was. More respectable activities were also possible: the
long-established choral tradition was still strong; few places did not have a brass
band or silver band; many occupants of terraced houses had become allotment
holders and vied with one another for prizes at produce shows. The shorter
working day, the increasing trend to make Saturday a half- or even whole-day
holiday, helped to encourage an ever-widening range of pastimes. Against the
backdrop of gathering economic doom, which we see with a hindsight denied
to those who lived at the time, it should not be forgotten that people sought to
lead normal lives and were keen to have a good time whenever they could.

THE DEPRESSION IN INDUSTRY

Even after the full impact of world recession set in from 1929 onwards, its worst
effects were contained in particular areas. The anthracite coalfield continued to
experience steady demand for its hard, smokeless coal, and unemployment
levels there never reached the heights known in the Rhondda and further east.
The non-ferrous metals industry of the Swansea-Llanelli area also maintained a
steady level of activity. Dockyard and transport workers were laid off. But the
most desperate cases were the mining communities in the old steam and bituminous coal mining districts. From 1928 the government had set up the Industrial Transference Board, intended to facilitate the movement of people from
areas of high unemployment to areas where new jobs were being developed.
South Wales was the most prominent area designated for this form of clearing,
though the scheme was essentially aimed at younger unmarried men, and a
high proportion of the south Wales unemployed were older and married. A
survey of the region was conducted in 1933, and its reporter recommended that
'surplus' men and youths up to the age of forty-five should be strongly encouraged to leave, and that a training centre for the purpose be set up. There was a
definite feeling in government and administrative circles that, just as these

towns had grown to serve an expanding industry, they should now be allowed to shrink and wither with the decline of that industry. Such extreme laisser-faire was never official policy, but the measures taken to alleviate unemployment were late, severely restricted in their scope, and inadequately funded. In 1934 the region was one of several designated 'Special Areas', but the commissioners appointed to promote new employment had little success.

By June 1932 there were almost 150,000 registered unemployed in south Wales. At that time, more than half the miners in the Rhondda could not find work, and three years later there was very little improvement. In June 1935 there were only 52.5 per cent of the working population of Merthyr actually in work, even if only part-time. For Dowlais the figure was 20 per cent – eight out of ten had no job.

The position was almost as bad among the iron and steel workers. For those parts of the country, the decade 1928–38 was a grim one. Independently of

---

'THE PLACES OF MY BOYHOOD'

There has always been an element of ambivalence in the way the industrial valleys have been seen and described. On the one hand there is the vibrant spirit of community which flourished in the close-packed streets; on the other the sense of a natural environment blighted by slag and smoke. Community, family and individual livelihoods were secured by long, laborious and dangerous work, far underground. 'Don't send your sons down the dark dreary mines,' ran a line from a folk song about the Gresford disaster: 'They'll be damned like the sinners in hell.' Yet without the mine, the community faced extinction. There was a grim irony in the situation, arousing a love-hate relationship, which is captured in Idris Davies's poem 'The Places of My Boyhood', written in the Depression years:

> In the places of my boyhood
> The pit-wheels turn no more,
> Nor any furnace lightens
> The midnight as of yore.
>
> The slopes of slag and cinder
> Are sulking in the rain,
> And in derelict valleys,
> The hope of youth is slain.
>
> And yet I love to wander
> The early ways I went,
> And watch from doors and bridges
> The hills and skies of Gwent.
>
> Though blighted be the valleys
> Where man meets man with pain,
> The things my boyhood cherished
> Stand firm, and shall remain.

---

government agencies, many people moved out in order to find, not only new jobs, but a standard of living and even a self-respect which they could no longer associate with the mining and steel towns. Some came back, but more than 60 per cent of those who left, stayed away. As late in the decade as 1937, unemployment levels in Merthyr Tydfil stood at nearly 36 per cent; in Pontypridd that year the level still exceeded 40 per cent. Of those, 17 per cent had been in the register for five years or more. This indicated the plight of men in their thirties or forties, probably with a family. Even as jobs became available, they found it hard to compete against younger men. On the showpiece new industrial estate at Treforest, which employed 2,196 people in June 1939, well over half the workers were aged eighteen or less.

THE EFFECTS OF THE DEPRESSION

The depression years left their deep mark on Welsh society. A generation that grew up in the late 1920s and 30s, and then found itself conscripted into a new European war, formed its own strong views about how society should be run. Other factors came into this shaping of opinion, too. Not only in the towns, but also in the countryside of Wales there was a great deal of squalor and disease. Though county councils had been democratically elected since 1892, the councillors tended to come from the prosperous mercantile Liberal element, and usually showed great reluctance to spend money or embark on any kind of social initiative. The most telling figures are those which compare the incidence of tuberculosis in Wales to that in the rest of Great Britain. In the national campaign to eradicate the disease, Wales fell far behind. In the period 1916–20, the death rate from TB in Scotland, at 147 per 100,000, was greater than that of Wales, at 144. By 1935, the rate in both countries had fallen, but Scotland's was 74 while Wales's was 92. The rural counties were sluggish in their efforts to improve water supplies and their medical service. In 1933, the seven counties of Britain with the highest TB mortality rates were all in Wales, including the country districts of Anglesey, Meirionydd and Cardigan. This reflected the poor state of much rural housing. Farmworkers' and estate workers' cottages were in many cases unimproved hovels without running water. Town councils had usually done little about slum clearance. Whilst councils found it extremely difficult to raise funds when their income from rates was falling, they showed little initiative in pursuing such government grants as were available, or even in agitating for more assistance.

A committee of inquiry into the Welsh anti-tuberculosis effort gave a damning report in 1939. Its chairman, Clement Davies, Liberal MP for Montgomery, produced a catalogue of shortcomings, delays and failures in provision which lay very much more in the record in local government of his own party than with the Labour-run towns, which had in most cases been more energetic and systematic in tackling the problem (though in the Rhondda, as in some counties, there were times when the TB mortality figures went up rather than down).

In the countryside, the farming communities too had to tighten their belts. They suffered from reduced demand and reduced prices. In turn this affected the rural industries that lived on agriculture. Already beginning to be hit by mechanisation, the local blacksmith, the farrier, the wheelwright began to close down. Farmers, few of whom yet had tractors, had to go further to find an artisan. Instead, more widely spread, there grew up the local garage and workshop, often with a couple of buses to operate local services. Migration out of the rural areas continued. From 1933 an increasing number of farmers went from arable and stock-rearing to dairy farming, encouraged by the setting up of the Milk Marketing Board, which gave a guaranteed price for fresh milk and ensured its distribution.

DECLINING LIBERAL PARTY FORTUNES

Through the 1930s, political life in Wales was not in accord with the state of the parties at Westminster. In 1931, following the resignation of Ramsay Macdonald's ineffective second Labour government, Wales provided sixteen of the forty-six Labour members at Westminster. Through the years of the national government and the Conservative administrations that followed it, Welsh constituencies returned a majority of Labour and Liberal members. The Liberals were far from united. Four 'National Liberals' supported the national government, four 'official Liberals' were to break away from it in 1932; four 'Lloyd George' Liberals, including of course the ex-premier himself, ranged themselves in opposition together with the surviving rump of the Labour Party. Despite the Liberal split, politics in Wales showed themselves to be less febrile than in England, where the national government found proportionately far greater support. In the 1935 election, Labour won eighteen of Wales's thirty-six seats. The Liberals still had Lloyd George, who remained a national figure in the British context and who in the 1930s was preaching the need for the kind of 'New Deal' in Britain that the presidency of Franklin Roosevelt had provided for the USA. He commanded respect and attention, but it was plain that his split and a much-reduced party could not provide the support and drive that his policies needed. In 1935, Labour salvaged itself from the disastrous Macdonald years and re-emerged as a party with its own policies and solutions. Among its most powerful orators was Aneurin Bevan, MP for Ebbw Vale, who articulated the need that so many people felt for a new society ordered on different principles to that which had led into the Depression. Another significant figure, very different to Bevan, was James Griffiths, president of the South Wales

Miners' Federation, who entered parliament in a by-election at Llanelli in 1936, beating a 'National Liberal' by 16,000 votes. Both would be Labour cabinet ministers, with sharply opposing views on what was best for Wales.

THE FOUNDING OF PLAID CYMRU

In 1925, in a temperance hotel in Pwllheli, during the National Eisteddfod, six men became the founders of a new movement, first called Plaid Genedlaethol Cymru, later simply Plaid Cymru. They did not invent the Nationalist movement on that day; the new organisation was a merger of two small groups, Byddin Ymreolwyr Cymru and Y Mudiad Cymreig, the Welsh Home Rule Army and the Welsh Movement respectively. Its original aims were chiefly concerned with promoting the use of Welsh as the administrative and official language of the country; the Welsh Movement strand taking priority rather than the Home Rule Army one. Nationalism within the British Isles was a live and current theme. In Ireland twenty-six counties had formed the 'Free State' since 1922, and a violent guerrilla movement, Sinn Fein, still fought for the six counties of Northern Ireland to be included. In Scotland, the Home Rule Association had been refounded in 1918, and in 1921 a Scots National League

---

ANEURIN BEVAN (1897–1960)

A miner's son from Tredegar who became a mineworker himself at thirteen, in the year of the Tonypandy riots, Bevan was chairman of his pit's union lodge by the time he was nineteen. In 1919 he went to attend the Central Labour College in London, where he was bad at getting up in the morning but an intense and original debater. Returning to the erratic employment of the 1920s, he resumed activity as a trade unionist and socialist orator and agitator, and in 1929 was elected Labour MP for Ebbw Vale, which he represented until his death. Never afraid to take an independent line, he began drilling squads of unemployed workers in the early 1930s, to resist attacks from police or fascists. His fierce but always cogently argued opposition to capitalism, and his ability to expound socialist policy made him an increasingly important figure in Labour circles. In 1945 he was appointed Minister of Health in the new Labour government, charged with bringing the National Health Service into being. This was duly achieved, despite heavy opposition from the medical establishment, in 1948. Always on the left wing of the party, Bevan resigned in April 1951 over the decision to impose charges for spectacles and dentures. The existence of the 'Bevanite' wing contributed to the disunity of the party in the 1950s, until an uneasy truce in 1957, when he became deputy leader. A major row with his own old colleagues on the left erupted when he supported Britain's possession of nuclear weapons, insisting 'We should not go naked into the conference chamber.'

Bevan's Welshness was never in doubt, but his belief in centralism, in the need for unity among the workers of Britain, in the strength of numbers, meant that he was hostile to any suggestion of self-government for Wales. Unlike Lloyd George, he could never have been described as an unofficial minister for Wales.

Aneurin Bevan with Huw T. Edwards at Corwen Pavilion, 1951

seeking full independence was set up. E.T. John, Liberal MP for East Denbighshire, had founded a Welsh National League before 1914, the year in which he introduced a Welsh Home Rule Bill, which never got beyond a first reading. (John has been castigated as 'desperately dull' but this is quite beside the point. Dull men can make revolutions in the right conditions. The conditions – not least in 1914 – were not right for E.T. John.) In its early years Plaid Cymru was not a political party, certainly not seeking political office. It was very small. If anyone in the political mainstream took note of it all, as Lloyd George did, it was only to deride it.

The days of Lloyd George's heavy flirtation with Cymru Fydd were long past. Especially in the 1920s and 30s, he was proposing Britain-wide solutions for what he saw as Britain-wide problems. From a different angle, this was also true of the Labour Party. Bevan saw the Labour movement as that of the whole British working class, and believed that only by acting collectively could it achieve its aims of a fair and just democratic society. It may be tempting to trace a thread of continuous connection from the founding of the Welsh National Party in 1925 to the establishment of a national assembly in 1999, and to trace a dotted line from there into the future … but it is only correct in so far as Plaid Cymru managed to lead a continuous existence. At certain times it commanded

SAUNDERS LEWIS

Of the six founders of Plaid Cymru, Lewis (1893–1985) was the most influential. He was actually born in Cheshire, of a Welsh-speaking family, and studied English and French at Liverpool University: his interest in France was central to his life. In 1922 he became lecturer in Welsh at University College, Swansea. In 1925, with the Rev. Lewis Valentine, Moses Gruffydd, H.R. Jones, Fred Jones, and D.J. Williams, he was a founder of Plaid Genedlaethol Cymru, and in 1926 became its president. Lewis was an accomplished writer of poetry and prose, and an excellent public speaker. With his friend Ambrose Bebb, another francophile, he was strongly influenced by the right-wing French writer and *homme politique,* Charles Maurras, whose Action Française movement he hoped to emulate in Wales. In 1932 he became a Catholic, though this was long kept secret; and in 1936 he was one of the saboteurs of Pen y Berth. Even before his conviction he was dismissed from his job. On trial at the Old Bailey in London, he refused to speak in any language but Welsh, and was jailed for nine months. After prison he made his living as a journalist, writer and part-time farmer. He resigned as leader of Plaid Cymru in 1939. In 1952 he was appointed lecturer in Welsh at Cardiff, retiring in 1957, and living in relative seclusion until his celebrated BBC broadcast lecture of 1962, *Tynged yr laith,* which stimulated the passionate action of the Welsh Language Society. Lewis became its president. A prolific writer in both Welsh and English, he wrote plays, novels, poems, essays and literary criticism; his last work, *Excelsior,* was published in 1980.

the attention of the whole country, but there was no continuous chain of action and reaction prompted by Plaid Cymru. With a membership in 1930 of 500, it was seen chiefly as a Welsh language pressure-group run by scholars, somewhat more political than the much more obviously successful Urdd Gobaith Cymru, the Welsh League of Youth, founded in 1922 by Ifan ab Owen Edwards. This too arose out of the perceived need to defend and promote the language, especially to the rising generation. It was to be very influential, through local branches, summer camps, *eisteddfodau*, organised games and books and magazines. Through it the first private Welsh-language school was started at Aberystwyth in 1939. By 1934, Urdd Gobaith Cymru claimed to have 50,000 members.

WELSH LANGUAGE AND THE BID
FOR SELF-RULE

In 1929, Plaid Cymru contested one seat in the general election, in Caernarfonshire, achieving a derisory result. From 1932, the party's stated aim became much more political. It was to gain self-government for Wales. The country would in effect be a dominion of the British Empire, like Canada or Australia, independent in every sense but still under the British Crown. A number of intellectuals and writers, like Kate Roberts, gave their support. Although the membership remained small, and the circulation of the two journals, *Y Ddraig Goch* and *Welsh Nationalist*, very modest, the views of Plaid Cymru activists were followed and known by many people who would have stopped short long before joining the party.

The events of 1936, when three senior Plaid Cymru members set fire to a controversial new RAF bombing school set up at Pen-y-Berth in the Llyn peninsula, gripped the nation for a time. After the sabotage, they gave themselves up. Instead of being tried in Wales, the case was transferred to London, causing indignation among many people with no great sympathy for their action. The three were sentenced to nine months' imprisonment. After this, the profile of Plaid Cymru was much higher. Such direct action was done on an individual basis and not as part of the party's programme, but a young member, Gwynfor Evans, got the party conference to agree to non-violent direct action in 1938. In K.O. Morgan's trenchant phrase, however, as far as the mass of the population was concerned, Plaid Cymru was 'a small esoteric group

Saunders Lewis

of Utopian fanatics' (p. 256) and would remain so for some decades.

For the Plaid Cymru members, the cause of the Welsh language and the cause of Welsh self-government became one. For many of them, the main reason for a government was to protect the language, rather than as the people's expression of identity. After all, unlike Scotland and Ireland, Wales had never had a parliament (other than Glyndwr's). There was no tradition to be restored. Such people need only to have looked across to independent Ireland to see that government backing could be the kiss of death to a minority language. And by now Welsh was very much the language of a minority of the population. By 1931 it was spoken by 37 per cent of the population. Many Welsh people were concerned for the survival of their language without feeling that independence was necessary to preserve it. In the 1930s, the growth of the Urdd movement offered some hope for the future, but it was clear that Welsh was being used less and less in any kind of general context. Industry, business and administration all used English. So did the schools and the colleges of the University. Newspapers and magazines were overwhelmingly in English. Then, as now, the great bulk of newspapers sold in Wales were published in England and (not as now) distributed across the country via the rail network. Political nationalism had its movement. Language nationalism, with many more adherents, had no single movement. The *eisteddfod* system provided this to some extent, but the focus of the National Eisteddfod on the past, on folklore, on a relatively narrow range of highly literary activity; indeed its whole robed and bardic ritual, separated it from the lively vernacular everyday Welsh spoken by those who attended it, with its neologisms needed to cope with twentieth-century life, from *telefon* to *psycho-analysis*. Individuals and spontaneously formed ginger groups hammered at the BBC, at the University of Wales, at the Ministry of Education, to do more for Welsh. But the slide in Welsh speaking went inexorably on.

THE LEGACY OF THE DEPRESSION

The 1930s were an unpleasant decade for Wales as for many other countries. Heavy industry was not killed off, and the mines and steel plants remained in place, to be fully activated again during the years of World War II. But particularly in the south, where the majority of the population lived, the Depression left a legacy which was only fully appreciated in the post-war years. Years which might have been spent in modernising and improving both industry and the living conditions of the people, were lost. Investment in new machinery, new buildings, new schools, new houses, was minimal. In the Denbighshire–Flintshire area, the problem was not so great. Its broader industrial base and its geographical links to England meant that the slump affected it less and for a shorter time. Road surfaces improved steadily throughout the decade – the commercial transport lobby had already come into existence, and private car ownership among the salaried class was becoming increasingly common as mass-production brought Fords and Austins into an acceptable price-bracket. The south had good railway links with England, via the Severn Tunnel and the south to north-west trunk lines, but its accessibility by road was poor. In 1936 a House of Commons Select Committee had declared that it saw no need for a road bridge across the Severn Estuary.

CHAPTER EIGHTEEN

World War II and After

WALES AT WAR

The politically aware among the Welsh people had closely followed overseas news during the 1920s and 30s, mostly with foreboding, as a renewed militarism took over in Italy and Germany, though sometimes too for inspiration. As a distinct people, if not in the political sense a nation, the Welsh felt an interest in the other small countries and peoples of Europe. A hundred and forty or so from among the most politically committed – almost all of them miners – went to Spain after 1936 to join the Republican cause in the Spanish Civil War. Even among the politically apathetic there was a growing realisation that war was coming and that, more obviously than in 1914, it was a 'just' war, in which countries with a belief in human rights and a tradition of civil liberty would have to fight to defend these rights not only on their own behalf but for others in other countries. As the British war machine was brought back into action and cranked up, so the gates of demand, so long half-closed, finally opened. Coal, iron, steel, metal products of all kinds, were wanted, urgently and in enormous quantities. The start of the war was embarrassing to the sizeable number of Communists in the mining valleys. The pact between Nazi Germany and Soviet Russia was hard to understand and harder to explain. For most people, however, there was no problem in identifying with the aim of the war.

For the first time since the farcical French invasion of 1797, war from the outside came to Wales, and this time it was no light matter. In 1940 and 1941, the factories and harbours of the south were targets for bombing raids. Between 19 and 21 February 1941, most of the centre of Swansea was destroyed by bombs and the subsequent fires. More than 11,000 houses in the city were damaged, and 387 people were killed. Cardiff, Newport and Pembroke Dock were also heavily bombed. In 1941, 985 civilians were killed in air raids. Here as elsewhere, the 'blitz' was stoically accepted and people went to extraordinary lengths to maintain business as usual.

As in World War I, government control reached into all key areas of industry and transport. Rationing was imposed on foodstuffs, clothing materials and petrol. One perhaps surprising result was that much of the population of Wales became better fed, on a more balanced and nutritious diet than they could have afforded during the 1930s. Women were once again welcomed – indeed drawn by every force the state could muster short of conscription – back into work.

New factories were built, for aircraft building in the north, for munitions in both north and south. The vast munitions complex at Bridgend, at its busiest, employed more than 37,000 people, the majority of them women. Airfields were laid out at many level sites near the coast, as part of the campaign to guard the Western Approaches. It was as a result of the wartime extension of RAF Valley that the Llyn Cerrig Bach hoard of weapons and iron implements came to light. The farmers, who had had a fairly lean time in the 1930s, were now encouraged to take more land into cultivation and to grow more crops, and national food distribution gave them a guaranteed price. 'British Summer Time' was extended by an extra hour, making it two hours out from Greenwich Mean Time; it could not extend the daylight but it gave a more effective agricultural working day.

The tradition of pacifism in Wales, which stemmed from the tenets of non-conformism, was not as strong as it had been in World War I, just as religion itself was not as strong. Although there was plenty of anti-German feeling, on the whole the animus of the war was ideological rather than national: Nazism, and its embodiment in Adolf Hitler, was the enemy, rather than Germans. There was less cheap and mindless 'patriotism' in World War II. A few strong-minded and high-principled people were jailed for expressing anti-war sentiments. Plaid Cymru, by opposing the war, heightened its distance from the average citizen. Its position was carefully thought out, and explained by its president, Professor J.E. Daniel: 'This is a clash of rival imperialisms from which Wales, like the other small nations of Europe, has nothing to gain but everything to lose … [Plaid Cymru] does not accept the right of England to conscript Welshmen into her army or regard it as the duty of Wales to help London beat Berlin.' As Welshmen trooped into the armed forces, and Welsh industry throbbed, roared, and lit up the night skies once again, this was an extreme minority view, and destined to stay such. Unlike Lloyd George, who eventually gained points for having opposed the Boer War, Plaid Cymru reaped no rewards from its anti-war stance. The Communists, on the other hand, became ardently and vocally bellicose once the German attack on Russia began.

TRADITIONS OF NON-CONFORMISM
ON THE WANE

One of the victims of the war was none other than the great Welsh non-conformist tradition itself. There was of course always a difference between non-conformity and the tradition with which it was associated, which carried so much non-religious freight, including the temperance movement and political anti-Toryism. There was also a difference between the group of non-conformist denominations, with their membership (still totalling over 400,000 in the

1920s), and the wider society, affected by the ethos which their beliefs, way of life and attitudes to others created. This ethos was shared by many who were not paid-up members of the chapel; and also by many Anglicans. A great many others lived under it, more or less restively or peacefully, accepting the social climate created by the clergy and their congregations. We have already met this sector of the population, slightly more than half of the total even in 1851, and by now an even greater proportion. Between 1926 and 1939, membership of the three main non-conformist sects fell by over 42,000.

By the 1930s much of the moral authority of the non-conformist ethos had broken down. Communities were open to many more external influences. People moved about far more readily and easily, and approval or disapproval within the community, whilst still important, was not as dominant a force as it once had been. A variety of new kinds of secular entertainment had grown up. Chapel purists might disapprove, but most people enjoyed them; again the influence of religion was weakened. In a world that had come to terms with Darwinism, that was absorbing the ideas of Sigmund Freud, and was beginning to learn something of the extraordinary thoughts of Albert Einstein, the funda-mental simplicities of the ministers were beginning to sound not only old-fash-ioned but irrelevant. The relaxations in the social framework that were accomplished during World War I were enhanced in the 1920s. In the crisis years of the 1930s, the chapels played a very minor role compared to elected councils, trade unions and government bodies. When 1939 initiated another six years of social upheaval, the change to a secular society was already well advanced. Indeed, it was remarkable to what extent the non-conformist tradi-tion, moth-eaten and frayed as it might be, often cloaking nothing but a cynical emptiness, clung on until the full advent of the consumerist, leisure-oriented, television-watching society of the 1960s and after.

POST-WAR WALES: SOCIAL AND POLITICAL CHANGE

With the end of the war in Europe, in May 1945, the people of Wales, as indeed throughout the rest of Great Britain, were ready for political change. In the general election of that year, the Labour Party won a comprehensive victory. In Wales, Labour had twenty-five seats and almost 60 per cent of the total votes cast. The Conservatives had four (including Caernarfon Boroughs, long the seat of Lloyd George, who had retired from the Commons and had been given an earldom shortly before his death). Liberals of various complexions had seven. Local government reflected the same pattern. As a constituent part of Great Britain, and as a Labour heartland, Wales was poised to accept and embrace swift social change.

The measures came in a steady flow. It was accepted that it was right for the state to own and control what Aneurin Bevan referred to as 'the commanding heights of the economy'. Only in this way could it also provide the benefits of the 'welfare state' proposed in the wartime Beveridge Report and eagerly awaited by millions of people for whom free medicine, free hospital treatment, free dentistry, had been an impossible dream. In some instances, Wales was recognised as a separate entity, as with the Welsh Gas Board, which took over all the town and city gas-works. There was also a South Wales Electricity Board, but the north was included with the Mersey region. Nationalising of the railways reflected the previous corporate pattern established in 1923: most of Wales fell into the Western Region of British Railways, with the Swansea–Shrewsbury and Holyhead–Chester lines in the London Midland region. The most triumphal moment was 1 January 1947, when the act nationalising the coal industry came into force. In 1947, the steel industry also was brought into public ownership, and work began on a vast new steelworks at Port Talbot.

Early 1947 was also the worst winter in living memory, with snow and ice over most of the country from January into March. Distribution of fuel, food and other essentials was difficult, and helped to form the memory of 'austerity' years, as, with rationing still enforced for many items, government and industry struggled to build a peacetime economy on the battered and frequently obsolescent manufacturing base inherited from six years of war and ten years of Depression before.

The pattern of the 1940s did not repeat that of the 1920s. Unemployment, though somewhat above the UK average, did not reach a critical level. Demand for the basic products of industrial south Wales remained steady. Government policy also sought to bring some balance into the industrial scene. The whole of south Wales was designated a development area, and manufacturing industries were steered towards it by a mixture of intervention and incentives. The vast munitions factories of Bridgend and Hirwaun were turned into industrial estates. 'Light industry' became an increasingly large employer, and, as did not happen in 1918, women remained a substantial element in the workforce. In 1946, though it still employed 116,000 people, the coal industry had been overtaken by general manufacturing as the largest source of employment.

NEW STIRRINGS OF NATIONALISM

English dissatisfaction with continuing 'austerity' brought about a minority Labour government in 1950 and a new Conservative administration in 1951. In Wales, however, Labour's fortunes were undiminished, with twenty-seven seats in the 1951 and 1955 elections. This massive disparity between the

TWO POETS

The two best-known poets of modern Wales were polar opposites in many ways, except that one wrote entirely in English, the other mostly in English. The elder and longer-lived, R.S. Thomas (1913–2000), born in Cardiff, always regretted his lack of cradle Welsh; he learned the language in his thirties as a country clergyman in north Wales. A fierce Welsh patriot and defender of Welsh culture, he often had harsh words for his fellow-citizens who did not seem to care if they were committing what he called 'cultural suicide'. He aroused controversy by supporting the burning of English-owned second homes: 'What is one death against the death of the whole Welsh nation?' His poetry is austere, questing, uncompromisingly opposed to a material civilisation; though it frequently opens up to a spare lyric beauty, his true concern is to get a sense of the nature of God.

Dylan Thomas (1914–53) was born in Swansea, where his father was English master at the grammar school; and he began writing verse while still a schoolboy. Restive in formal education, he left at sixteen and became a journalist. His first poems were published in 1934, the year he moved to London. In 1949 he and his wife came to live in Laugharne. He never learned Welsh and had no interest in Welsh politics, but his background profoundly influenced his work and the rhythms and cadences of spoken and sung Welsh are integral to it. His poems are expressive and often lush in their phrasing, with a vibrant vitality quite unlike the other Thomas's asceticism. His prose works have a strong poetic element, especially *Under Milk Wood* and *Portrait of the Artist as a Young Dog*. Though Dylan Thomas led a notably bohemian life, he was a meticulous literary craftsman. His premature death, in New York, was a direct consequence of heavy drinking.

wishes of the Welsh electorate and that of England, twenty times larger, might have prompted the question of devolution to arise again. In fact it did not, to any great extent. There was a portent of things to come, however, when in 1946 Plaid Cymru polled 20 per cent of the votes in a by-election at Aberdare. With Labour not only the party of government, but the party of the 'establishment' in Wales, the protest vote was moving to the Nationalists. Some senior Welsh Labour figures, notably James Griffiths, were sympathetic to the idea of devolved government in Wales, but Bevan, still immensely influential despite his resignation from the cabinet in 1951, was among those wholly opposed to it. In 1948, with Griffiths' keen support, and against Bevan's opposition, an Advisory Council for Wales was set up, combining local authority, employers' and trade unions' representatives, but it was powerless. The British Labour Party, needing its phalanx of Welsh MPs, just as the Liberal Party had needed its Welsh supporters seventy years before, took a poor view of any plan that might reduce their number. The first government to create a separate Welsh ministry was Churchill's Conservative administration of 1951, though it could not find a suitable minister in any seat nearer than Liverpool. In 1954 the 'National Liberal' Gwilym Lloyd George took on the role for two years; though his own Welsh credentials were of the highest order, he actually represented a seat in Newcastle upon Tyne. The cosmetic nature of these appointments was underlined by the government's rubber-stamping, in 1957, of the flooding of the Tryweryn Valley in Meirionydd to provide water for Liverpool, despite intense opposition from Wales, and by the government's persistent ignoring of the proposals and recommendations made by the Advisory Council for Wales.

From 1949 to 1956, a 'Parliament for Wales' movement rose and fell. Open to all, irrespective of party, it included Socialists, Communists, Liberals and Conservatives, but in small numbers and on an individual basis. The only party to involve itself was Plaid Cymru. By this time, under the leadership of Gwynfor Evans, it was losing its old image of the party of a small intellectual and rather eccentric group, proudly waiting in the cold for the Welsh to wake up and join its cause. It was beginning to take an interest in local issues, and cultivate the 'grass roots' of support. There was still a long way to go, and its electoral fortunes during the 1950s did not offer much hope, although the trend of support was slowly upwards.

WELSH LANGUAGE MILITANTS AND SUCCESS FOR PLAID CYMRU

The contrast between linguistic and political nationalism was heavily underscored in 1962. A BBC talk by Saunders Lewis, a founder of Plaid Cymru back in 1925, but for some years self-exiled from the political scene, created a sensation. *Tynged yr Iaith*, 'The Fate of the Language', was his theme, and with it he returned to the original motivation of 1925, the protection and promotion of the language as the crucial definer of Welsh identity. The census of the previous year had shown that only a quarter of the population spoke Welsh. Lewis foresaw its disappearance into limbo with Manx and Cornish unless 'revolutionary methods' were employed. The timing was right. In June 1962 Cymdeithas yr Iaith Gymraeg, the Welsh Language Society, was founded, at a Plaid Cymru summer school. Lewis was made its president. Somewhat to the embarrassment of the Nationalist party, the movement took off with dramatic speed and a vigour not seen in Welsh political life since 1945. Its tactics were based on direct action, confrontation, and harassment of officialdom. It was a youth movement, but one more akin to the revolting students of Paris a few years later than to the demure hymn-singers and games-players of Urdd Gobaith Cymru in the 1920s (soon the militants were in Urdd as well). In the words of Gwyn A. Williams: '... young people stormed all over Wales, staging sit-ins, wrecking TV masts, generally making life hell for any kind of official ...' (p. 288). The campaign went on for several years and was at least partly responsible for the 1967 Welsh Language Act, based on a report on the status of the Welsh language by the Hughes-Parry Committee – which a Tory government had set up in 1961 – and which gave equal validity within Wales to Welsh and English. By 1971, however, the ratio of Welsh speakers was significantly down again, at 20 per cent.

Many people who would not themselves have daubed road signs or blockaded post offices nevertheless felt that in some way the agitators were doing the right thing. The success of *Tynged yr Iaith* perhaps prompted the actions of a very small group, the Free Wales Army, who sought to introduce terrorism for political ends, on the model of the Irish Republican Army. Bombs went off at government offices and public buildings. A child was seriously injured. With no roots in Welsh tradition, and a widespread sense of alarm and revulsion, it had no hope of securing the kind of community support that sustained the Republican movement in Northern Ireland.

In successive elections the voters continued to remain indifferent to Plaid Cymru. In 1964 Labour returned to power at Westminster, and the new cabinet included the first Secretary of State for Wales, in the person of James Griffiths. A Welsh Office was set up, with limited powers extending over housing, local government, roads; other areas would follow in 1969, including health, agriculture and education. There was no Welsh budget, and the Treasury and Home Office were reluctant to yield any of their authority. But it was an important development. From it stems the large, well-paid and vocal administrative cadre which characterises present-day Cardiff. In 1966, in the Carmarthen by-election following the death of the Liberal-turned-Labour Lady Megan Lloyd George, Gwynfor Evans, who had long nursed the seat for Plaid Cymru, was elected as the party's first Westminster MP, where he took the oath of allegiance in Welsh. This success was maintained in by-elections at Caerphilly and Rhondda in 1967 and 1968, where in each case huge and seemingly perpetual Labour majorities were brought down to a danger margin by Plaid Cymru candidates. The party had come in from the cold, and in from the rural fastnesses, in a big way. In the 1970 general election, when a Conservative government was returned, it fell back again, losing Carmarthen to Labour. But it was now definitely the party of protest, the people's alternative, and the future no longer seemed so bleak.

THE CHANGING PATTERN OF LIFE AND WORK

There was a great deal for the people to protest, or at least feel concern, about. Through the 1940s and 50s, the pattern of life, industry, and business in Wales was still very much on the pre-war model. Colliery winding gear still rattled and spun above the rooftops of the valley towns. Steam trains ran through the mountains, linking Carmarthen to Aberystwyth, the Cambrian Coast to Wrexham, Brecon to Swansea. Motor cars, usually black in colour, were owned only by the better-off. Football league teams recruited players from their own towns, and paid them a workman's wage. Horse-drawn milk-carts went through the streets. Working men wore flat caps. Housewives in turban-like headscarves scrubbed their doorsteps daily. The town grammar schools were attended by neatly uniformed girls in gym tunics and boys in short trousers. Holidays were spent staying with relations or in the boarding houses and hotels of places like Tenby, Porthcawl, Rhyl and Prestatyn. Few homes had refrigerators or washing machines. Central heating was for public buildings only. The sound of singing in Welsh could still be heard from High Street chapels on a Sunday morning. And on that day the pubs stayed shut. Signs of novelty and change were present – new factories, television sets from the early 50s, the travel agent offering holidays in France – but the general pattern was a familiar and well-established one.

Through the 1960s and 70s this pattern changed with almost bewildering rapidity. In 1960 the number of mine workers was 106,000. In 1979 this was down to 30,000 and it was clear that there were further losses to come. Coal, synonymous with Wales for more than a century and a half, was now a minor element in the Welsh economy, its market eroded by the huge expansion in the use of oil, natural gas and nuclear power. Expensive to extract, Welsh coal could not compete against the Yorkshire collieries and foreign imports. It was a sad irony that the cost of modernising Welsh pits and improving their safety facilities, tasks tackled more vigorously under public ownership, added to their operating costs and helped to make them uneconomic. Meanwhile the oil complex around the Milford Haven anchorage grew steadily until there were six refineries in the area, and in terms of tonnage it was among the world's major ports. In the mid-1960s, Wales lost more than half its railway lines and stations. Though many were uneconomic and under-used, this caused great disruption across the country and helped to inflame the reputation of Wales for bad communications, which worked against new commercial and industrial investment. Up to the 1960s, the steel industry remained in a vibrant condition, with much new investment at Port Talbot, Velindre and Trostre. Another giant steelworks arose at Llanwern, east of Newport. But in the 1970s, world supply of steel began to exceed demand, and the price of Welsh steel was undercut by output from Germany, Japan and Korea. Older steel plants like East Moors and Ebbw Vale shut down; newer ones went on to short time and began to trim their work-force to a minimum in order to reduce costs. In south Wales, especially, such drastic decline could have led to a replication of the 1930s, but by now a much more diversified industrial base had been established. 'Inward investment', subsidised by government money, lay behind most of these new factories. American, European, Japanese and Korean companies set up branch factories in Wales. British or Welsh enterprises tended to be in the service sector. Many of the new developments, whether light industry or commercial, offered most jobs to women, and the proportion of women in the total workforce rose steadily.

Social change happened on a corresponding scale. The two-tier system of grammar and secondary modern schools, established by the 1944 Education Act, was changed to one of comprehensive schools, a development pioneered in Anglesey. In 1961, 10.1 per cent of Welsh secondary schoolchildren attended comprehensive schools; by 1985, it was 99 per cent. With so many women at work, the mother-centred pattern of family life changed. Often it was the husband who became the partner staying at home. An increased divorce rate and the rapidly growing number of one-parent families, along with a growth in population, put pressure on the housing stock. Many town houses were converted into flats. The mass production of domestic appliances saved labour and shopping time. A fast-growing 'personal finance' industry made it possible for people to buy items otherwise beyond their means – fridges, cars, dish-washers, and, for a time, the rapid inflation of money-value in the 1970s made hire-purchase relatively painless. As the Welsh became a nation of consumers, so the pattern of retailing changed. Hundreds of small specialist shops, drapers, haberdashers, corner grocery stores, ironmongers, fishmongers, bakers, closed down as supermarkets began to appear, followed by out-of-town shopping centres.

RESTRUCTURING – OR DISMANTLING?

In 1974 another set of landmarks was removed as the system of boroughs and counties was re-formed into a small number of regional and urban authorities. The names of ancient kingdoms were borrowed to colour the change with a sense of historic continuity – Gwynedd and Powys reappeared, though Dyfed was favoured over Deheubarth. In the north-east there was Clwyd; in the south-east Gwent. Glamorgan was split into west, mid, and south. The new disposition found few admirers. Meanwhile a wider political dimension was opening up. In the referendum held the following year, two-thirds of Welsh voters came out in favour of joining the European Common Market. In this choice they ignored the advice of most of their politicians.

Farming in Wales benefited from British membership of the Common Market (as it then was). The Common Agricultural Policy almost doubled the subsidies to Welsh agriculture between 1977 and 1985, though the 'administration' required of farmers went up by an even greater degree. For a time farm incomes went up and there was much investment in new mechanical equipment. Many farms increased in size, by acquiring smaller, less economically viable holdings, and the overall number of farms fell from 48,000 in 1970 to around 30,000 in 1990. From 1985, Welsh farming went into decline.

Restrictions on production, with cultivable fields being 'set aside', reductions in subsidies, the squeezing of basic purchase prices by the supermarket chains, all had a cumulative effect. In addition, the industry was buffeted by a succession of disasters – the Chernobyl nuclear fall-out of 1986; the 'mad cow disease' crisis that began in 1989 and resulted in the disappearance of the export market; the foot-and-mouth disease epidemic of 2001. The morale of the agricultural community was badly hit by these shocks, which had serious consequences for the economy of large areas like Powys, where almost a quarter of the working population were directly dependent on farming, and many others indirectly.

One historian calls it 're-structuring'; another calls it 'dismantling'. By 1980, society in Wales had changed greatly, and in many ways for the better, though the puritan might say such changes were exclusively material and were counterpointed by a spiritual decline. The definition of poverty accepted then would have brought a bitter smile to anyone who remembered the 1930s. The majority of people in the latter decades of the twentieth century were better-housed, better-clothed, better-fed and better-informed than they were in the 1950s.

Consumers had a vastly extended range of purchases, though charity shops and everything-under-a-pound shops reflected a substantial element of poverty as well as a healthy thriftiness. The Welsh took more foreign holidays, drank more alcohol, owned more cars, than ever before. Children stayed at school for longer and when leaving had a far wider choice of higher education options, within Wales and beyond, than previous generations. Many chose to go out of Wales; the University of Wales by contrast attracted English students in large numbers and by the 1990s more than half the undergraduates were English. These developments caused much concern in Welsh educational circles and also in the Welsh Language Society. Before or after their higher education, many students would spend a year travelling or working abroad, an opportunity almost impossible before the arrival of the jumbo jet.

Greater awareness of, and concern for, the fragility of the environment had led to much change in the old industrial landscape. The clearing or planting of colliery spoil tips was speeded up after the horrifying disaster at Aberfan in 1966, when a primary school was engulfed in slurry and more than a hundred children were killed. Townscapes, too, changed. Soot-encrusted buildings were scrubbed, the results surprising many who had supposed they were made of black stone. Many of the worst slum streets were demolished. There was much undistinguished new architecture of shopping centres and public buildings. In 1966, the first Severn Bridge was opened, at last giving south Wales a direct road link into England and extending the 'M4 corridor' of new industry into Monmouthshire and Glamorgan. Harri Webb's satirical lines commemorate the event:

The second Severn Bridge

Two lands at last connected
Across the waters wide,
And all the tolls collected
On the English side.

SELF-GOVERNMENT REJECTED

Despite these signs of prosperity, the pace of change, and the nature of many of the changes, brought about a sense of anxiety, even of decline, which was not confined to the linguistic nationalists. There was a general perception that an old order – which perhaps seemed more steady in retrospect than it had been in reality – was passing very fast, while the country was ill-prepared to assess and take up new options. Volatility at the polls was one sign of this uncertainty. In 1974 Labour, with twenty-four seats, saw its share of the total vote drop below 50 per cent for the first time since before 1945, and Plaid Cymru won Caernarfon and Meirionydd; in the second election of that year they again took Carmarthen, as well. In 1979, Labour was down to twenty-one seats, the Conservatives had eleven, Plaid Cymru two, the Liberals one. Between these two years, in 1975, the Nationalist movement suffered a traumatic blow when a referendum rejected the proposal for a Welsh Assembly by a huge majority, with only 11.8 per cent of the entire electorate supporting an Assembly and 46.5 per cent (or over 78 per cent of those voting) against. Even the two constituencies with Plaid Cymru MPs voted heavily against. After everyone, especially the Nationalists, had got their breath back, there was no shortage of explanations, including the somewhat toothless nature of the proposed Assembly, though no one could say whether the people would have been any more in favour of a body with greater powers. A complex pattern of attitudes and prejudices under-lay the devastatingly simple result. Cultural, linguistic, economic and political factors all played a part, pulling together or conflicting with each other in a way that has not yet been fully analysed and perhaps (given the 1999 result) never will be. What the referendum showed beyond doubt was that an absolute majority of Welsh voters did not want to take a step towards self-government.

THE DECLINE OF STEEL AND COAL

From 1979 the monetarist policies of Mrs Margaret Thatcher's Conservative government accelerated the decline of heavy industry and created the most serious post-war recession to affect Wales, with unemployment rising to over 13 per cent of the total workforce in 1984. There was a drastic reduction of workers in the steel industry, where in four years between 1979 and 1983, two thirds of the 63,000 employees of the British Steel Corporation lost their jobs as the industry was restored to private capital and underwent a restruc-turing. The coal miners, now organised in the South Wales branch of the National Union of Mineworkers, forewarned of the closure of seven pits, went on strike in 1981, the action spreading from south Wales to the rest of Britain. The strike brought reluctant concessions from the government and gave the NUM an illusory confidence in the strike weapon for the future. Having over-whelmingly rejected devolution, Wales once again found itself at the receiving end of policies which the majority had not voted for. Caught between the hard place of devolution and the rock of Thatcherism, the electorate seemed to have nowhere to turn to. In the election of 1983, the swing towards the Tories continued. They had their best result of the century, with fourteen Welsh seats to Labour's twenty, and capturing 31 per cent of the votes against Labour's 37.5 per cent. Meanwhile the government's war against the trade unions had dramatically reduced the number of days lost through industrial action and was steadily sapping the numerical strength and bargaining power of the unions themselves. The crisis came in 1984–85, with a mineworkers' strike that began in March 1984 and lasted for a year. Always the most militant of the coalfields, the miners of south Wales had not failed to notice that virtually no investment was planned for development of their area's reserves, compared to the industrially more placid (and more easily workable) Yorkshire field. In 1984 they numbered 20,000, down by over four-fifths in twenty years. Their future was at stake, and they knew it. This was a confrontation the government had no intention of losing, and it brought all the resources of anti-union legislation, and a massive police presence, to bear. On 1 March 1985, the miners voted to return to work, having gained nothing for a year of painful endurance. Their solidarity had been remarkable, even as the last expression of a remarkable tradition of cohesion and co-operation. By the end of 1986, more than half of them had been declared redundant, and nine more pits had closed.

LABOUR'S RECOVERY AND
THE WELSH ASSEMBLY

The general election of 1987 marked the end of the swing towards the ideological Conservatism of Mrs Thatcher, with Labour reclaiming four of its lost seats, perhaps aided by the fact that its leader since 1983, Neil Kinnock, was a Welshman and Welsh MP. Kinnock was a long-standing opponent of Welsh devolution, but, as D. Gareth Evans remarks in *A History of Wales, 1906–2000*, the Labour Party 'had manifested an enviable ability to renew itself.' The massive 'No' of 1975 had not silenced the Nationalist movement. In the 1992 election, Plaid Cymru took four seats, all in the Welsh-speaking rural regions, but it made minimal impact in the urban areas. Through the 1990s, however, there was a shift in the public perception of devolution. Its potential economic benefits were strongly argued. Conservative governments' fondness for unelected administrative bodies controlling many areas of public life from the water supply to industrial training and health care – the so-called quangos – attracted much opposition in Wales; and central government exercised control over most functions of the enlarged county councils. A Welsh Assembly was seen as one way of reclaiming Wales from Whitehall. These were pragmatic, debatable political points, far removed from the language issue. The European Union also began to be seen as a source of opportunity; its regional programmes, its familiarity with and official support for dual languages and minority languages, showed the value of some form of Welsh representation in Brussels. Even under the anti-devolutionist Tories, a Wales–European Centre was established in Brussels in 1992. John Major's Conservative administration also passed a new Welsh Language Act in 1993, confirming the equal status of Welsh and English.

In 1994 the twenty-year life of the 'regional' county councils was brought to an end by a local government act which replaced them with twenty-two 'unitary authorities', responsible for most aspects of local administration.

THE EMBLEMS OF WALES

The flag of Wales shows *y ddraig goch* ('the Red Dragon'), *passant*, on a ground divided into two horizontal strips of equal size, white above and green below. The dragon emblem is believed to have been introduced to Wales by the Romans, who used it as a military ensign. It was used by Cadwaladr in the seventh century, and before that may have been used on tribal war banners; hence the title 'Pendragon' for a war leader. It was one of the heraldic supporters in the coat of arms of the Tudor kings.

The origin of the leek as a national plant is lost in legend. It is associated with St David, and also with even earlier use as a druidic symbol. The wearing of a leek on St David's Day was well known by Shakespeare's time. In *King Henry V*, Gower asks Fluellen: 'But why do you wear your leek today? St Davy's Day is past.' One tradition relates it to Cadwallon's victory over the Northumbrians in 633, when his men plucked leeks from a field and wore them in order to identify themselves to one another in the battle. The victory, under the patronage of St David, was associated with this symbol, and the leek was then worn to commemorate the Saint's day each year.

The daffodil has only recently assumed the position of national emblem. The flower was very popular during the nineteenth century and its status was elevated by Lloyd George who wore it on St David's Day and used it in 1911 in ceremonies to mark the investiture of the Prince of Wales at Caernarfon.

Emblems of Wales: the Welsh dragon

Emblems of Wales: the leek　　　　　*Emblems of Wales: the daffodil*

Gwynedd and Powys continued to sprawl across the ancient and thinly populated counties of Anglesey, Carmarthen and Meirionydd, and Radnor, Montgomery and Brecknock; but most other authorities were more compact. Monmouthshire reappeared, and a new district of Conwy was formed out of parts of Denbighshire and the eastern edge of Gwynedd. In the first elections for these councils, a resurgent Labour Party took control of fourteen, a portent for the general election of 1997 in which its share of the vote once again went over 50 per cent, and it took thirty-four out of forty Welsh seats. Plaid Cymru had four seats, the Liberals two. For the first time since the Liberal landslide of 1906, Wales returned no Conservative MPs at all.

Labour was pledged to hold a new referendum on a Welsh Assembly, and did so speedily. The poll, on 18 September 1997, gave a knife-edge result: 50.3 per cent of those voting said 'Yes'; 49.7 per cent said 'No'. Just over half the eligible voters turned out. A simple majority was all that was needed. The Assembly was agreed. In 1985, a pessimistic Gwyn A. Williams wrote that: 'the Welsh electorate in 1979 wrote *finis* to nearly two hundred years of Welsh history.' Now a new page was turned. In May 1999 the first Assembly elections, under a system of proportional representation, were held, and provided a rude shock to Labour. Although much the largest party, with twenty-eight of the sixty seats, it was not in a majority. And Plaid Cymru, with seventeen seats (and also strongly established in many local councils), was the major opposition party. It had scored

253

remarkable victories in the Rhondda and Llanelli, among other places. The Conservatives had nine seats; the Liberals (who formed a coalition with Labour) had six.

Welsh and English were designated official languages of the Assembly (with instantaneous interpretation available for the numerous members with no command of Welsh). For a body with very little economic power, its first years had their stormy moments. In 2000 a vote of no confidence led to the resignation of the First Secretary, Alun Michael (who had suffered by being seen too obviously as Downing Street's man for the job), and his replacement by Rhodri Morgan. In early 2001, the possible closure of the Llanwern Steelworks, as a direct consequence of the strength of the pound sterling, became the first major test of the Assembly's ability to manage the country's economy. Among its eighteen devolved policy fields, economic development is included, as well as agriculture, health, housing, education, social services, and, of course, the Welsh language.

WELSH IDENTITY AT THE END OF THE MILLENNIUM

By the 1990s, what had seemed an irreversible slide in the number of Welsh speakers was at last arrested, or at least, the rate of decline was greatly slowed. The percentage of Welsh speakers in 1981 was 18.9; ten years later it was 18.6. Distribution of Welsh speakers was still heavily tilted towards the countryside. They formed 61 per cent of the inhabitants of Gwynedd, but only 6.5 per cent in South Glamorgan and 2.4 per cent in Monmouthshire. An important aspect concealed within those figures is an increase in the numbers of young people able to speak Welsh. Educational initiatives such as Mudiad Ysgolion Meithrin, the Welsh nursery school movement, the establishment of Welsh-medium primary and secondary schools, and the inclusion of Welsh as a core subject in the national curriculum, appear to be having an effect.

Intense debate still goes on as to what kind of national community Wales is; and what, in the twenty-first century, constitutes Welshness. By the end of the twentieth century, great changes had taken place. One historian notes that: '… all the evidence suggests that Welsh society has entered a post-Christian phase' (D. Gareth Evans, *A History of Wales, 1906–2000*). Wales also seemed to be entering a post-industrial phase, with most of the new jobs available being in service industries such as telephone call-centres, financial services companies and in the social services. In 1997 the combined workforce of the coal, steel and non-ferrous metals industry accounted for less than 3 per cent of the total numbers employed. A hundred years ago, there were still many isolated, small rural communities. Many of these are now abandoned, and none are beyond

The new Welsh Assembly Building under construction in Cardiff Bay

the reach of the motor car. The electricity grid reaches everywhere, and television, telephone and the Internet link every part of the country with instant global communication. Although their numbers are very small, new Welsh children are being born into Sikh, Moslem, Hindu, Chinese and other immigrant communities, and the number of Welsh residents born in England also continues to increase.

Chapter Sixteen looked at the historical perspective, both ahead and behind, of a sixty-year-old Welsh person in 1880. That person's great-great-grandchild, born in 1930, and aged seventy in 2000, could look back on an at least equally dramatic era of change in industry and technology; and an even more radical pattern of change in Welsh society. Of the future to be anticipated by today's ten-year-olds, any prediction is likely to look foolish in a few years' time. The community that is Wales is less static than at any time in its past. The only confident predictions that can be made are that change will continue, and so will the Welsh people.

> A vineyard placed in my care is Wales, my country,
> To deliver unto my children
> And my children's children
> Intact: an eternal heritage.
>> Saunders Lewis, *Buchedd Garmon*, translated by D.M. Lloyd

A Chronology of Events in Wales

43
- Claudian invasion of Britain.

50
- Romans fighting the Ordovices, Silures and other tribes.

51
- Caratacus defeated in Ordovician country.

60
- Paullinus undertakes the conquest of Mon (Anglesey).

78
- South Wales completely occupied by the Romans.
- Agricola conquers Mon.

212
- All free men in the Roman Empire are made Roman citizens.

255
- Rebuilding of the Roman barracks at Caerleon.

367
- Picts and Scots overrun the province of Britannia.

383
- Magnus Maximus (Macsen Wledig) made emperor in Britain.

409
- End of Roman Imperial rule.

429
- St Germanus visits Britain; 'Alleluia' victory over the Picts.
- About this time St Patrick writes to Ceredig Wledig, ruler of Strathclyde.

461
- A British bishop attends a church gathering at Tours.

c.500
- The battle of Mount Badon is fought around this time.

c.537
- Battle of Camlan said to have been fought around this time; death of Arthur.

c.540
- Gildas writing *De Excidio et Conquestu Britanniae*.

c.550
- St David is at work converting the pagans of Dyfed.
- The poem *Y Gododdin* is composed.
- Outbreaks of plague occur.

c.555
- St Samson, born in Wales, is a bishop in Brittany around this time.

575
- Rhydderch defeats Gwenddoleu ap Ceidio in the battle of Arthuret in Cumberland.

577
- Battle of Dyrham leaves south Wales exposed.

c.588
- St David dies around this time.

c.602
- St Augustine, Archbishop of Canterbury, meets the Welsh bishops.

c.615
- Aethelfrith of Northumbria defeats the Britons at Chester.

633
- Cadwallon, in alliance with Penda of Mercia, defeats the Northumbrians.

634
- Defeat and death of Cadwallon, in battle with Oswald of Deira.

655
- Oswiu defeats the Britons at the Winwaed river; Cadfael of Gwynedd deserts the day before. Britons of north and south now separated.

664
- Synod of Whitby: debate between Roman and Celtic church practices.

682
- Plagues this year; one victim is Cadwaladr, son of Cadwallon.
- From around this time, Aberffraw

becomes the main seat of the kings of Gwynedd.

722
- The Welsh win two battles over the Mercians in south Wales.

c.730
- Around this time, Seisyll, King of Ceredigion, conquers Ystrad Tywi to form the kingdom of Seisyllwg.

768
- Welsh church accepts Roman date for Easter and Roman tonsure.

c.790
- Offa's Dyke constructed.

c.800
- The *Historia Brittonum*, attributed to Nennius, is written.

812
- Degannwy is burned by lightning.

822
- Powys is overrun by the Anglo-Saxons.

844
- Rhodri Mawr becomes King of Gwynedd.

850
- First recorded attacks by the Vikings.

853
- 'Black Danes' ravage Anglesey.

855
- Cyngen, King of Powys, dies on a pilgrimage in Rome.

878
- Death of Rhodri Mawr.

881
- Anawrad's army turns back an English raid at the Conwy.

c.893
- Asser writes *De Rebus Gestis Aelfredi*.

896
- Great Viking raids into Brycheiniog, Gwent and Gwynllg.

915
- Vikings raid the south and capture Bishop Cyfeiliog of Llandaf, who is ransomed by Edward the Elder, King of Wessex.

918
- Hywel Dda offers submission to Edward the Elder.

926
- Athelstan, King of England, summons the Welsh rulers to a meeting at Hereford.

928
- Hywel Dda goes on pilgrimage to Rome.

942
- Hywel Dda takes the kingships of Gwynedd and Powys.

945
- Around this time, the 'Laws of Hywel Dda' are compiled.

950
- Death of Hywel Dda; battle of Nant Carno inaugurates an era of warfare.

972
- Godfrey, King of Man, overruns Anglesey.

973
- Homage is paid by Welsh kings to Edgar, King of England, at Chester.

980
- Vikings raid the Welsh coast repeatedly around this time.

987
- Vikings take two thousand slaves from Anglesey.

999
- Vikings raid St Davids for the third time and kill the bishop.

1039
- Gruffudd ap Llywelyn becomes King of Powys as well as of Gwynedd.

1042
- Hywel ab Edwin, Lord of Dyfed, defeats a Danish army at Pwll Dyfach.

1052
- Gruffudd ap Llywelyn takes over wide territories in the Wye Valley.

1055

- Gruffudd ap Llywelyn adds Deheubarth to his kingdom.
- Gruffudd ap Llywelyn, in alliance with Aelfgar, sacks Hereford.

1056

- Gruffudd ap Llywelyn defeats the army of the Bishop of Hereford, near Glasbury.

1063

- Death of Gruffudd ap Llywelyn.

1067

- William fitzOsbern made Earl of Hereford; Norman colonisation begins.

1073

- Building of the Norman castle at Rhuddlan. Normans ravage Ceredigion and Dyfed.

1081

- Battle of Mynydd Carn, between Gruffudd ap Cynan with Rhys ap Twedwr, Trahaearn, Meilir and Caradog ap Gruffydd.
- William the Conqueror visits St Davids.

1090

- *Life of St David* written by Rhygyfarch of Llanbadarn.

1093

- Founding of Pembroke Castle by Arnulf.

1094

- Rising of the Welsh against the Normans.

1098

- King Magnus Barefoot defeats the Earls of Chester and Shrewsbury.
- Priory of Pembroke founded.

c.1105

- Bernard of Neufmarché founds Brecon.

1108

- Consecration of Llanthony Abbey.

1109

- Carmarthen appears as site of a royal castle.

1115

- Bishopric of St Davids acknowledges rule of Canterbury.
- Abbey of St Dogmaels founded around this year.

1116

- Abbey of Llanbadarn Fawr founded.

1120

- Bishop Urban transfers the remains of Dyfrig (Dubricius) from Bardsey to Llandaf.

1128

- Bishop Urban of Llandaf goes to Rome to promote the interests of his see.

1130

- Around this year Bishop Bernard

begins campaign to make St Davids an archbishopric.
- Neath Abbey founded.

1131
- Basingwerk and Tintern Abbeys founded.

1136
- Uprisings against Norman rule in south Wales.

1137
- Death of Gruffydd ap Cynan. Accession of Owain Gwynedd.

1139
- First known copy of Geoffrey of Monmouth's *Historia Regum Britanniae* ('History of the Kings of Britain').

1140
- First Welsh Cistercian monastery founded (established at Trefgarne from 1144).

1141
- Ewenni Priory founded around this year.

1146
- Giraldus Cambrensis born around this year.

1147
- Margam Abbey founded.

1152
- Geoffrey of Monmouth is made Bishop of St Asaph.

1164
- Monastery of Ystrad Fflur (Strata Florida) founded.

1165
- Henry II driven back from the Berwyns; twenty-two Welsh hostages mutilated.

1167
- Owain Gwynedd wins Rhuddlan Castle
- First movement of Normans into Ireland.

1169
- Robert fitzStephen and other Normans sent into Ireland by the Lord Rhys.

1170
- Death of Owain ap Gwynedd.
- Abbey of Strata Marcella founded.

1171
- The Lord Rhys makes his peace with Henry II and becomes his ally.
- Lord Rhys builds a castle at Aberteifi.
- 'Strongbow' sails for Ireland.

1175
- Giraldus Cambrensis becomes Archdeacon of Brecknock.

1176
- The Lord Rhys holds a great *eisteddfod* at Aberteifi, the first to be definitely recorded.

1177
- Many Welsh kings and chiefs swear fealty to Henry II at Oxford.

1188
- Giraldus Cambrensis tours Wales with Archbishop Baldwin of Canterbury.

1190
- Around this time, the nunneries of Llanllyr and Llanllugan are founded.

1191
- Giraldus Cambrensis' *Itinerary of Wales* appears.

1197
- Death of the Lord Rhys.
- Gwenwynwyn comes to power in south Powys.

1198
- Defeat of Gwenwynwyn by the English at Painscastle.

1201
- Llywelyn the Great swears fealty to King John.
- Valle Crucis Abbey founded.

1202
- Clergy intervention averts war between Llywelyn and Gwenwynwyn.

1211
- King John invades Wales against Llywelyn the Great.

1212
- Anti-Norman uprisings across Wales.

c.1215
- Around this year, Ednyfed Fychan, ancestor of the Tudors, becomes seneschal to Llywelyn.

1216
- Llywelyn the Great's overlordship accepted at Aberdyfi.

1240
- Death of Llywelyn the Great

1241
- Dafydd ap Llywelyn surrenders to Henry III.

1244
- Gruffudd ap Llywelyn dies trying to escape from the Tower of London.
- Warfare between England and Wales.

1245
- War ends inconclusively.

1246
- Death of Dafydd ap Llywelyn.
- Resumption of warfare with England.

1247
- The Peace of Woodstock: four-year truce with England.

1254
- Prince Edward is invested with the Crown possessions in Wales.

1256
- Llywelyn II conquers the north as far as Chester.

1257
- Welsh defeat a royal army at Cymerau.

1258
- Llywelyn II accepts homage of lesser

Welsh chiefs and styles himself Prince of Wales.

1259

- Llywelyn II conquers the east border-lands as far as Brecknock.

1263

- Llywelyn II secures allegiance of Gruffydd ap Gwenwynwyn; all Welsh lords now accept his overlordship.

1267

- Llywelyn II acknowledged as Prince of Wales by Henry III at Montgomery.

1268

- Earl of Gloucester begins building of Caerffili Castle.

1274

- Welsh abbots defend Llywelyn II against the Bishop of St Asaph's charges.
- Llywelyn II conquers southern Powys.

1275

- An earthquake is recorded in September.

1277

- Edward I begins military campaign against Llywelyn II.
- Llywelyn II forced to agree to Edward's terms in the Peace of Conwy.

1278

- Llywelyn II marries Eleanor de Montfort in Worcester Cathedral.

1282

- Anti-English rising instigated by Dafydd ap Gruffudd.
- Llywelyn II is killed on the banks of the Irfon.

1283

- Edward I's conquest of Wales.

1284

- Statute of Rhuddlan imposes English laws.

1294

- Revolt of Madog ap Llywelyn.

1301

- The future Edward II is made Prince of Wales.

1322

- Forty-eight Welsh members recorded at parliament in York.

1327

- Twenty-four Welsh members recorded at parliament in Westminster.

1349

- The Black Death strikes across Wales, killing up to a third of the population.

1372

- Abortive expedition of Owain Lawgoch from France.

1378

- Assassination of Owain Lawgoch.

1399

- Richard II is captured at Flint.

1400
• Rebellion of Owain Glyndwr.

1404
• Owain Glyndwr's alliance with France.
• Glyndwr holds a parliament at Machynlleth.
• French land at Milford Haven.

1405
• The Tripartite Indenture, between Glyndwr, Mortimer and Northumberland.

1406
• The 'Pennal Policy' published.

1408
• Fall of Harlech and Aberystwyth Castles.

1410
• Owain Glyndwr's last raid into England.

1415
• Owain Glyndwr refuses Henry V's offer of pardon.

c.1428
• Around this year, Owen Tudor secretly marries the dowager Queen Catherine of Valois.

1430
• An *eisteddfod* is held at Carmarthen.

1453
• Edmund Tudor is made Earl of Richmond; Jasper Tudor, Earl of Pembroke.

1455
• 'Wars of the Roses' begin.

1461
• Battle of Mortimer's Cross; Jasper Tudor defeated.

1483
• Failed revolt and execution of the Duke of Buckingham.

1485
• Henry Tudor lands at Milford Haven; becomes King Henry VII after battle of Bosworth.

1489
• Prince Arthur is made Prince of Wales.

1498
• Insurrection in Meirionydd.

1501
• Council in the Marches of Wales is formally constituted at Ludlow.

1525
• Princess Mary made Princess of Wales, with a court at Ludlow.

1526
• Sir Mathew Cradock leases coal mines at Kilvey and in Gower.

1531
• Execution of Rhys ap Gruffudd.

1532
• Anne Boleyn made Marchioness of Pembroke.

1534

- Rowland Lee is made Lord President of the Council in the Marches of Wales.

1535

- Act passed for the making of justices of the peace in Wales.

1536

- First Act of Union passed.
- First regular representation of Welsh shires and towns in parliament.
- Most Welsh monasteries suppressed.

1541

- Grammar school founded in Brecon.

1542

- Four law-court circuits established in Wales.
- Haverfordwest is made a county.

1543

- Second Act of Union passed.
- Grammar school founded in Abergavenny.

1547

- William Salesbury publishes *Oll Synnwyr Pen Cymro*, Welsh proverbs.

1549

- Laws passed permitting clergy to marry.

1553

- Accession of Mary I restores Catholicism.

1555

- Execution of Robert Ferrar at Carmarthen for heresy.

1556

- Ordnance foundry set up at Abercarn.

1557

- Grammar school founded at Bangor.

1558

- Accession of Elizabeth I.

1559

- Acts of Supremacy and Uniformity restore Protestantism.

1562

- Shrewsbury Drapers acquire monopoly of Welsh cloth trade.

1563

- Parliament passes an act authorising translation of the Bible into Welsh.

1564

- The Sidney family open a forge and ironworks near Cardiff. Digging of iron ore becomes quite widespread in this decade.
- Elizabeth I grants rights to exploit copper and precious metals to Thomas Thurland and Daniel Hochstetter.

1565

- Grammar school endowed at Presteign.

1567

- Publication of the New Testament and Book of Common Prayer in Welsh.

1568

- The last great *eisteddfod* at Caerws (until the *eisteddfod* at Corwen in 1789).

1571

- Foundation of Jesus College, Oxford, often referred to as the 'Welsh College'.

1572

- Minstrels excepted from the Poor Law setting out punishment of vagrants.

1576

- Grammar School founded at Carmarthen.

1584

- Company of Mines Royal sets up smelter for Cornish ore at Neath.
- Richard Gwyn is first Welsh Catholic martyr.
- *Historie of Cambria* is published by David Powel.

1588

- Translation of the Bible into Welsh by William Morgan.

1592

- Publication of Dr Sion Dafydd Rhys's *Welsh Grammar*.

1595

- Dr Gabriel Goodman founds a grammar school at Ruthin.

1603

- With the Stewart accession, the Welsh dragon is replaced by the unicorn in the royal coat of arms.

1616

- William Vaughan of Torycoed buys land in Newfoundland for a planned Welsh settlement, Cambriol.

1621

- Publication of Dr John Davies's *Welsh Grammar*.

1630

- Publication of the *Beibl Bach*, first cheap edition of the Bible.

1632

- Publication of Dr John Davies's *Welsh Dictionary*.

1637

- Thomas Bushell is authorised to set up a mint at Aberystwyth, to stamp coins from Welsh silver.

1639

- William Wroth and William Erbury set up first church outside the established church.

1641

- Council in the Marches of Wales is abolished by parliament.

1642

- Civil War begins.

1643

- Royalists under Earl of Carbery advance into the south-west.

1644

- Rowland Laugharne breaks out from Pembroke Castle but is forced back by Colonel Gerard's royalist army.

1645
- After Naseby, Charles I retreats temporarily to south Wales.
- Parliament regains control of the south.

1646
- Royalist rising in Glamorgan is crushed.

1647
- Fall of Harlech Castle confirms parliament's supremacy in the north.

1648
- Second Civil War breaks out in south and north, suppressed by parliamentary forces; battle of St Fagans; Cromwell obtains surrender of Pembroke Castle.

1649
- Establishment of Sequestration Committees in north and south.

1650
- Act for the Better Propagation and Preaching of the Gospel in Wales is promulgated.

1651
- Anti-government riots in Cardiganshire.

1652
- John Taylor, 'the Water Poet', tours Wales.

1653
- Quaker preachers sent to the Wrexham area.

- Vavasor Powell protests against Cromwell becoming Lord Protector.

1655
- Penruddock Rising in the south-west is put down.

1657
- George Fox, Quaker leader, visits Wales.

1659
- *The Distressed Oppressed Condition of the Inhabitants of South Wales* is published, attacking the corrupt practices of Philip Jones and others.
- Sir Thomas Myddelton joins the failed Cheshire Rising in favour of Charles II.

1660
- Restoration of Stewart kings with Charles II.

1664
- Conventicle Act forbids gatherings of more than five persons outside of church.
- Menai ferry capsizes; seventy-nine passengers drowned.

1670
- The population is estimated at 341,000.
- Rebuilding of Tredegar House in the Baroque style.

1673
- Explosion recorded at Mostyn Colliery, Flint.

1674

- Henry Morgan, ex-pirate, is knighted and made Deputy-Governor of Jamaica.
- The Welsh Trust, for establishing schools, is founded.

1679

- Thomas Jones from Shrewsbury acquires right to publish an annual *Welsh Almanac*.

1681

- From this year, numerous Welsh Quakers emigrate to North America.

1686

- Sir Humphrey Mackworth builds a wooden-railed tramway at Neath.

1688

- Flight of James II, accession of William and Mary.
- Catholics and Protestants stage a battle in Welshpool.
- Toleration Act ends persecution of dissenters.

1690

- Discovery of the Gogerddan silver deposits.

1693

- Landowners win mineral rights to their property from the Crown.

1694

- Death of Sion Dafydd Las of Nannau, last of the family bards.

1697

- First of a succession of years of bad harvests, hunger and unrest.

1700

- Population estimated at 406,000.
- Sir Humphrey Mackworth establishes Company of the Mine Adventurers.

1707

- Edward Lhuyd publishes *Archaeologia Britannica*.

1709

- Anti-dissenter riots in Wrexham.

1710

- Welsh Jacobites found the Cycle of the White Rose.

1715

- Foundation of Honourable and Loyal Society of Ancient Britons.

1717

- Mechanical pumps in use in Mansel's coal pits at Swansea.
- Copper smelting starts at Langyfelach, near Swansea.

1718

- First Welsh printing press established by Isaac Carter, at Trefhedyn, near Carmarthen.

1722

- Death of Bartholomew Roberts (Barti Ddu), said to be the first pirate to use the skull-and-crossbones flag.

1723

- Publication of Henry Rowlands's

Mona Antiqua Restaurata, on the druids of Anglesey.

1727
• An epidemic of typhus increases the death rate until 1731.

1728
• Payne's method of rolling tinplate introduced.
• Potatoes recorded as being grown in Wales.

1732
• Discovery of the mineral springs at Llandrindod.

1736
• Wynnstay mansion rebuilt in the Palladian style between this year and 1739.

1737
• First recorded turnips grown in Wales.

1739
• Failed harvests and bad weather cause great hunger and hardship this year and into 1741.

1741
• The Pembroke Literary Society founded.

1745
• On one night in October, Cardigan Bay fishers net 1,386,500 herrings.

1746
• The Jacobite, David Morgan, is executed after the defeat of Culloden Moor.

1747
• A smallpox epidemic rages across the country.

1750
• Population estimated at 493,000.

1751
• Food shortages cause riots this year and in the next two years.
• Foundation of the Honourable Society of Cymmrodorion.

1752
• First turnpike road in Wales, joining Wrexham to Shrewsbury.
• Epidemics of smallpox and typhus.
• Eleven days removed from September to regularise the calendar.

1755
• First Welsh county society established in Brecknockshire.

1756
• William Edwards's bridge over the Taff at Pontypridd has the widest single span in Europe (145 ft / 44 m.).

1764
• Publication of Henry Rowlands of Llanidan's *Idea Agriculturae*, on farming improvement (written 1704).
• Publication of Evan Evans's *Some Specimens of the Poetry of the Antient Welsh Bards*.

1766
• Food shortages cause riots.

1767

* A proper road links Cardiff and Merthyr.

1768

* Discovery of copper lodes in Parys Mountain, Anglesey.

1770

* The Gwyneddigion Society is founded.

1771

* Wynnstay is equipped with its private theatre.

1773

* Publication of the first edition of Thomas Pennant's *Tours in Wales*.

1785

* Fifty-four people swept away in Menai ferry disaster.

1787

* Seventeen miners killed in a gas explosion at Llansamlet Pit.

1788

* First Welsh colonists in Australia, two men and two women convicts in the 'First Fleet'.

1789

* Revival of the *eisteddfod* at Corwen.

1793

* Food riots at Swansea.
* First periodical in Welsh, *Cylchgrawn Cymmraeg*, published by Morgan John Rhys.

1794

* Glamorganshire Canal completed (begun 1790).

1797

* French invasion foiled at Fishguard.

1799

* Widespread riots against grain shortages.

1800

* Population estimated at 587,000.

1801

* Population of Merthyr is over 7,700.
* First volume of the *Myvyrian Archaiology* published by the Gwyneddigion Society.

1804

* Horse-drawn railway along Swansea Bay is authorised by parliament (opens 1806, claimed as first passenger rail line in the world).
* First Welsh weekly paper, *The Cambrian and General Weekly Advertiser*, at Swansea.

1809

* John Vivian opens a copper works at Hafod, Swansea.

1811

* Methodists break with Anglican church and appoint their own ministers.

1812

* Brecon and Monmouthshire Canal completed.

1815

- End of Napoleonic Wars heralds a major trade and industrial depression.
- Telford's Waterloo Bridge at Conwy opens.

1816

- Troops disperse a Merthyr ironworkers' demonstration.
- Beginnings of the 'Scotch Cattle' workers' movement in Monmouthshire and Breconshire.

1817

- First known hospital in Swansea.

1819

- Attachment of the Gorsedd of Bards to the *eisteddfod* at Carmarthen.
- Methodists break away from the Church of England.

1822

- Collapse of the Cardiff Bank.

1823

- The 'Red Lady' is excavated at Paviland Cave, Gower.

1826

- Completion of Telford's suspension bridges over the Menai Strait and at Conwy.

1827

- Foundation of St David's College, Lampeter, for the training of Anglican clergy.

1830

- Courts of Great Sessions abolished.

1831

- The Merthyr Rising: twenty-six demonstrators shot dead by troops.
- Richard Lewis (Dic Penderyn) hanged in Cardiff Gaol.

1832

- The Reform Act raises the number of Welsh constituencies from twenty-seven to thirty-two.
- Walter Coffin begins exploitation of coal pits in the Lower Rhondda.
- At Holywell, first Welsh Temperance Society.

1834

- The Poor Law Amendment Act causes outrage.
- Lady Llanover (Augusta Hall) publishes *On the Advantages Resulting From the Preservation of the Welsh Language and the National Costume of Wales*.

1835

- Swansea Museum founded.

1836

- Tithe Commutation Act replaces tithes with money payments.
- Working Men's Association founded by William Lovett and Henry Hetherington.

1837

- Welsh Manuscript Society founded.
- David Thomas smelts iron using anthracite at Yniscedwyn Works, Ystradgynlais.

1838

- First Chartist meeting in Wales at Newtown.
- Publication of 'The People's Charter'.
- Lady Charlotte Guest begins publication of *The Mabinogion*.

1839

- Opening of the Bute West Dock at Cardiff.
- Narberth Workhouse set on fire.
- First of the 'Rebecca' attacks which continue until 1844.

1840

- Formation of the Liberation Society.

1841

- Taff Vale Railway built.

1842

- Repeal of government duty on coal carried on British ships.
- Women, and children under ten, forbidden to work underground.

1846

- Cambrian Archaeological Society founded.

1848

- Wales produces 631,000 tons of iron.
- Public Health Act passed, establishing local health boards.
- Cricket first played at Cardiff Arms Park.

1849

- Fifty-two miners killed in a colliery explosion in Aberdare; sixty-five at Middle Dyffryn Colliery.

1849

- Opening of the north coast railway to Bangor.

1850

- Robert Stephenson's Britannia Tubular Bridge across the Menai Strait opens; completion of the railway line to Holyhead.
- First Cardiff Waterworks Act.

1851

- The population is 1,153,000.
- Non-conformist chapels claim 80 per cent of church-going population.

1854

- Opening of Rhymney Railway.

1855

- First medical officer of health appointed to Cardiff.

1856

- The Police Act brings about general policing of communities.

1858

- Bangor 'Normal' College, for teacher training, founded.
- First *eisteddfod* on a national scale, at Llangollen.

1859

- Opening of the Bute East Dock at Cardiff.

1861

- The new 'tonic sol-fa' system greatly popularises choral singing.

1865
- The Mid-Wales Railway from Shrewsbury to Swansea opens.
- Opening of Penarth Dock.
- Welsh colony in Patagonia established.

1867
- Electoral Reform Act enlarges the electorate.

1870
- First Welsh-speaking bishop since Queen Anne's time is appointed, to St Asaph.

1871
- Opening of Aberystwyth University College.
- An act is passed to authorise construction of the Severn Railway Tunnel.

1872
- The Ballot Act provides for secret balloting at elections.

1873
- John Bateman establishes that 571 persons own over 60 per cent of Welsh land.
- Coalowners' Association of Wales founded.

1874
- North Wales Quarrymen's Union established.

1875
- Public Health Act.

1880
- Formation of National Eisteddfod Association.

1881
- Legislation forces closure of Welsh pubs on Sundays.
- Aberdare Committee highlights lack of secondary education in Wales.
- Welsh Rugby Union formed in Castle Hotel, Neath.
- First Wales–England rugby international, won by England.
- Population of Cardiff reaches 106,164.

1883
- University College, Cardiff, founded.
- Second Wales–England rugby international won by England.

1884
- University College, Bangor, founded.
- Electoral Reform Acts of this year and 1885 redraw Welsh constituencies and substantially enlarge the electorate.
- England win rugby international.

1885
- Open-hearth steel plants established at Brymbo and Shotton.
- Severn Railway Tunnel completed, linking London, Bristol and south Wales.
- Marquess of Bute buys Glamorgan and Aberdare Canals for conversion to railways.
- Society for the Utilisation of the Welsh Language founded.
- Grandstand at Cardiff Arms Park is built.
- England win rugby international.

1886
• England win rugby international.

1887
• Opening of Roath Docks, Cardiff.
• Wales and England draw in rugby international.

1888
• Miners awarded a monthly day off: 'Mabon's Day'.
• Discovery of the Roman villa at Llantwit Major.

1889
• Opening of Barry Docks.
• Inauguration of elected county councils.
• Welsh Intermediate Education Act passed: government money for secondary schools.
• First lecturer in Welsh at a Welsh college: John Morris-Jones at Bangor.
• Peak year of slate production, with 16,000 workers.

1890
• David Lloyd George elected Liberal MP for Caernarfon Boroughs.
• First Welsh win in a rugby international against England.
• South Wales Soccer League set up.

1891
• Census records a population of 1,577,000, plus over 228,000 Welsh people residing in England.
• 54.4 per cent of the adult population recorded as Welsh-speaking.
• Tinplate production reaches 586,000 tons.
• England win rugby international.

1892
• England win rugby international.

1893
• Royal Commission on Welsh Land sits until 1895.
• University of Wales receives its charter.
• Wales wins its first Triple Crown.

1894
• Parish and district councils introduced.
• Cymru Fydd established as a national league.
• Keir Hardie launches the South Wales Branch of the Independent Labour Party.
• 250 miners killed at the Albion Colliery, Cilfynydd.
• England win rugby international.

1895
• Royal Commission on Welsh Land produces a divided report and no action.
• England win rugby international.

1896
• John Summers Steelworks erected at Hawarden.
• Snowdon Mountain Railway opens; first and only fatal accident on first day (6 April).
• England win rugby international.

1897
• Wales win rugby international against England.

1898
• Opening of Port Talbot New Docks.

- Six-month coal strike; 'Mabon's Day' abolished.
- South Wales Miners' Federation founded.
- England win rugby international.

1899

- Wales win rugby international against England.

1900

- The Penrhyn slate 'lock-out' lasts till 1903.
- Welsh collieries raise 42 million tons of coal.
- Wales win rugby international against England and the Triple Crown.

1901

- Population is 2,019,000.
- Wales win rugby international against England.

1902

- Welsh councils resist implementation of the Education Act.
- Mond Nickel Works established at Clydach: world's largest.
- Taff Vale judgement enables owners to claim damages as a result of strikes.
- Vale of Rheidol Railway (narrow gauge) opens .
- First electric tramcars in Cardiff.
- Bangor Eisteddfod marks a revival of Welsh literature.
- Wales win rugby international against England and the Triple Crown.

1903

- Wales win rugby international against England.

1904

- Evan Roberts sparks off a religious revival.
- Draw in rugby international with England.

1905

- Cardiff is given city status.
- The government authorises the Welsh National Library at Aberystwyth and National Museum at Cardiff.
- Wales beat the All Blacks and England at rugby and win the Triple Crown.

1906

- In the general election, Liberals win thirty-three out of thirty-four Welsh seats; the odd one is Merthyr, won by Keir Hardie for Labour.
- South Wales Branch of the Workers' Educational Association founded.
- Opening of the Law Courts at Cathays Park, Cardiff.
- Wales beat England in rugby international.

1907

- First organisation for Women's Suffrage in Wales is formed at Llandudno.
- A Welsh Department of the Board of Education is set up.
- First motor buses in Cardiff.
- Wales beat England in rugby international.
- Wales win UK soccer championship.

1908

- Cardiff and District Women's Suffrage Society formed.
- Wales beat England in rugby interna-

tional and win the Grand Slam (Five Nations).

1909
- Implementation of the eight-hour day for coal miners.
- King's Dock opened at Swansea.
- Cardiff Corporation Act.
- Construction of Llwyn-On Reservoir begins.
- The 'Plebs' League founded in the Rhondda.
- Wales beat England in rugby international and win the Grand Slam.

1910
- Riots in Tonypandy (November) during a coal strike; troops are sent in; one man killed and much damage done.
- Welsh National Memorial Association founded to promote health and hygiene.
- The first 'kinema' opens in Aberdare.
- England win rugby international.

1911
- Population of Cardiff is 182,259.
- Two railwaymen shot dead by troops at Llanelli during a rail strike.
- Anti-Jewish riots in South Wales.
- Sir John Edward Lloyd's *History of Wales to the Edwardian Conquest* is published.
- The Prince of Wales is invested at Caernarfon.
- Wales beat England in rugby international, and win the Grand Slam.

1912
- Welsh Council of Agriculture set up.
- Tinplate production reaches its peak at 848,000 tons.

- Rhiwbina Garden Village founded.
- England win rugby international.

1913
- At Senghennydd, 439 men die in Wales's worst mine disaster.
- 485 collieries are operating in Wales, 323 of them in Glamorgan.
- Barry overtakes Cardiff as the world's biggest coal-exporting port.
- 823,000 tons of tinplate are produced this year.
- John Morris Jones publishes his *Welsh Grammar*.
- England win rugby international.

1914
- Disestablishment of the church in Wales approved by parliament.
- E.T. John introduces a Home Rule Bill to parliament.
- 242,000 men are employed in the coal industry.
- Frederick Thomas ('Freddie Welsh') becomes world lightweight boxing champion.
- A new Welsh Division created in the British Army, following the start of the First World War.
- Wales beat England in rugby international.

1915
- Welsh miners go on successful strike for higher pay.
- Caradoc Evans's controversial story collection, *My People*, is published.
- First Welsh branch of the Women's Institute, at Llanfairpwll.

1916
- David Lloyd George is first Welshman to become British prime minister.

- Ocean Colliery at Treharris is one of the two first collieries in Britain to provide pithead baths.
- Jimmy Wilde becomes world flyweight boxing champion.

1919
- Welsh Board of Health set up.
- Wales win UK soccer championship, 1919/20.

1920
- University College, Swansea, founded.
- 271,516 men are engaged in the coal industry; the maximum recorded number.
- Miners' Welfare Fund established to support miners' institutes.
- First Archbishop of Wales elected in the newly disestablished church.
- Gregynog Hall music festivals begin.
- Wales beat England in first post-war rugby international.

1921
- National Coal Strike.
- Cyfarthfa Steelworks at Merthyr close.
- Oil refinery established at Llandarcy.
- England win rugby international.

1922
- Welsh Highland Railway takes over most narrow-gauge lines in north Wales.
- The slate industry employs 9,523 people; output is 231,410 tons.
- *Y Llenor*, influential literary journal, founded by W.J. Gruffydd.
- Wales beat England in rugby international.

1923
- Labour win twenty out of thirty-six seats in the general election.
- BBC begins broadcasts from Cardiff.
- Railway amalgamation brings most Welsh lines into the Great Western system.
- England win rugby international.
- Wales win UK soccer championship, 1923/24.

1924
- Labour win sixteen seats in general election, Conservatives nine and Liberals eleven.
- Ramsay Macdonald (then MP for Aberavon) is second MP for a Welsh constituency to become prime minister of Great Britain.
- National Council of Music established under Sir Walford Davies.
- Wales beat England in rugby international.

1925
- Unemployment in Wales rises to 16.5 per cent of the insured population.
- Kate Roberts publishes *O Gors y Bryniau*, a novel set in slate-mining country.
- University of Wales Press, and Board of Celtic Studies founded.
- Welsh League of Youth, Urdd Gobaith Cymru, founded by Sir Ifan ap Owen Edwards.
- England win rugby international.

1926
- The General Strike, May 1926, followed by a prolonged miners' strike.
- Draw in the Wales–England rugby international.

1927
- 23.3 per cent of insured working population is unemployed.
- Labour take twenty-five out of thirty-six seats at the general election.
- Formal opening of the National Museum.
- Coleg Harlech for working men founded by Thomas Jones and the WEA.
- Bedwellty Board of Guardians suspended for overspending on Poor Relief.
- England win rugby international.
- Cardiff City FC win the FA Cup.
- Wales win UK soccer championship, 1927/28.
- Rioters prevent Sunday golfing at Aberdyfi.

1928
- Welsh National Orchestra founded.
- England win rugby international.

1929
- Aneurin Bevan elected Labour MP for Ebbw Vale.
- Swansea and Mumbles Tramway electrified.
- Steel-making ceases at Ebbw Vale (until 1938).
- England win rugby international.

1930
- 27.2 per cent of insured working population is unemployed.
- Steel-making ends at Dowlais and Brymbo.
- St Lythan's Reservoir opened to supply Barry with water.
- Bus service competes with Cardiff–Merthyr trains.
- England win rugby international.

1931
- 'National' government elected at Westminster: Labour hold sixteen seats in Wales; the Conservatives gain five.
- Welsh National School of Medicine receives its charter.
- Census records 37.2 per cent of the population as Welsh-speaking.
- Draw in the Wales–England rugby international.

1932
- Merthy Tydfil records 63.3 per cent unemployed.
- Wales beat England in rugby international.
- Wales win UK soccer championship, 1932/33.

1933
- Establishment of the Milk Marketing Board.
- Last tram runs in Llanelli.
- All seven counties with the highest rate of tuberculosis in Britain are in Wales.
- Wales beat England in rugby international, 1933/34.

1934
- Disaster at Gresford Colliery kills 243 men; 2,000 miners are laid off.
- Swansea Guildhall completed.
- Dylan Thomas's first collection, *Eighteen Poems*, published.
- D. Gwenallt Jones publishes *Plasau'r Brenin*, a novel based on his wartime imprisonment.
- England win rugby international.

1935
- First broadcast in Welsh, from Bangor.

- 'Stay-down' strikes at Bedwas Colliery.
- Draw in the Wales–England rugby international.

1936
- Reconstruction Association set up to bring industry to depressed districts.
- East Moors Steelworks set up at Cardiff.
- Three senior Plaid Cymru activists jailed at the Old Bailey for setting fire to an RAF bombing school at Pen-y-berth in Llyn.
- King Edward VIII visits Dowlais.
- Spanish Civil War begins; 174 Welsh volunteers take part on the Republican side.
- Draw in the Wales–England rugby international.
- Wales win UK soccer championship, 1936/37.

1937
- Closure of Welsh Highland Railway.
- Last tram runs in Newport.
- Separate broadcasting begins with 'Welsh Home Service'.
- England win rugby international.

1938
- Completion of the Temple of Peace in Cardiff.
- 76,000 private cars are licensed in Wales.
- Idris Davies publishes *Gwalia Deserta*.
- Wales beat England in rugby international.
- Wales tie with England and Scotland in UK soccer championship, 1938/39.

1939
- Steel strip mill opens at Ebbw Vale.

- Last tram runs in Rhondda Valley.
- Establishment of Treforest, an early trading estate.
- Bridgend has largest ammunition plant in Britain, eventually employing 37,000 workers.
- The slate industry employs 7,500 workers.
- England win rugby international.

1940
- First major air raid on Swansea (1 September) with thirty-three deaths.

1941
- German bombing raids kill 985 people in Newport, Cardiff and Swansea.
- Undeb Cymru Fydd is founded.

1942
- Welsh Court Acts allow the use of Welsh in litigation.
- Trolleybuses begin to replace trams in Cardiff.

1943
- T. Rowland Hughes publishes *O Law I Law*, set in the Caernarfonshire slate quarries.

1944
- Welsh Council of Peace formed.

1945
- Welsh Arts Council established.
- Youth Orchestra of Wales founded.

1946
- Nationalisation of transport, gas and electricity.
- Welsh National Opera Company founded.

281

- R.S. Thomas publishes *The Stones of the Field*.

1947
- Nationalisation of the coal industry.
- Formation of the Steel Company of Wales.
- Wales Gas Board established.
- Unemployment stands at 5.2 per cent of the adult working population.
- Agriculture Act stabilises farm prices and gives subsidies to hill farmers.
- England win first post-war rugby international.

1948
- Advisory Council for Wales and Monmouthshire is established.
- Draw in Wales–England rugby international.

1950
- Eighteen foreign-owned companies employ around 14,000 people in manufacturing.
- Last tramcar runs in Cardiff.
- Wales beat England in rugby international and win the Triple Crown and the Grand Slam.

1951
- A new steel mill, largest in Britain, established at Port Talbot.
- 28.9 per cent of the population is Welsh-speaking.
- New *eisteddfod* rules begin.
- Wales beat England in rugby international.

1952
- Establishment of the new town of Cwmbran.

- Dylan Thomas's *Under Milk Wood* broadcast by the BBC.
- Wales beat England in rugby international and win the Triple Crown and the Grand Slam.
- Wales tie with England in UK soccer championship, 1951/52.

1953
- Dilys Cadwaladr becomes first woman to win a bardic crown at the National Eisteddfod.
- Dylan Thomas dies in New York; he is brought to Wales for burial.
- England win rugby international.

1954
- England win rugby international.

1955
- Cardiff is made capital city of Wales.
- Wales beat England in rugby international.

1956
- Llandudno–Colwyn Bay tram line closes.
- Wales beat England in rugby international.
- Wales tie with England, Scotland and Northern Ireland in UK soccer championship, 1955/56.

1957
- Pit closures on a large scale begin.
- England win rugby international.

1958
- Cardiff plays host to the Empire Games.
- Draw in Wales–England rugby international.

1959

- Car plants set up at Cardiff and Llanelli.
- Yr Academi Gymreig, The Welsh Academy, founded.
- Wales beat England in rugby international.

1960

- 106,000 men are employed in the Welsh coal industry.
- Sheep stock of Wales is 5,196,000; cattle, 1,127,000.
- Publication of *Welsh History Review* begins.
- England win rugby international.
- Wales tie with England and Scotland in UK soccer championship, 1959/60.

1961

- Opening of the Llanwern Steelworks at Newport.
- Opening of a BP oil terminal at Milford Haven.
- Wales has 1,889 miles of railway track and 538 railway stations.
- Welsh Books Council begins work.
- Local polls reduce the number of 'dry' Sunday areas.
- Census records the proportion of Welsh speakers at 26 per cent.
- Wales beat England in rugby international.

1962

- Formation of the Welsh Language Society, Cymdeithas yr Iaith Gymraeg.

- Draw in Wales–England rugby international.

1963

- Impending closure of many rural railway lines and stations is announced.
- England win rugby international.

1964

- First appointment of a Secretary of State for Wales (James Griffiths); the Welsh Office is set up.
- A Ford motor plant set up at Swansea.
- BBC Wales set up.
- Number of Welsh students in the University of Wales falls below 50 per cent.
- Lynn Davies wins gold medal for the long jump at Tokyo Olympics.
- Draw in Wales–England rugby international.

1965

- Last big pit disaster, at the Cambrian Colliery, Tonypandy.
- Controversy arises over a reservoir for Birmingham at Clywedog, Montgomery.
- *Poetry Wales* is launched.
- Wales beat England in rugby international, and win the Triple Crown.

1966

- Council for Wales ceases to function. Welsh Economic Council set up.
- In the general election, Labour takes thirty-two out of thirty-six Welsh seats.
- Cledwyn Hughes is appointed Secretary of State.
- Gwynfor Evans wins Carmarthen by-election for Plaid Cymru.
- First Severn Bridge built.

283

- A colliery tip at Aberfan slumps, killing 144 people, 116 of them schoolchildren.
- Wales beat England in rugby international.

1967

- Welsh Language Act gives Welsh and English equal status.
- Leasehold Enfranchisement Act passed.
- Gittins Report recommends that primary school children be given the opportunity to be bilingual.
- Welsh Arts Council restarted.
- Cardiff Festival of Twentieth-Century Music founded.
- Wales beat England in rugby international.

1968

- After local polls, only Anglesey, Caernarfon, Meirionydd and Ceredigion remain 'dry' on Sundays.
- The Royal Mint is moved to Llantrisant.
- Draw in Wales–England rugby international.

1969

- Investiture of Prince of Wales at Caernarfon Castle.
- Swansea is given city status.
- Only one working pit (Maerdy) is left in the Rhondda.
- Wales beat England in rugby international and win the Triple Crown.

1970

- Rio Tinto Zinc establishes an aluminium plant near Holyhead.
- Fire closes Menai Tubular Bridge; it is rebuilt as an arched bridge.

- Last trolleybus runs in Cardiff.
- Wales beat England in rugby international.
- Wales tie with England and Scotland in UK soccer championship.

1971

- Census records the proportion of Welsh speakers at 20.8 per cent.
- 33.7 per cent of workers are employed in manufacturing; 49.1 per cent in services (see 1996).
- First transatlantic flight from Cardiff Airport.
- Welsh Nursery School movement, Sefydlu Mudiad Ysgolion Meithrin, founded.
- Wales beat England in rugby international and win the Grand Slam.

1972

- Less than 1,000 men now employed in the slate industry.
- Cardiff College of Advanced Technology becomes a college of the University of Wales (University of Wales Institute of Science and Technology) and St David's College, Lampeter, also becomes a constituent college, making seven in total.
- Commercial Bank of Wales launched (later Bank of Wales).
- North Wales Music Festival founded.
- Wales beat England in rugby international.

1973

- The Kilbrandon Report recommends an elected Assembly for Wales.
- Formation of the Welsh Trades Union Congress.
- Wales beat England in rugby international.

1974

- Local government is rationalised into eight regional counties.
- Driver and Vehicle Licensing Centre (later Agency) set up at Swansea.
- Swansea Sound begins independent radio broadcasting.
- Oriel Gallery opens in Cardiff.
- England win rugby international.

1975

- In a referendum, 66 per cent approve of entering the Common Market.
- Wales beat England in rugby international.

1976

- Welsh Development Agency set up.
- James Callaghan is the third Welsh MP (though not a Welshman) to be prime minister of Britain.
- Plaid Cymru take control of Merthyr Tydfil and Rhymney councils.
- Theatr Clwyd set up in Mold.
- Wales beat England in rugby international and win the Grand Slam.

1977

- Development Board for Rural Wales established.
- Radio Cymru and Radio Wales start broadcasting.
- Wales beat England in rugby international and win the Triple Crown.

1978

- The Welsh Bill is passed by parliament, but a referendum is required before election of an Assembly.
- 550 men are employed in the slate quarries of Gwynedd.
- Wales beat England in rugby international and win the Grand Slam.

1979

- Devolution referendum: 956,330 vote against limited devolution, 243,048 support it.
- 30,000 men are employed in the Welsh coal industry.
- Major job cuts in the steel industry at Port Talbot and Llanwern announced.
- Wales beat England in rugby international and win the Triple Crown.

1980

- A spate of arson attacks on 'second homes' in Wales.
- England win rugby international.

1981

- Census records 79.4 per cent of the population as born in Wales; 17 per cent of residents are English-born.
- 18.9 per cent of the population are Welsh-speaking.
- 10.4 per cent of the working population is unemployed.
- Miners strike against plans to shut down seven pits.
- Wales beat England in rugby international.

1982

- Sianel Pedwar Cymru (S4C) is established.
- Pope John Paul II visits Cardiff.
- England win rugby international.

1983

- The official opening of St David's Hall in Cardiff.
- Draw in Wales–England rugby international.

1984

- Coal miners embark on a year-long strike.
- Unemployment stands at 13.2 per cent of the adult working population (British average 10.6 per cent).
- CADW, Welsh Historic Monuments organisation, established.
- Wales beat England in rugby international.

1985

- Wales has 916 miles of railway track and 180 stations.
- Tourism provides around 90,000 jobs, mostly seasonal.
- Wales beat England in rugby international.

1986

- Fallout from the Chernobyl nuclear disaster makes Welsh hill grazing radioactive for a time.
- England win rugby international.

1987

- Wales beat England in Rugby World Cup at Brisbane and in home international.

1988

- A national curriculum for education introduced.
- Unemployment stands at 7.3 per cent of the adult working population (British average 6.2 per cent).
- Wales beat England in rugby international and win the Triple Crown.

1989

- Outbreaks of BSE ('mad cow disease')

begin to have an adverse effect on the stock-rearing industry.
- Wales beat England in rugby international.

1990

- England win rugby international.

1991

- The population, at 2,800,000, is the highest ever recorded.
- 18.6 per cent of the population are Welsh speakers.
- More than 67,000 people employed in manufacturing by foreign-owned companies.
- England win rugby international.

1992

- England win rugby international.

1993

- Unemployment at 10.3 per cent conforms to the British average.
- Welsh Language Act confirms equal status of Welsh and English.
- Welsh Film Council set up.
- Wales beat England in rugby international.

1994

- Cardiff is voted 'world's best-value city' for the seventh time in a row.
- Cardiff Airport is used by over 1,000,000 passengers for the first time.
- England win rugby international.
- Wales's biggest international rugby score: 102 points against Portugal's 11.

1995

- Local government is reorganised into 21 'unitary authorities'.
- 475,000 women in employment (including part-time); 471,000 men.
- England win rugby international.

1996

- Unemployment in Wales is at 8.2 per cent.
- 21.5 per cent of workers employed in manufacturing; 71.1 per cent in services.
- Second Severn Crossing opens.
- The tanker *Sea Empress* hits rocks entering Milford Haven; 72,000 tons of oil are leaked.
- England win rugby international.

1997

- General election: Labour take 34 out of 40 Welsh seats, Plaid Cymru 4, Liberals 2; no seats are held by the Conservatives.
- Referendum on a national assembly results in 50.3 per cent in favour, 49.7 per cent against.
- Only two deep collieries remain open in south Wales.
- England win rugby international.

1998

- Government of Wales Act is passed at Westminster.
- Ron Davies, Secretary of State, resigns.
- Coal production in south Wales is around 3 million tons, mostly from open-cast sites.
- England win rugby international.
- Wales's biggest international rugby defeat: 13 points against South Africa's 96.

1999

- First elections for Welsh Assembly: Labour win 28 out of 60 seats and form coalition with Liberals (6 seats); Plaid Cymru have 17 seats, Conservatives 9 seats. Alun Michael is First Secretary.
- Welsh whisky begins to be distilled in Brecon.
- Welsh Rugby Union hosts the Rugby World Cup.
- Wales beat England in rugby international (Six Nations).
- Opening of Millennium Stadium in Cardiff, first in UK to have closing roof.

2000

- Alun Michael resigns as First Secretary (February), replaced by Rhodri Morgan, whose title from October is First Minister.
- Storm brings highest-ever river levels and flooding to the north-east.
- England win rugby international.
- Death of R.S. Thomas, poet and priest.

2001

- Analysis of census figures (published 2003) shows population at 2,903,085; proportion who speak, read and write Welsh has gone up from 13.6 per cent to 16.3 per cent since 1991.
- General election: Labour hold 34 seats, Plaid Cymru 4, Liberal Democrats 2, Conservatives none.
- Outbreak of foot-and-mouth disease affects Welsh stock-rearing industry.
- Closure of tin-plate works at Ebbw Vale and cut-down in steel production at Llanwern are announced.

- Death of Roderick Bowen, former Liberal MP.

2002
- Go-ahead is given for biggest onshore wind farm in Britain, at Cefn Croes.
- Newport is given city status.
- Lease is signed for Welsh International Centre in New York.
- Explosion of blast furnace at Llanwern kills three people.
- England win rugby international.

2003
- Assembly elections give half the seats to Labour; a Labour-only adminstration is formed. The Welsh Assembly is the only elected national assembly in the world in which half the members are women.
- Welsh Office in Whitehall to close; Peter Hain is new Secretary of State, combining this post with the post of Leader of the House of Commons.
- Five members of North Wales police force resign after exposure of racist attitudes.
- Race riots against Kurdish refugees in Wrexham: 74 people arrested.
- Dr Barry Morgan is elected Anglican Archbishop of Wales.
- University of Wales at Bangor is awarded £5 million to set up a Management Development Centre.
- Prince of Wales opens Phase 3 of Welsh Highland Railway project (Waunfawr–Rhyd Ddu).
- England win rugby international.

2004
- European Parliament elections: Wales has 2 Labour MEPs, 1 Plaid Cymru MEP and 1 Conservative MEP.

- The Richard commission on Assembly powers and election methods proposes increase of AMs from 60 to 80, and election by single transferable vote.
- Wales and Latvia sign a co-operation agreement, the first between Wales and a full EU member state.
- Corus steel company announces £150 million expansion plans for Port Talbot and Llanwern.
- A total of £387,000,000 has been paid to ex-miners and their families.
- Work begins on renewing Vale of Glamorgan Railway between Barry Town and Bridgend.
- Deaths of Lord Geraint of Ponterwyd (Geraint Howells, ex-Liberal Democrat leader); John Charles, footballer; Islwyn Ffowc Ellis, writer.
- England wins rugby international.

2005
- Welsh Development Agency merged into Department of Enterprise, Innovation and Networks.
- National Assembly Building is formally opened on St David's Day.
- General election: Labour down to 29 seats, Liberal Democrats 4, Conservatives 3, Plaid Cymru 3, Independent 1.
- National Waterfront Museum opens in Swansea.
- Gwyneth Lewis is named as first 'National Poet for Wales'.
- Deaths of Sir Glanmor Williams, historian; James Callaghan, former prime minister; Gwynfor Evans, former leader of Plaid Cymru.
- Wales win rugby international against England and their first grand slam for 21 years.

2006

- Labour defeated by Independent candidates in Blaenau Gwent by-elections for Westminster and the National Assembly.
- Government of Wales Act provides for increased powers for the Welsh Assembly government.
- Plaid Cymru shortens its campaigning name to Plaid; adopts the yellow Welsh poppy as its new logo.
- Gwenno Teifi Ffransis is jailed for damaging Radio Carmarthenshire's Narberth studio in a protest at the lack of Welsh-language broadcasts.
- Rhodri Morgan inaugurates the Anglesey coastal path.
- Deaths of Merlyn Rees, Labour politician; Leslie Norris, poet; Stefan Terliszki, hotelier and Conservative politician.
- England win rugby international.

2007

- Elections for the Assembly result in 26 seats for Labour, 15 for Plaid Cymru, 12 for Conservatives, 6 for Liberal Democrats, one Independent; Labour and Plaid form a coalition administration under Rhodri Morgan.
- Welsh Climate Change Commission is inaugurated.
- The Welsh Baccalaureate, new school-leaving qualification, is extended nationally after three years of pilot tests.
- Corus Steel is taken over by the Indian Tata steel company.
- The Chief Medical Officer launches a campaign to reduce child obesity.
- Sir Martin Evans of Cardiff University is awarded the Nobel Prize for Medicine.

- Holy bulls at a Hindu community are condemned because of bovine TB.
- Plans are announced to introduce a zebra herd at Cwmduad, Carmarthen, for animal behaviour research.
- Forty-four beaches are given EU Blue Flag accreditation.
- The country's largest sculpture is erected at Aberavon Beach.
- Deaths of Roland Mathias, poet; Ivor Emmanuel, actor; Peter Prendergast, artist; Brian Williams, rugby player.
- England win rugby international by widest-ever margin, 62-5.

2008

- Peter Hain resigns as Secretary of State after failure to report political donations. Paul Murphy is appointed.
- Welsh is spoken for the first time at an official EU event in Brussels, by Heritage Minister Alun Ffred Jones.
- Latest life expectancy figures for Wales are: men 76.7 years; women 81.1 years.
- South Wales police are the only force in the UK to record an increase in crime, 2007–08.
- Gwynedd County Council inaugurates a Welsh Language Charter to promote the use of Welsh.
- 22 million smuggled cigarettes are seized by Cardiff customs officers in the biggest-ever haul of its kind in Wales.
- Health survey statistics show that 36% of adults consume more than the advised daily limit of alcohol, and 36% of children are obese.
- The number of people killed or seriously injured on the roads is 1,395,

31% down on the average 1994–98 figures; 37% of deaths are in the 16–25 age group.
- By November, the average house price has fallen 11.7% to £126,181, from November 2007.
- Deaths of Leo Abse, politician; Vernon Handley, conductor; Alun Hoddinott, composer; John Ellis Williams, novelist.
- Wales win rugby international, and the Grand Slam.

2009
- European Parliament elections: Wales returns one member each from Conservative, Labour, Plaid and UKIP parties.
- Rhodri Morgan resigns as First Minister; succeeded by Carwyn Jones.
- Peter Hain is reappointed Secretary of State.
- Cardiff International Sports Stadium opens.
- Corus announce the mothballing of the Llanwern hot strip steel mill and No. 4 blast furnace at Port Talbot (January).
- A new Local Development Fund, to promote 4000 small enterprises, is announced, using £23 million of European Development Fund money.
- Welsh Assembly government backs the Broughton Airbus assembly plant with an investment of £28.66 million.

- 32-storey Bay Pointe apartment development at Cardiff Harbour is abandoned.
- No. 4 blast furnace at Port Talbot restarts in September.
- Unemployment reaches 125,000 (8.7%), compared with UK average of 7.8%.
- Four people die in a mid-air plane collision near Kenfig.
- Theatr Clwyd closes at Bangor.
- Deaths of Jackie Bowen, rugby international; Vic Crowe, footballer; Eluned Phillips, poet and writer; Aeronwy Thomas, poet and writer.
- Wales win rugby international.

2010
- A BBC poll in March finds 56% of electors in favour of increased law-making powers for the Assembly; 35% against.
- A quarter of eligible students will sit the Welsh Baccalaureate exams this year.
- Glyndwr University in St Asaph participates in the building of the world's largest telescope.
- Wales has thirteen active vineyards.
- Death of Micky Jones, guitarist.
- England win rugby international.
- Wales this year is to host the Ryder Cup golf competition at Newport (October).

Bibliography

Bede, *A History of the English Church & People*, translated by Leo Sherley-Price. Harmondsworth, 1955

Black, R., Gillies, W., and Ò Maolalaigh, R., *Celtic Connections*. Phantassie, 1999

Borrow, George, *Wild Wales*. London, 1862

Chadwick, Nora, *The Celts*. London, 1971

Cunliffe, Barry, *The Ancient Celts*. Oxford, 1997

Davies, John, *A History of Wales*. London, 1990

Durkacz, V. E., *The Decline of the Celtic Languages*. Edinburgh, 1983

Elwyn Jones, Gareth, Modern Wales: *A Concise History*. New ed., Cambridge, 1994

Elwyn Jones, Gareth and Smith, Dai, *The People of Wales*. Llandysul, 1999

Etheridge, K., *Welsh Costume*. Ammanford, 1958

Evans, D. Gareth, *A History of Wales*, 1906–2000. Cardiff, 2000

Frere, Sheppard, *Britannia*. New ed., London, 1978

Giraldus Cambrensis, *Itinerary Through Wales*, translated by Sir Richard Colt Hoare. London, 1908

Hawkes, Jacquetta, *Prehistoric Britain*. London, 1948

Jackson, Kenneth, *Language and History in Early Britain*. Edinburgh, 1953

Jenkins, Geraint, *The Foundations of Modern Wales*, 1642–1780. Oxford, 1987

Jones, J. Gwynfor, *Wales and the Tudor State*. Cardiff, 1989

Jones, Edward, *Musical and Poetical Relicks of the Welsh Bards*. London, 1808

Jones, Thomas (ed.), *Brut y Tywysogion*. Cardiff, 1955

Koch, J.T., and Carey, J., *The Celtic Heroic Age*. Malden, Mass., 1995

Lloyd, Sir John, *A History of Wales*. 2 vols., London, 1911

Lloyd, Sir John, and Jenkins, R.T., *Dictionary of Welsh Biography*. London, 1959

MacKillop, James, *Dictionary of Celtic Mythology*. Oxford, 1998

Matthews, John, *The Bardic Source Book*. London, 1998

Morgan, Kenneth O., *Rebirth of a Nation: Wales 1880–1980*. Oxford, 1981

Price, Glanville, *The Languages of Britain*. London, 1987

Rhys, John and Brynmor-Jones, David, *The Welsh People*. London, 1906

Ross, Anne, *Pagan Celtic Britain*. London, 1971

Ross, Anne, *Druids*. Stroud, 1999

Salway, Peter, *Roman Britain*. Oxford, 1981

Smith, Dai, *Aneurin Bevan and the World of South Wales*. Cardiff, 1993

Stenton, Sir Frank, *Anglo-Saxon England*. Oxford, 1971

Thomas, David (Ed.), *Wales: A New Study*. Newton Abbot, 1977

Thomas, Hugh, *A History of Wales, 1485–1660*. Cardiff, 1991

Walker, David, *Medieval Wales*. Cambridge, 1990
Williams, Glanmor, *Owain Glyndwr*. Cardiff, 1993
Williams, Gwyn A., *When Was Wales?* London, 1985

Index